The Mosquito Confederation

EARLY
AMERICAN
PLACES

ADVISORY BOARD

Vincent Brown, *Duke University*
Cornelia Hughes Dayton, *University of Connecticut*
Nicole Eustace, *New York University*
Amy S. Greenberg, *Pennsylvania State University*
Ramón A. Gutiérrez, *University of Chicago*
Peter Charles Hoffer, *University of Georgia*
Karen Ordahl Kupperman, *New York University*
Mark M. Smith, *University of South Carolina*
Rosemarie Zagarri, *George Mason University*

The Mosquito Confederation

*A Borderlands History
of Colonial Central America*

DANIEL MENDIOLA

The University of Georgia Press
ATHENS

© 2025 by the University of Georgia Press
Athens, Georgia 30602
www.ugapress.org
All rights reserved
Set in 10.5/13.5 Adobe Calson Pro Regular
by Rebecca A. Norton

Most University of Georgia Press titles are
available from popular e-book vendors.

Printed digitally

Library of Congress Cataloging-in-Publication Data

Names: Mendiola, Daniel, author.
Title: The Mosquito Confederation : a borderlands history of colonial
Central America / Daniel Mendiola.
Description: Athens, Georgia : University of Georgia Press, 2025. |
Series: Early American places | Includes bibliographical references and index.
Identifiers: LCCN 2024033886 (print) | LCCN 2024033887 (ebook) |
ISBN 9780820369648 (hardback) | ISBN 9780820369624 (paperback) |
ISBN 9780820369655 (ebook) | ISBN 9780820369662 (pdf)
Subjects: LCSH: Mosquitia (Nicaragua and Honduras)—
Politics and government. | Mosquitia (Nicaragua and Honduras))—History—
18th century. | Miskito Indians)—Politics and government. |
Miskito Indians)—History)—18th century.
Classification: LCC F1529.M9 M463 2025 (print) | LCC F1529.M9 (ebook) |
DDC 972.85/303)—dc23/eng/20241202
LC record available at https://lccn.loc.gov/2024033886
LC ebook record available at https://lccn.loc.gov/2024033887

CONTENTS

PREFACE xi

INTRODUCTION 1

CHAPTER 1.
The Formation and Expansion of the Mosquito Confederation, 1687–1713
25

CHAPTER 2.
Consolidating the Mosquito Imperial System, 1713–1729
46

CHAPTER 3.
New Challenges and the Recovery of the Confederation, 1728–1749
73

CHAPTER 4.
Mosquito Aggression and Reconciliation with Costa Rica, 1747–1763
95

CHAPTER 5.
The Mosquito Confederation and New Internal Tensions, 1763–1775
120

CHAPTER 6.
The Mosquito Confederation and Civil War, 1776–1791
145

CONCLUSION AND HISTORIOGRAPHICAL CONSIDERATIONS 171

EPILOGUE 185

ACKNOWLEDGMENTS 189

NOTES 191

BIBLIOGRAPHY 225

INDEX 231

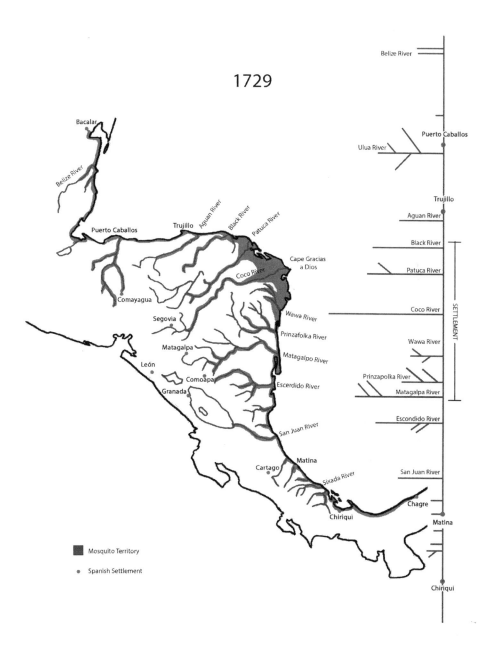

PREFACE

Perhaps the most fundamental misunderstanding of the Mosquito Kingdom has been the presumption that it was in a state of constant war with the Spanish. Whereas the historiography has long benefited from vigorous debates on other topics, such as the nature of the Mosquito kingship or the degree of autonomy that the Afro-Indigenous Mosquito maintained vis-à-vis European colonial powers, studies overwhelmingly have taken for granted that a constant barrage of Mosquito attacks against Spanish settlements was simply the norm throughout the eighteenth century, with peace negotiations playing virtually no role in this relationship. Furthermore, the historiography has typically treated Costa Rica as the epicenter of this onslaught, with some studies even generalizing that the Mosquito attacked Spanish settlements in Costa Rica's Matina Valley twice per year during most of the eighteenth century.[1]

The myth of constant warfare is so pervasive, in fact, that when I began this project as a graduate student my original plan was to write a dissertation focusing on Mosquito raiding. Having focused much of my graduate training on colonial borderlands, I was curious whether conditions in Central America at the southern fringes of New Spain might be comparable to the classic borderland examples in the north. More specifically, I wondered if the rapid expansion of the Mosquito Kingdom and its supposed incessant raiding might be comparable to the expansion of the powerful Comanches, who in the assessment of Pekka Hämäläinen created an "empire."[2] Accordingly, I decided to travel to Costa Rica, hoping to find sources describing the constant attacks that supposedly happened twice per year. Given that Costa Rican sources barely appeared in previous studies, I assumed there probably was not much to find, and I wondered whether the trip would be a waste of limited time and resources. But in the interest of being thorough, I decided to go and managed to obtain a small travel grant from my home department at the University of Houston to cover expenses for about three weeks of research.

I was doubly surprised, therefore, when I arrived at the National Archive of Costa Rica (ANCR) and began digging through collections related to the Mosquito. To begin, the sheer number of relevant documents was enormous—far more than I could read in three weeks—and the sources were filled with previously uncited original reports and eyewitness accounts describing concrete events. Even more surprising, however, these documents told a completely different story: instead of describing constant warfare, they often portrayed peaceful interactions and ongoing negotiations. In fact, for most of the eighteenth century, the Mosquito considered Spanish Costa Rica an ally, and when violence did occur, it was usually in response to specific provocations with the purpose of pressuring the Spanish province back into the alliance.[3] As a caveat, the Mosquito did not consider free Indigenous peoples living within what would be present day Costa Rica to be Spanish, and these peoples did suffer heavily from Mosquito raiding. But it is still indisputable that Mosquito attacks on Spanish Costa Rica were far less common than peaceful interactions, and when violence outbursts did occur, they were usually not raids so much as instances of gunboat diplomacy.

This discovery demanded a complete rethinking of the Mosquito Kingdom's role in colonial Central America, and after compiling my initial findings, I applied for and received a Fulbright research grant that allowed me to spend a full ten months carefully reading through this massive trove of new information. I also received additional grants from my department to travel to archives in Guatemala and London to supplement my core research in Costa Rica, and as I continued to find new information, more of the prevailing assumptions regarding Mosquito history began to unravel. For example, the commonsense explanation for the alleged barrage of Mosquito attacks on the Spanish was that the Mosquito became caught in a desperate cycle of raiding and trading, leading to the additional conclusion that the Mosquito way of life depended on access to European manufactures, such as firearms supposedly needed for these raids.[4] However, the firsthand descriptions of Mosquito activities that I found in Costa Rican sources contradicted this characterization. Mobility, manpower, and alliance building—all possible because of Indigenous knowledge—were far more important for Mosquito power than European goods. Indeed, Mosquito expansion was never a desperate measure to fill subsistence gaps but rather a calculated geopolitical project that Mosquito leaders enacted from a position of stability and strength. And the cornerstone of this geopolitical project remained the system of internal alliances that came to constitute a highly unified Mosquito Confederation. In light of this new evidence, the core narrative of Mosquito history needed to be entirely rewritten.

The *Mosquito Confederation* is the culmination of the described research. Its primary purpose is to offer a detailed, chronological, archivally grounded retelling of Mosquito history. While this story is the central thrust of the book, I have also sought to include robust historiographical discussions tracing how earlier ideas about the Mosquito originated and to explain why new evidence demands their reassessment. Ultimately, this book offers a new approach for thinking about the colonial history of Central America and the Caribbean: an approach that centers the Mosquito Confederation.

INTRODUCTION

Watching in horror while Mosquito forces overwhelmed his home village, Christobal de Guadalupe decided that he would rather risk his life escaping than continue to abet his captors. It was April 1719, and for the past three years, Christobal had served as a guide for the Mosquito Kingdom's southern fleet. Born sometime in the late seventeenth century in a Guaymi village along the Cocle River, Christobal had found himself absorbed by the imperial orbit of the Spanish early on: accepting baptism, serving in the remote militia outpost at the mouth of the Cocle River, and learning Spanish. In 1716, however, a passing Mosquito fleet occupied the militia outpost while Christobal was on watch. Recognizing Christobal's linguistic and geographic knowledge, his captors forced him to serve as a guide. This service contributed to the massive 1719 raid on Christobal's home further inland, in which the Mosquito decimated the village and enslaved dozens of Christobal's friends and family, including his wife. Unable to bear the situation any longer, Christobal plotted with his wife to escape, and when the Mosquito fleet stopped at another Spanish outpost in Costa Rica's Matina to trade for supplies for the return voyage, they fled to a nearby forest to hide. Then, after waiting several days to be sure that their captors had left, they turned themselves in to Costa Rican authorities.[1]

The story of Christobal de Guadalupe offers a window into the world that was forming along the Caribbean coast of Central America in the early eighteenth century: a world shaped by competing conquests. Some of these conquests are likely more familiar than others. Speaking Spanish, professing

Christianity, and even serving in the colonial militia, Christobal certainly bore the hallmarks of the Spanish conquest, which Central American authorities had taken up with renewed vigor in the late seventeenth century in order to "pacify" the countless Indigenous peoples who continued to live free of Spanish rule. But the Spanish were not the only conquerors in Central America, and by the start of the eighteenth century, the Indigenous Mosquito Confederation was embarking on its own expansion.

The Mosquito Confederation, often referred to as the "Mosquito Kingdom," was a powerful alliance of Amerindian and African-descended communities that dominated Central America's Caribbean coast throughout the eighteenth century. The Mosquito emerged as a burgeoning power in the late seventeenth century when the leaders of several Miskitu-speaking bands united under a central council. The resulting confederation coordinated this increased manpower to assemble a powerful navy, along with a strategic body of well-informed guides, translators, and negotiators, thus providing the basis for an expansionist vision. This program notoriously included raids on Indigenous and Spanish settlements along the coast. Yet, significantly, raiding was only one component of a broader set of conquest practices. Directed by the council members, these included intelligence gathering, treaty negotiation, gunboat diplomacy, maritime logistics, and trade. The result of these activities was the creation of an empire-like system that left nearly the entire Caribbean coast of Central America under varying degrees of Mosquito influence, and which endured for nearly the entire eighteenth century. However, after a series of internal conflicts, the principal factions of the confederation descended into a bitter civil war. In the aftermath, the Mosquito remained fiercely independent. Nonetheless, the Mosquito Confederation never recovered its former power, and its imperial phase came to an end.

Significantly, the Mosquito Confederation reshaped landscapes of Indigenous power relations, creating a quasi-imperial power center in a region long characterized by diffused power. Moreover, the Mosquito played a critical role in shaping how European interlopers such as the Spanish and English attempted their own Central American conquests. The Mosquito rise to power did not take place in a vacuum, and the confederation maintained varying degrees of contact with Europeans throughout its expansion. However, Mosquito power never depended on European support, and its success derived primarily from Mosquito knowledge, manpower, and technology. European colonial projects, on the other hand, did become dependent on Mosquito support as the Europeans tried to expand their presence into the Caribbean side of the Central American isthmus. These overarching power dynamics characterized Mosquito relations with Europeans until the end of the eighteenth century. Arguably, one of the most important consequences of the confederation's demise was to attenuate the subordinate status that European colonizers in the region had long endured in their interactions with the Mosquito.

The use of the term "conquest" requires some explanation. In this book, conquest refers broadly to packages of long-term practices and processes that ultimately result in the expanded territorial influence of specific political units. In this view, military campaigns are only a small component of conquests, and this book focuses primarily on how quotidian networks of communication, diplomacy, coercion, and trade shaped imperial outcomes over time. This distinction is important given that other scholars have wisely cautioned that the term "conquest" is problematic in many colonial contexts, especially in describing early encounters between Spanish and Amerindian groups since the term might imply that Spanish expansion was a foregone conclusion. Matthew Restall, for example, has observed that calling Cortes's 1519 expedition "the Conquest of Mexico" reinforces a myth-laden narrative of triumph, and in his 2018 study *When Montezuma Met Cortés*, he instead uses the more accurate name "Spanish-Aztec War." In the present study, however, the word "conquest" remains useful because the objects of analysis are different. Rather than analyzing specific military encounters within a relatively narrow time frame, this book describes long-term processes of territorial expansion. Both the Spanish and the Mosquito deployed a variety of practices to contest each other's influence in Central America throughout the eighteenth century, and the English eventually joined the fray as well, hoping to extend their island-based Caribbean colonization project into the mainland. Each of these three competing conquests has a place in this book, but highlighting the centrality of the Mosquito Kingdom remains a key theme throughout. Accordingly, this book is designed to demonstrate how the Mosquito themselves shaped the policies, practices, and outcomes of these conquests, their own included.

The book addresses a straightforward set of questions: Who were the principal actors facilitating these conquests? What specific practices did they implement? And how did these processes shape relations of power for the people involved? The specific answers vary in different places and times, yet the overarching argument is that the rise and decline of the Mosquito Kingdom—a process that depended far more on the novel practices of Mosquito leaders than on outside support—was the driving force shaping imperial outcomes in the region. The confederation's influence was of course most evident in the Caribbean borderlands, where European interlopers and Indigenous peoples alike found the conditions of their lives shaped by Mosquito expansion. But the Mosquito Kingdom shaped history in even broader ways, affecting the imperial playing field and thereby influencing how officials in distant colonial centers imagined, discussed, and planned their own imperial designs. True, these distant actors were not always conscious of how much the Mosquito influenced their decisions. Yet frequently they *were* aware, and the historical record is full of examples of would-be colonizers openly recognizing the Mosquito as protagonists in the geopolitical processes of the region.

In describing these processes, this study excavates the roles of diverse peoples in Central America's Caribbean borderlands: thoughtful Mosquito leaders who balanced complex geopolitical considerations; Afro-descended Central Americans who shaped Spanish and English responses to the Mosquito; and Amerindians who moved among Spanish, English, and Mosquito worlds. Moreover, this book challenges the common assumptions that the Mosquito Kingdom depended on European support from its inception and that the principal cause of the confederation's decline was a breakdown in this support. Taking for granted that Mosquito power must have depended on "superior" European technologies, such as firearms and metal tools, the prevailing grand narrative in the historiography is that the Mosquito became increasingly dependent on outside trade to maintain their way of life, leading to Mosquito history characterized by an unstable, reactionary cycle of raiding and trading.[2] However, new archival evidence overturns several key assumptions of this narrative. For example, firsthand descriptions of specific events throughout the eighteenth century demonstrate that Mosquito advantages in military power did not actually depend on European material support, nor was Mosquito raiding simply intended to extract tradable resources. In fact, the Mosquito acquired advantages by relying on Indigenous knowledge, technologies, and manpower—whether through internal alliances among the Miskitu people or through enslavement of Indigenous laborers, translators, and guides—and their military activities often were not raids at all but rather strategic interventions in service of more complex geopolitical considerations. Ultimately, this new evidence leads to new explanations for the confederation's eighteenth-century rise and decline.

The Mosquito "Conquest" of Central America

This book uses the term "Mosquito Confederation" to refer to the political unit constituted by Miskitu-speaking Amerindian and Afro-descended inhabitants of Central America's Mosquito Coast, and which came to be characterized by an empire-like propensity to expand. This expansion did not occur by overland conquest of two-dimensional spaces, nor was the Mosquito conquest land-centric at all. In this sense, the confederation might be aptly compared to Southeast Asian river kingdoms since Mosquito expansion progressed by channeling the polity's coercive capacities almost exclusively along waterways.[3] In both creating and maintaining this sphere of influence, Mosquito leaders deployed a range of imperial practices, including protection agreements, tribute demands, and demonstrations of force in addition to outright raiding. By these means, the confederation's central leaders managed to exert broad influence over a region long characterized by dispersed, localized power. In other words, the Mosquito Confederation's effective project of imperial expansion was unlike anything the region had ever seen.

Researchers have never conclusively determined how the name "Mosquito" originated, but by the start of the eighteenth century, this name—along with several alternate spellings such as Moskito or Musqueto—had become the most common way of referring to the Indigenous peoples of the Cape Gracias a Dios region in written sources. In the current historiography, the name has become standardized under two variants: *Mosquito* and *Miskitu*. These spellings are almost interchangeable since they both refer to the same people, though to some extent they signal different historical periods. Since "Miskitu" emerged as the preferred spelling after the language was phoneticized in the nineteenth century, this spelling is commonly used in studies emphasizing the national period. On the other hand, "Mosquito" was the standard spelling in both British and Spanish sources during the eighteenth century, so researchers of the colonial era tend to use this spelling. Following this pattern, I have elected to use the spelling Mosquito when referencing the people and the confederation since this book examines events in the colonial period, though I do use the spelling "Miskitu" when specifically referring to the language.

Whereas Spanish colonial institutions became well established in population centers such as Mexico City and Guatemala, the predecessors of the Mosquito remained well-insulated from these processes. Spanish adventurers began arriving in Central America as early as the 1490s, yet they explored only minimal portions of the Caribbean side of the isthmus and left no permanent settlements.[4] Accordingly, the early Indigenous inhabitants of the Mosquito Coast had no sustained contact with the Spanish world, even though they may have had isolated encounters with passing ships, shipwrecked sailors, and possibly a few wayward missionaries who died soon after arriving.[5] Moreover, even when the Mosquito did eventually take an interest in the economic opportunities of the colonial world, they looked not to the Spanish world of the mainland but rather to the burgeoning trade networks of the Caribbean. This is evident in the early trade carried out with the English settlers of nearby Providence Island, which dated back as early as the 1630s.[6] The Mosquito also deployed their strategic position on the coast as a supply depot for pirates and contrabandists, with Mosquito men sometimes even joining ships' crews.[7]

Caribbean contacts did eventually lead to visible changes in Mosquito society. One such change was the incorporation of a significant population of people of African descent. It remains unclear exactly how frequently runaway African slaves from Spanish frontier colonies or British logwood settlements may have joined the Mosquito, but several eighteenth-century sources allude to a major influx of shipwrecked slaves around 1640. Some chroniclers claimed that these newcomers were simply assimilated through intermarriage.[8] Other sources said that the new arrivals had to violently displace Indigenous inhabitants in order to permanently settle.[9] What is certain, however, is that even though these African-descended groups adopted Mosquito cultural attributes such as the Miskitu language, their descendants ultimately maintained a distinct ethnic affiliation, known throughout the eighteenth century as *Zambo-Mosquito*. On the other hand, those who associated themselves primarily with Amerindian ancestry came to be called *Tawira-Mosquito*.[10] The use of the term "Zambo" is well documented throughout the eighteenth century in English and Spanish sources, though the term "Tawira" may be anachronistic since written sources do not confirm its use until the nineteenth century. This does not necessarily mean, of course, that the term did not exist in the colonial period, and it is entirely possible that it was common among Miskitu speakers and simply never written down in English or Spanish sources. Regardless, the "Tawira" has become a commonly accepted way to talk about the Mosquito who primarily identified with their Amerindian ancestry, and the present study follows this convention.

An even more consequential change in Mosquito society, however, was the unification of several Miskitu-speaking groups into a confederation directed by a central council. After participating in Caribbean trade networks for several decades, the Mosquito leaders well understood that the coercive power of a strong military would give them an advantage in controlling valuable sites of resource extraction and exchange. In the sparsely populated Caribbean lowlands, however, developing such a military force required more than simply fighting prowess: it also required alliance-building on an unprecedented scale. Without any major population centers, the Caribbean side of the Central American isthmus had long been characterized by the diffusion of power among scattered peoples.[11] The architects of the Mosquito Confederation radically altered this situation by unifying the scattered Zambo and Tawira bands into a coastal confederation, a political innovation that came to have resounding implications for Central America's geopolitical landscapes. With the emergence of the Mosquito Confederation, an expansionist project took root in the Caribbean lowlands for the first time, supporting a vast expansion in economic and political power. Providing a detailed narrative of this expansion is the primary purpose of the chapters that follow.

Early elements of the Mosquito Confederation emerged in the late seventeenth century as an alliance among three principal factions: a *king's* faction near Cape Gracias a Dios with its principal settlement of Sandy Bay in present day Nicaragua, a *general's* faction along the northern coast in present day Honduras, and a *governor's* faction that extended south toward Costa Rica. Throughout the eighteenth century, the king and the general were reputed to have large Zambo followings, whereas the governor led primarily Tawira populations. Later, in the 1730s, a fourth district emerged even farther south, in the Pearl Key, which was headed by the *admiral* and reputed to be primarily Tawira.[12]

Since there were no documents written in the Miskitu language in the eighteenth century, it is difficult to assess to what extent the commonly used titles of king, governor, general, and admiral were full loan words or English translations of Miskitu terms. In Spanish documents, these titles are usually translated to the Spanish equivalents—for example, *rey* for king, *gobernador* for governor—though interestingly, there are some examples of transliterations of English titles appearing in Spanish documents, perhaps indicating that the Mosquito themselves used these terms. The Mosquito admiral Dilson, for example, was occasionally called "Almoral" in Spanish.[13] As this example indicates, another source of spelling discrepancy in the historiography concerns the names of Mosquito leaders, who appear alternately in English and Spanish sources with anglicized or Hispanicized names. King Jeremy II, for example, was called "Bernabé" in Spanish sources, and his close ally Governor Hannibal was called "Aníbel." For clarity, this book typically uses the anglicized spellings for names and titles to refer to Mosquito leaders.

Regarding the political organization of the Mosquito, a tendency emerged early in the historiography to use the word "kingdom" when discussing Mosquito politics of the eighteenth century. This convention accords with the terminology used at the time. Throughout the period of this investigation, the most prominent lineage of Mosquito leaders held the title of "king," and some English documents signed by Mosquito leaders did explicitly refer to a "kingdom."[14] Accordingly, most studies reasonably continue to use the conventional title Mosquito Kingdom when referring to the political unit, though as a caveat, recent works have wisely cautioned that this traditional title is misleading since Mosquito political practices did not align well with current definitions of the term kingdom. For example, whereas kingdom implies a strong degree of centralization under a specific sovereign with far-reaching command power, evidence suggests that power within the Mosquito Kingdom was spread among allied factions with no central ruler.[15]

This book proposes another term that more accurately describes Mosquito political organization: the Mosquito Confederation. To be clear, I have never seen the word "confederation" or a literal translation used to describe the Mosquito in eighteenth-century documents. Nonetheless, I argue that invoking the term here is not anachronistic because the current meaning of confederation accurately describes the Mosquito Kingdom's political practices. Notably, the Mosquito Kingdom was composed of distinct factions that never disappeared, even though the blocs remained closely allied under a representative council that met regularly to coordinate activities. And while the king was arguably the most powerful of the leaders who met on the council, he did not alone rule the other factions. Accordingly, this study prefers the name Mosquito Confederation, though this newer name is used interchangeably with the more common title Mosquito Kingdom.

I also use similar reasoning for invoking the concept of imperialism. While it remains unclear whether the Mosquito themselves—or any other contemporary observers for that matter—would have used some version of the noun "empire" to label the Mosquito Kingdom, the broader concept of imperialism is still useful because the Mosquito did participate in a variety of activities associated with how empires work in practice. This way of thinking engages the work of other scholars who similarly approach imperialism as a way of practicing power relations, as opposed to limiting the concept to European archetypes of government structures. For example, Burbank and Cooper identify two categories of ruling practices that characterize imperialism: the tendency to expand through conquest and the tendency to incorporate conquered peoples into hierarchical systems of unequal status.[16] As the following chapters illustrate, the Mosquito Kingdom engaged in both of these practices in various ways throughout the eighteenth century. Consequently, whereas this study does not necessarily argue that the Mosquito Confederation should be labeled an empire, it does assert that the adjective "imperial" accurately describes many characteristic Mosquito practices.

Characterizing the geopolitical practices of the Mosquito Confederation as empire-like also builds recent approaches in the historiography of colonial borderlands, especially the work of Pekka Hämäläinen, who similarly invokes empire in describing Amerindian confederacies in North America. As Hämäläinen explains, "The Iroquois, Comanches, and Lakotas may not have understood themselves as unified empires, and they lacked centralized bureaucracies, standing armies, and other traditional hallmarks of empires. Yet, for a long while, and more successfully than the Europeans around them, they did what empires do."[17] The present study demonstrates that the Mosquito Confederation oftentimes "did what empires do," paralleling the Iroquois, Comanches, and Lakotas of Hämäläinen's research. To highlight these parallels in imperial practices, I intentionally describe Mosquito activities using a variety of terms that are discursively affiliated with European imperial practices such as "occupation," "gunboat diplomacy," and "monopoly on violence." On the other hand, I tend to avoid other terms such as "tribe," "chief," or "warrior" that risk obscuring similarities between Amerindian and European practices by placing them into arbitrary discursive realms with racialized connotations.

The geography of Mosquito territory relative to the rest of the isthmus also requires some explanation. Overland travel was exceedingly difficult in the region, and while English settlers on the Mosquito Coast often discussed trying to cut a road to Guatemala, no known overland routes connected Mosquito territory to Spanish Central America throughout the eighteenth century.[18] In fact, many Spanish documents even refer to Mosquito territory as an island, especially when planning expeditions to try and attack the Mosquito. Though not literally true, it was not completely wrong either for the Spanish to call Mosquito territory an island since they could only reach it by boat, almost making it an island in practice.[19]

Significantly, this geographical positioning compounded the overland distance between the Mosquito and the interior Spanish provinces, and any land-based invasion by Spanish forces was never a real threat. On the other hand, effective distances contracted along the Caribbean coast as the nimble watercraft of the Mosquito passed riverine and coastal waters quickly, and entire fleets with hundreds of men could reach Costa Rica's Matina Valley in less than a week. For comparison, express couriers traveling from Matina to the Costa Rican capital of Cartago took about four days on average, and larger groups with troops or supplies usually took two or three times as long. Moreover, traveling from Costa Rica to Guatemala took even longer, with correspondence usually taking over a month to arrive.[20] These effective distances played an important role in shaping how the Mosquito and Spanish conquests intersected. For example, though perhaps not obvious from a bird's-eye map, effective travel times meant that Costa Rica's Matina Valley remained a remote outpost of the Spanish imperial world, yet a nearby coastal neighbor for the Mosquito. Accordingly, Matina became a site of intense interaction, with the Mosquito Confederation exerting enormous influence locally and oftentimes dictating the terms of negotiation.

Regarding territorial expansion, this study evaluates the Mosquito conquest by tracking not only the confederation's core settled territories but also its wider spheres of influence. Here I find it useful to distinguish between "power" and "influence." Both terms refer to one's propensity to serve as a causal force, acting upon others to bring about tangible changes. Nonetheless, whereas power refers more specifically to the ability to accomplish desired ends, influence refers more broadly to one's capacity to cause change in general, even if the effects may not necessarily be intended.[21] Mosquito fleets routinely traveled up and down the Caribbean coast far beyond the confederation's settled territories, and while these fleets did not necessarily subordinate these distant territories to daily administration, they did exert enormous influence as Amerindians and Europeans alike were forced to confront Mosquito fleets through varying processes of accommodation and opposition. This influence was strongest in places where Mosquito mariners, diplomats, and traders visited directly, forcing local populations to respond to these power imbalances even if Mosquito leaders did not necessarily institute a traditional imperial system of day-to-day governance. Yet Mosquito influence also extended far beyond the sites of their tangible activities, as officials in distant colonial centers such as Guatemala, Jamaica, Madrid, and London were likewise forced to come up with ways to confront the Mosquito conquest.

The Spanish and English "Conquests" of Central America

From the Spanish perspective, what we today call Central America fell under the jurisdiction of the Viceroyalty of New Spain as a subunit called the

"Captaincy General" or "Audiencia" of Guatemala. This subunit included the province of Guatemala, which contained the capital city of Santiago de Guatemala, as well as the subordinate provinces of Chiapas, Nicaragua, El Salvador, Honduras, and Costa Rica. The entire Audiencia was administered by a Crown-appointed president, who also served as the governor of the immediate territory of Guatemala. Each of the other provinces had its own governor, who reported to the president.[22]

In contrast to Mosquito expansion, which created a new, linear space by spreading along aquatic channels of efficient transportation, the Spanish typically tried to build upon the previously established population centers of inland Indigenous societies. These patterns reflected the divergent interests of the Spanish and Mosquito conquests. Whereas the Mosquito Confederation displayed little interest in incorporating subjects beyond the slaves taken back to Mosquito territory and opted for a more hands-off approach to conquest by stressing transportation routes and sites of exchange, the Spanish conquest did prioritize acquiring new subjects. Indeed, conquistadores saw little value in unoccupied lands, and from the earliest stages of the conquest, they concentrated their efforts on finding population centers where ready sources of labor facilitated economic exploitation and previously established government infrastructures facilitated the transition to colonial rule.[23] This emphasis also corresponded to the conquerors' missionary zeal, in which they sought moral justification by adding converts to the Catholic fold. Accordingly, two of the most important institutions of Spanish colonial rule were the *encomiendas*, which gave conquistadores the right to Indigenous labor, and the *reducciones*, which reorganized Indigenous converts under the authority of missionaries and royal officials.[24]

In practice, however, Spanish colonial power did not extend as far as these theoretical jurisdictions claimed. European explorers sailing nominally under the Spanish Crown began arriving in Central America as early as the 1490s, though at first attempts to establish permanent settlements were few and ephemeral. Other than the struggling Darién settlement in present day Panama, colonies remained elusive, and the primary activity of Spanish adventurers in Central America was simply to cruise the coasts looking for unsuspecting Amerindians to capture and enslave.[25] The Spanish did become more established in Central America in the 1520s as footholds in Panama and Mexico allowed more sustained invasions into the isthmus from both the north and the south. Still, even these invasions concentrated on the Pacific highlands, where larger Amerindian populations provided ready pools of labor, knowledge, and precedents for government infrastructure.[26]

Referring to this colonial project as "Spanish," or even a "project," can be misleading without proper contextualization. In the first place, Spain's conquest in Central America was only Spanish in the sense that its participants nominally professed loyalty to Iberian monarchs and maintained at least some formal connection with governing institutions such as the Catholic Church. However, only a small portion of these participants were actually from the Iberian Peninsula, whereas Amerindian and African-descended people constituted the bulk of the population. Significantly, these non-Peninsular peoples played vital roles in sustaining nominally Spanish conquest institutions, sometimes providing forced labor as slaves or tributaries, though just as often serving in more specialized roles such as translators, guides, soldiers, craftsmen, and even local officials. Consequently, when this book uses the term "Spanish," it is referring inclusively to the diverse historical actors who participated in the nominally Spanish project of imperial expansion in Central America.

Additionally, it is important to clarify here that this "project" was not, as the term might suggest at first glance, a centrally planned scheme organized in the Iberian Peninsula. Rather, the Spanish imperial project in Central America would be better characterized as a piecemeal series of practices and events driven primarily by local actors. From the perspective of the Iberian Peninsula, therefore, calling the Spanish conquest a "project" might overstate Iberian agency. I still use the term, however, because from the local perspective of Spanish Central Americans, the conquest was indeed an intentional, organized effort. This is especially evident from the ongoing "Spanish" initiatives to press the Caribbean frontier throughout the eighteenth century, which local Central American authorities attempted to coordinate.

In contrast, whereas the Spanish conquest emphasized control over Indigenous subjects, the English conquest followed a settler colonial model that focused less on controlling Indigenous subjects and more on creating and populating profitable enclaves. In this sense, the rise of the Mosquito Confederation created opportunities for the English by providing a stable, widespread governing system capable of recognizing English land grants and facilitating trade. The military power of the Mosquito Confederation also created an opportunity for the English to acquire slave labor, both through raids to capture new enslaved people to sell, as well as through the coercive power to keep slaves from escaping or rebelling. In theory, English colonizers hoped to use these early concessions on the part of the Mosquito in order to establish footholds and eventually bring new territories under English control. Nonetheless, English colonization efforts never managed to shed their dependence on Mosquito support, making dependency a defining characteristic of the English conquest throughout the eighteenth century.

The Providence Island venture of 1629 was one of the first examples of English imperial expansion into the Caribbean using the settler colonialism model. It was also the first English encounter with the Mosquito. Even though the colony's creation was orchestrated by the private initiative of its Puritan founders, the venture was officially part of the English imperial system since the colonization company's charter was recognized by the English Crown. In this regard, the colony mirrored the practices of Spanish conquistadores, whose exploits were not centrally organized by the king yet were still official conquests since they were Crown-sanctioned. A major difference, however, was that instead of focusing their efforts on subjugating local populations for the purposes of taxation and labor tributes, the English colonizers selected Providence Island because it was relatively unpopulated, creating an opportunity to fill the colony with White settlers and their African slaves.[27] Of course, this did not preclude contact with Indigenous groups, and in fact the settlers of Providence Island carried on a regular trade with the Indigenous inhabitants of the Mosquito Shore.[28] Accordingly, the colony provided an early foothold for English efforts to expand into Central America's contested Caribbean borderlands.

The Providence Island colony was short-lived: a Spanish invasion forced the settlers to evacuate in 1641.[29] Nonetheless, the English established a more lasting base of operations in Jamaica after seizing the island from its Spanish occupiers in 1655. This venture was more centrally planned than the Providence Island colony, carried out by the Royal Navy as part of a broader effort to expand the English empire at the expense of the Spanish. And while the English settlers occupying Jamaica feared that an overwhelming Spanish invasion might make the venture just as short-lived as the Providence Island colony, the English succeeded in defending the island from Spanish counterattacks.[30] Jamaica then gained official recognition as an English colony under the terms of the Treaty of Madrid ("American Treaty") of 1670, adding a degree of stability.

As with the Spanish case, the English conquest was never a centrally planned project but rather a piecemeal series of local initiatives that came to be nominally subsumed into a wider British imperial network. Still, the terms "English" and "conquest" are both still relevant when describing these processes since these settler outposts provided footholds that did indeed facilitate the expansion of an imperial system that functioned nominally under the English monarchy. In some cases, these outposts remained informal, yet they still provided economic support to formal colonies nearby, implicating them in practice into the English imperial sphere. In other cases, these settlements fell officially within English jurisdictions, shaping formal territorial claims. English settlements on the Mosquito Shore in particular provide excellent examples of these long-term processes of conquest. Though originally informal, they provided economic opportunities to Jamaica, helping to sustain English occupation after the island's military takeover in 1655. Furthermore, English officials eventually recognized the Mosquito Shore itself as an English "intendency," thus contesting the broad claims of the Spanish conquest. These processes were not necessarily a conquest in the traditional sense of a series of battles to subjugate local peoples, but they did constitute a broader package of social, economic, and legal practices that were supported in varying degrees by the coercive power of the state, which facilitated the geographic expansion of English influence in the long term. The concept of settler colonialism is also relevant since the English model was territory-centric, focusing on establishing territorial footholds and sending settlers to replace Indigenous inhabitants, as opposed to the subject-centric Spanish model, which sought to keep Indigenous peoples on the lands while replacing only the leadership.

Accordingly, whereas the day-to-day practices of settler colonialism may not look like conquests when viewed in the short term, the concept of conquest is still relevant when considering how in the long term these practices fit into conscious efforts at coercive colonial expansion. Establishing English imperial authority through gradual settlement was certainly the English intention in Central America's Caribbean borderlands, and so this study treats English activities within a framework of settler colonialism, characterizing them as a third conquest competing with those of the Mosquito and the Spanish.

It is also important to clarify that not all agents on the ground doing the work of English imperialism were themselves English, or even White Europeans at all. As Jamaica's plantation economy developed after the English conquest, the island remained heavily dependent on the labor and knowledge of Africans and Amerindians, both enslaved and free alike. With the image of sugar plantations ingrained in the popular image of Jamaica, most people would probably not be surprised to hear that it quickly became a majority enslaved colony. What is perhaps more surprising, however, is that according to population records Black River—the largest nominally English settlement on the Mosquito Shore—was also a majority enslaved colony.[31] Again, I use "English" as convenient shorthand for this colonial project, though the intention is not to obscure the presence of non-European peoples who did much of the work that made the English conquest a tangible reality.

Archival Sources and Historiographical Trends

This book offers a new perspective on the historical significance of the Mosquito Kingdom, not only by questioning the explanatory power of previous terms and paradigms but more importantly by incorporating an extensive body of new archival evidence into the analysis. These sources allow for the most thorough account of Mosquito colonial history to date, and the following chapters offer a cohesive narrative of chronological events covering most of the eighteenth century. In so doing, I expand many previous lines of research, though at the same time, I demonstrate that certain formative ideas about the Mosquito deserve rethinking.

Several influential ideas about the Mosquito—such as their presumed dependence on European goods, or the idea that they constantly raided Spanish settlements—took shape in late nineteenth- and early twentieth-century survey works, such as Ayón's 1882 *Historia de Nicaragua*, Dolores Gámez's 1915 *Historia de la Costa de Mosquitos*, and Salvatierra's 1939 *Contribución a la historia de centroamérica*. It is difficult to quantify the amount of archival sources used in the early historiography since citation conventions were not yet established, though it is clear that the source base for characterizing the Mosquito was relatively small given that discussions of the Mosquito occupied only a small space in these works, which overall tended to focus far more on Spanish and English activities.[32] In contrast, their assessments of the Mosquito tended to rely on uncritical characterizations and racialized discourses rooted in a relatively small set of published travel narratives and document collections.

In the 1960s, historical monographs on the region expanded the archival source base for studying the Mosquito Coast, though as in earlier surveys, these studies did not necessarily focus on the Mosquito themselves. As such, they tended to accept previous assumptions about the Mosquito unquestioningly while using new sources to add nuance to analyses of English and Spanish activities. Floyd's 1967 book *The Anglo-Spanish Struggle for Mosquitia*, for example, emphasized Spanish sources, drawing from dozens of archival documents from Spain and Guatemala, along with several sources from published document collections on Central America.[33] A far denser archival research project on the Mosquito Coast was Sorsby's 1967 thesis "The British Superintendency of the Mosquito Shore," which made meticulous use of archives in England and Spain, citing over nine hundred archival sources in order to document colonial policies. These studies are both seminal works that continue to be cited, though again, the fact that they incorporated a broader source base overall did not mean that these sources offered new insights into the history of the Mosquito themselves, since this was not the purpose of either study. Consequently, while these investigations went a long way toward understanding the English and Spanish prerogatives in the region, they tended to repeat many of the stock characterizations of the Mosquito from earlier works.

Also significant, both studies fit the pattern of drawing primarily on sources from the second half of the century. Sorsby's work, for example, begins its periodization in the 1740s, and 85 percent of the documents cited are from the second half of the century, thus leaving earlier periods unexamined. This approach made sense for studying the Spanish and English initiatives in the region since English efforts to colonize the Mosquito Shore accelerated in the 1740s, and Sorsby's periodization reasonably followed these processes. However, some of the most important processes in the history of the Mosquito Kingdom occurred earlier—most notably, the formation of the confederation and the implementation of the unified fleet system to back economic, diplomatic, and geopolitical objectives—so even research as detailed as Sorsby's did not cover these vital events, instead relying on generalized assumptions for background context.[34]

Following these seminal works on European empires in the region, a major new line of inquiry emerged in the late 1960s that did attempt to center the Mosquito Kingdom. However, the primary source base for this new wave of critical investigation remained limited, so even these new approaches continued to rely heavily on conjecture and extrapolation. Most notably, Mary Helms, Phillip Dennis, and Michael Olien published a series of articles in the 1970s, '80s, and c90s analyzing the culture, economy, and politics of the Mosquito Kingdom, and while they advanced critical analysis of the Mosquito by incorporating innovative theoretical frameworks, the most influential works in this section of the historiography together relied on about thirty published primary source documents and no archival sources.[35] Accordingly, these works did not necessarily challenge core details of the narrative attributed to the Mosquito so much as reformulate these early premises within more sophisticated explanatory frameworks. Later studies remained hesitant in challenging these frameworks, though researchers such Karl Offen and Barbara Potthast did begin the important work of adding archival sources into the analysis.³⁶ Offen's prolific work on the colonial-era Mosquito is especially noteworthy, significantly expanding the archival document base used to study the colonial era Mosquito and providing a more thorough analysis of published primary sources than previous researchers had used. These studies still stopped short of challenging many formative ideas such as the presumed Mosquito dependence on foreign imports and subsequent cycle of raiding and trading, yet Offen's expanded source base made other major contributions that revitalized the field, for example by popularizing the use of the term "Tawira" and clarifying the existence of this ethnic distinction within the Mosquito Kingdom.³⁷

Two other authors who stand out for their contributions to archival research on the Mosquito Kingdom are Caroline Williams and Eugenia Ibarra. Williams's 2013 article "Living between Empires" drew from dozens of new archival documents—primarily from the Archivo General de Simancas (AGS) in Spain—to offer a detailed description of the Mosquito civil war at the end of the eighteenth century. This is one of the most archivally dense studies previously published on the Mosquito Kingdom, though significantly, the sources concentrated on a narrow period in the late 1780s and early 1790s, forcing the analysis to rely on less robust secondary works for earlier context and thus leaving most overarching assumptions about the Mosquito Kingdom unchallenged.

Ibarra's 2011 *Del arco y la flecha a las armas de fuego* has the distinction of being the only book-length scholarly publication to center the colonial Mosquito Kingdom, with a bibliography citing around 180 archival documents primarily from the Archivo General de Centroamerica (AGCA) in Guatemala and the National Archives (TNA) in London. Ibarra's book offers an excellent synthesis of previous research, as well as useful analysis of the cultural dynamics of the Mosquito from an anthropological perspective. Similar to Williams's work, however, Ibarra draws on sources primarily from the later eighteenth century, with over two thirds taken from the 1760s or later. Perhaps for this reason, even this relatively large source base did not lead Ibarra to question formative ideas about the Mosquito. Tellingly, the central argument of the book is that Mosquito dependence on firearms was a defining characteristic of the kingdom from its inception in the seventeenth century, yet the book only cites one archival document in direct support of this claim, and this document was written much later in the 1780s.³⁸

In contrast, the present study provides a chronological narrative of the rise and decline of the Mosquito Kingdom by emphasizing concrete practices and specific events, many of which have never appeared in previous studies. In the process, this book incorporates nearly 350 previously uncited archival documents that fill key gaps in previous knowledge, especially in the first half of the eighteenth century when the distinctive characteristics of the Mosquito Confederation first emerged. This archival basis draws most heavily from collections in the ANCR in San José. Costa Rica was the Spanish province nearest to Mosquito territory, and the Mosquito maintained regular contact with Costa Rica throughout the eighteenth century as the coastal port of Matina fell along the route of the Mosquito Confederation's southern fleet. Consequently, the ANCR houses an extensive collection of detailed, original testimonies: either written in Matina based on eyewitness accounts and forwarded to the Costa Rican capital of Cartago; or created in Cartago based on interviews with eyewitnesses sent from Matina to testify in person. The size of these collections alone is significant. Whereas the narrower archival bases of earlier works on the colonial-era Mosquito have required researchers to extrapolate Mosquito history based on a few scattered events—usually starting with relatively well-documented events in the later eighteenth century and then making inferences about the first half of the century—the extensive use of ANCR sources in the present study fills in the gaps by reconstructing Mosquito history according to a more comprehensive series of contextualized, chronological processes, including specific events in the first half of the eighteenth century that show the early practices of the confederation. Moreover, the reports stored in the ANCR provide uniquely detailed insight into Mosquito activities. Not only do these sources include thick descriptions of specific events, but they also include abundant testimonies of experts: escaped captives with years of experience living among the Mosquito, released captives representing Mosquito leaders as ambassadors, and translators who frequently interacted with Mosquito visitors. The archive even holds letters attributed to Mosquito leaders themselves.

The importance of ANCR sources is even more apparent when considered alongside sources from the Seville's General Archive of the Indies (AGI), which this book also utilizes as a valuable supplement. Whereas AGI sources are useful for assessing Spanish colonial policies, they tend to provide far less detail about events happening on the ground. This is because when higher colonial officials such as provincial governors received original reports or eyewitness declarations from the frontier, these reports often never made their way up the chain of command to end up on the Peninsula. And even when they did, governors rarely forwarded the original reports in their communications with the Peninsula, instead opting to forward summaries that often focused more on their proposed actions than on the original events. An illustrative example occurs in the documents regarding the critical period from 1721 to 1724, when the governor of Costa Rica tried to formalize a treaty with the Mosquito, culminating in a Mosquito attack when the negotiations fell apart. The AGI contains hundreds of pages of documents about these negotiations, but almost all are written by the Costa Rican governor, who had no first-hand experience with the Mosquito himself, and whose main focus is defending his own responses with only vague references to the specifics of the events.[39] In contrast, ANCR holdings for the same period include extensive reports and eyewitness testimonies from the coast where events were occurring, clarifying key details regarding Mosquito practices that never appear in the governor's reports.[40]

This book also makes extensive use of the TNA in London, where the colonial Jamaica file likewise documents numerous direct encounters with the Mosquito. These sources do shed light on English interactions with the Mosquito throughout the eighteenth century, though they are most insightful for documenting processes in the second half of the century when English officials worked to establish an official English colony on the Mosquito Shore. These efforts led to more intense interactions between the English and Mosquito conquests, and consequently, more detailed documentation. My research further draws from the AGCA in Guatemala City, Guatemala, whose colonial files contain various reports from frontier settlements in Nicaragua and Honduras documenting Mosquito encounters in other zones such as the northern coast of Honduras. AGCA documents also provide vital context for assessing Spanish perspectives on the Mosquito, even if these sources are less insightful than ANCR collections in describing the Mosquito people themselves.

A Note On Silences

While the Mosquito Confederation and other competing conquests remain the central objects of investigation, this book recognizes that this history does not belong to the conquerors alone. Just as Mosquito, Spanish, and English agents worked to expand imperial spaces, free Indigenous peoples likewise worked to forge zones of refuge. This way of thinking about conquest engages James C. Scott's 2009 study *The Art of Not Being Governed*. As Scott explains, "civilized" kingdoms and empires did not represent a linear evolution in society that "barbarians" naturally embraced as they became more advanced; rather, empires emerged as they forced free peoples to join unwillingly. In Scott's view, therefore, the history of state expansion is synonymous with the history of nonstate peoples. In fact, the two processes are mutually constructing, yet research has obscured the importance of nonstate peoples by focusing disproportionately on empires and kingdoms.[41]

Bearing this caution in mind, this book as much as possible seeks to highlight the presence, contributions, and experiences of nonstate peoples in Central America whose lives and livelihoods came to be caught up in these competing conquests. In my view, this study is most successful in this goal through its attention to the go-betweens and informants on whom these conquests relied. The story of Christobal de Guadalupe and his wife, recounted at the beginning of this chapter, is a compelling example. The book includes many more characters who like Christobal were neither Spanish, nor English, nor Mosquito, yet whose lives became intimately intertwined with the violent processes of imperial expansion. Still, while I recognize that this history belongs to them just as much as to the conquerors, I also recognize that there are so many more stories that remain absent in this book because they were not written down or stored in colonial archives. Christobal's story only survives here because he and his wife managed to escape Mosquito captivity during the return voyage, successfully arriving at Costa Rica's Matina Valley and recounting their harrowing experiences. But this couple's escape was exceptional, and so many other stories remain unrecorded. Unfortunately, this book can only do so much to fill these silences. Nonetheless, by at least naming them, it is my hope that this book will not be guilty of simply reproducing these lacunae.

Along with the missing voices of nonstate peoples, it is also important at the outset of this study to name the silences of women. As Susan Kellogg explains in *Weaving the Past*, a sweeping 2005 study on Indigenous women in the Americas, women have never played a passive role in Latin American history, either before nor after the arrival of Europeans. Indeed, Kellogg shows that despite gender asymmetries, women have always been active in shaping history, not only through vital domestic labor but also in the broader economic, political, and social spheres. Historical studies have frequently obscured these contributions, however, "in part because until relatively recently, women have not been able to shape or help create a historical record."[42]

The story of Christobal and his wife is again instructive in demonstrating Kellog's point. When the pair arrived in Costa Rica after escaping the Mosquito convoy, officials gathered testimony from only Christobal. In fact, documents do not even record his wife's name. Recognizing that the tendency to overlook women's contributions is a major problem in the historical discipline, this book calls attention to the presence of women whenever they do appear in the sources. Unfortunately, this is not very often, so this book admittedly does little to add to our knowledge of the contributions of women. Still, by naming this silence, I hope that my work will at the very least avoid normalizing the skewed perspective that these sources generate.

Chapter Summaries, Arguments, and Contributions

The overall organization of this book is designed to center the history of the Mosquito Confederation itself, first describing this history according to its own logic and periodization and then explaining its impact on competing conquests in Caribbean Central America. Accordingly, the chapters progress chronologically through the eighteenth century, and within each chapter, the analysis begins by first recounting Mosquito activities during a specific period, followed by sections reexamining their implications for the Spanish and English conquests.

Chapter 1 examines events in Central America's Caribbean borderlands from roughly 1687 to 1713. This period was characterized by the rapid expansion of Mosquito power as the internal alliances of the confederation solidified and Mosquito leaders began to pursue a more aggressive geopolitical program. These developments were especially evident in the confederation's interactions with the Spanish province of Costa Rica, which by 1711 faced pressure from Mosquito leaders to ally with the Mosquito in service of the confederation's expansionist program. In describing these processes, this chapter demonstrates that Mosquito expansion derived primarily from novel Indigenous practices such as the political restructuring that centralized power under the confederation council and the confederation fleet system, which pooled manpower and drew from an extensive network of allies and informants. This argument constitutes a major revision to the current historiography, which overwhelmingly presumes that the confederation's initial rise to power depended on access to European materials such as firearms and metal tools.[43]

Chapter 2 evaluates key events in Mosquito history from roughly 1713 to 1729. During this period, the Mosquito Confederation established the core practices that would come to define its empire-like relations with the rest of Caribbean Central America, such as seizing control of foreign ports, establishing norms of trade, enacting gunboat diplomacy, and carrying out these activities with the unified manpower of the entire confederation. In describing these processes, this chapter likewise provides a close narrative of the confederation's activities, which were characterized by diplomatic overtures and peaceful interactions toward Spanish Costa Rica, even while the Mosquito continued to raid Indigenous groups in the area. This complicates previous narratives, which have typically presumed that the Mosquito treated the Spanish as enemies and vice versa.[44] In reality, the relationship was far more ambiguous as frontier outposts such as Costa Rica's Matina Valley came to depend on the Mosquito for protection.

Chapter 3 analyzes the activities and impacts of the Mosquito Confederation from roughly 1730 to 1749. Even though this period began with a brief lapse in Mosquito power caused by a smallpox epidemic, the core institutions of the confederation remained strong, and the 1730s saw a resurgence as the Mosquito revived the fleet and continued a familiar pattern of turtle hunting, slave raiding, protection agreements, and gunboat diplomacy. During this time, the Mosquito alliance with the English became more formalized as English agents worked even more closely with confederation leaders to establish formally recognized colonies on the mainland. On the other hand, Mosquito relations with the Spanish became increasingly strained as anti-Mosquito policies hardened, even in Costa Rica's Matina Valley where frontier actors had previously shown more flexibility in negotiating. Ultimately, whereas most research has presumed that the Mosquito became economically and culturally dependent on the English, this chapter shows that the English were far more dependent on the Mosquito than the other way around.[45] Moreover, even though previous research has typically treated Mosquito hostility toward the Spanish as a static constant, this chapter shows that hostilities varied according to specific circumstances, most notably Spanish recalcitrance in the face of Mosquito treaty proposals.

Chapter 4 examines Mosquito practices from roughly 1747 to 1763. On the one hand, this period represented the height of hostilities with the Spanish, and Mosquito attacks in Costa Rica became more frequent than ever before. However, Mosquito leaders initiated a reconciliation with Costa Rica in 1763, ushering in a new era of diplomacy that became the norm in Costa Rica for the rest of the century and even created precedents for other Spanish provinces to negotiate with the Mosquito as well. Overall, the core features of the confederation, including the centrality of the council and the unified fleet system remained visible, though interestingly, there is also some evidence that the council exercised looser control over the confederation during this period. For example, a new trend was that private raiding ventures—often in conjunction with English allies—became more frequent. At the same time, however, the English remained dependent on the goodwill of Mosquito leaders, and English agents found themselves unable to control Mosquito war-making or peacemaking. Accordingly, this chapter further highlights how English efforts at colonial expansion continued to attach themselves to the knowledge, manpower, and political structures of the Mosquito.

Chapter 5 evaluates major developments in the history of the Mosquito Confederation from roughly 1763 to 1775. In terms of foreign relations, this period was characterized by expanding peace negotiations with the Spanish, which not only included the reconciliation with Costa Rica but expanded to other provinces as well as higher authorities became more amenable to Mosquito treaty proposals. This created new fears among English settlers, however, and Mosquito leaders had to devote more time and energy to reassuring their English allies that the confederation would not suddenly betray them. Regarding internal politics, this period saw increasing friction among Mosquito council members. Whereas previous generations of confederation leaders had always put forth a united front when talking to foreign allies, they increasingly criticized each other while addressing English fears during this period. Thus, this chapter provides important historical context for the coming and process of the Mosquito civil war, which was still far from inevitable during this period, although visible tensions were already eroding the core institutions of the confederation.

Chapter 6 analyzes Mosquito history from roughly 1776 to 1791, emphasizing the critical series of events leading up to the Mosquito civil war. This period was characterized by increasing negotiations between the Mosquito and the Spanish, though these negotiations temporarily became more complicated when the English and Spanish governments declared war in 1779. The Mosquito provided support for their longtime English allies in select campaigns, though they strategically limited involvement and maintained ongoing negotiations with Spanish allies such as the Costa Ricans. The tone of these negotiations shifted in the early 1780s, however, as Mosquito leaders increasingly negotiated individually rather than on behalf of the entire confederation. Ultimately, this chapter finds that just as the rise of the Mosquito Confederation had less to do with European support and more to do with internal alliances, so too did the confederation's decline. Moreover, contradicting the prevailing narrative in previous research, the sources examined in this chapter provide no evidence that disruptions in English support created new economic pressures that drove Mosquito disunity.[46]

The next chapter, "Conclusion and Historiographical Considerations," provides an overview of the book's key findings, as well as a discussion of how these provide key updates to previous research. In particular, this chapter discusses previous explanatory frameworks for Mosquito history such as the premise that Mosquito power originated from foreign technology, the presumption that the Mosquito became dependent on constant access to European trade, the idea that constant raiding resulted from this dependency, and the assumption that the Mosquito were overwhelmingly hostile to the Spanish. Ultimately, the chapter elaborates how these earlier ideas originated in the historiography, as well as the new archival evidence of this book contradicting these claims.

The book ends with a short epilogue reflecting on the role of conquest in the Americas. Whereas the Mosquito Confederation and other borderland powers highlight the extent to which the Spanish failed to complete their conquest, it is also true that these Indigenous groups no longer exert the same influence that they had during the colonial era. Consequently, their histories also highlight the disturbing extent to which later nation-states continued the conquest even more vigorously. And for many of the present day Miskitu people, this is not simply an abstract rethinking of history but in fact a lived reality.

CHAPTER 1

The Formation and Expansion of the Mosquito Confederation, 1687–1713

As the guards brought in the recently kidnapped Costa Rican captives, King Jeremy understood that this was a strategic opportunity. It was May 1711, and while Mosquito expeditions regularly passed along Costa Rican shores, Mosquito leaders had yet to establish any diplomatic contact with the province's Spanish authorities. Speaking through his team of Spanish translators—captives taken from other Spanish territories and missions in previous years—Jeremy first expressed respect for the king of Spain and even showed interest in learning about the Catholic faith. Jeremy then went on to explain his interest in opening commercial relations with Costa Rica and promised that if Matina ports remained open to supplying Mosquito convoys with food such as plantains, then he would place Matina under Mosquito protection. After the meeting, Jeremy arranged an armed escort to carry the captives back to Matina in two separate delegations, the first arriving in June, and the second in August. With these actions, Jeremy began a new phase of Mosquito expansion that would shape geopolitics in Central America's Caribbean borderlands for decades to come: with Matina as an allied port, the Mosquito Confederation would become more powerful than ever before.[1]

This chapter examines Mosquito history during the period from roughly 1687 to 1713, an era characterized by the emergence of the Confederation and its growing assertiveness in Central American geopolitics. In describing these processes, the chapter argues that Mosquito power did not derive from sudden access to European technologies such as firearms or metal tools as many studies have assumed.[2] In fact, Mosquito power depended far more on

Indigenous innovations: novel political arrangements among the Mosquito themselves to coordinate manpower, strategic pooling of linguistic and geographic knowledge gathered mostly from other Indigenous groups, and the maintenance of large numbers of nimble watercraft that were well-suited to the environment. These factors enabled the confederation to assemble a system of centrally coordinated fleets that forcefully backed Mosquito claims to an ever-expanding network of transportation routes, turtle-hunting grounds, supply ports, and slave-raiding sites.

Within this system, Costa Rica's Matina Valley emerged as a strategic supply depot connecting Mosquito territory to the turtle-rich waters of Bocas del Toro in present-day Panama. In asserting their influence over the Matina coast, the unified leaders of the Mosquito established many of the core practices that would characterize the geopolitical expansion of the confederation. In response, Spanish Central America reacted with contradictory policies: while distant authorities in Guatemala and the Iberian Peninsula took a hardline stance against the Mosquito in theory, local actors in Costa Rica largely accepted Mosquito peace offerings in practice. Throughout these processes, the Mosquito maintained close ties with English allies as well, though English actors in the region were well aware of their dependence on Mosquito goodwill for material and political support. Given these circumstances, the confederation's ongoing negotiations with Costa Rica would eventually become a source of fear for English actors in the region.

In telling this story, I do not pretend to be able to perfectly reconstruct Mosquito thought processes. After all, this investigation relies heavily on sources created by outside observers, so deeper levels of Mosquito thoughts and motivations remain elusive. Even the anecdote at the start of this chapter describing Jeremy's meeting with the Costa Rican captives had to be reconstructed according to later declarations by these same captives. Nonetheless, by using these sources to excavate, compile, and contextualize the concrete practices of specific Mosquito leaders, this narrative at the very least humanizes the Mosquito, presenting them as real, thoughtful people who shaped the history of Central America's Caribbean borderlands through ambitious, imperial initiatives. Moreover, in humanizing these processes, the purpose of this analysis is certainly not to romanticize this imperial drive. For the Mosquito, these processes meant an expansion of power that in many ways placed them above European interlopers in the region's geopolitical arrangements. However, for other peoples who suffered Mosquito attacks, these same events often meant violence, enslavement, the loss of loved ones, or even death. Ultimately, even while centering the Mosquito Confederation, this chapter seeks to humanize other historical actors, offering new insights into the messy realities of Mosquito conquest.

Jeremy I and the Early Mosquito Confederation, 1687–1711

The 1711 negotiations with Costa Rica represented a transitional moment in the rise of the Mosquito Confederation, as the policy of using Costa Rican ports as a base to fortify southern expeditions would characterize Mosquito geopolitics for much of the century. Nonetheless, the burgeoning power of the Mosquito had already been visible for some time. Specifically, it was during the reign of Mosquito king Jeremy I that key components of Mosquito imperial power became common practice. The precise years of Jeremy I's tenure as king remain unknown, but he became a visible figurehead of the Mosquito in 1687 when he led a diplomatic expedition to Jamaica. The purpose of the visit was to seek official recognition of his title as king, thus solidifying the informal alliance that the Mosquito already maintained in practice through trading relationships.[3] The English governor of Jamaica balked at signing a formal treaty, yet the visit succeeded in strengthening ties with Jamaica, with Jeremy reportedly even sending Mosquito soldiers to the island a few years later to help catch runaway slaves.[4]

Significantly, the published travel account of an English sailor known only as M. W. who visited the Mosquito Coast in 1699 provides further evidence to corroborate that the distinctive features of the Confederation emerged during the period of Jeremy I. Regarding military power, M. W. specifically mentioned the Mosquito carrying out raids on settlements as far south as the "Carpenter River," the English name for the Matina River on Costa Rica's Caribbean coast.[5] Earlier travel writers had mentioned that the Mosquito were skilled fighters who sometimes joined European pirate crews, but M. W.'s account is the first indication of Mosquito headmen pooling their resources to organize their own long-distance expeditions.

The timing of this territorial expansion is then corroborated by the few Spanish archival documents that exist from the time. Whereas Spanish officials never mentioned Mosquito raids before Jeremy I's tenure as king, reports slowly began to accumulate in the 1690s. At the turn of the eighteenth century, the Mosquito began outfitting expeditions to travel upriver, raiding inland settlements such as Segovia in Nicaragua, and they even began exploring the San Juan River that connected the Caribbean to Lake Granada.[6] Mosquito fleets also traveled down the coast as far as the Matina Valley in Costa Rica and traveled up the coast past San Pedro de Sula in Honduras and perhaps even as far as Peten in present day Belize.[7] Moreover, evidence suggests that this expansion of Mosquito military power accompanied negotiations with Indigenous allies. For example, according to the testimony of Micaela Gomez, a Nicaraguan "free mulata" woman who spent ten years as a Mosquito slave from 1707 to 1717, the original raid that had resulted in her capture was not executed by the Mosquito themselves but rather by an allied Indigenous group known as the Jicaques.[8] The Mosquito reportedly even had allies among various Indigenous settlements at the edge of Lake Granada who traded strategic knowledge by helping the Mosquito navigate the San Juan River.[9]

In addition to indicating the expanded geographic reach of Mosquito activities at the turn of the eighteenth century, M. W.'s account also hints at the increasing collaboration among Mosquito leaders. By the time he met King Jeremy I in 1699, Sandy Bay had already achieved a reputation as the most important Mosquito settlement. Additionally, after describing his meeting with Jeremy, M. W. went on to list several other headmen who were already on friendly terms with Jeremy. Among the leaders mentioned was a powerful chief to the south named Hannibal, who would later appear frequently in both English and Spanish sources with the title of governor.[10] M. W. did not describe any meetings that these leaders may have had in Sandy Bay, but significantly, the British smuggler Nathaniel Uring did. After visiting the Mosquito Shore in November 1711—a few months after the Mosquito had opened diplomatic relations with Costa Rica—Uring reported that "the most important Mosquito chiefs" frequently congregated at the residence of the king in the town of Sandy Bay. At these meetings, Mosquito leaders planned long-distance raiding expeditions, pooling manpower from their respective factions and sharing strategic intelligence gathered from slaves and informants.[11]

Given that previous studies have placed great emphasis on slave-raiding as a defining characteristic of the Mosquito Kingdom, it is worth adding some additional details here regarding what Mosquito slavery looked like in practice. Whereas the Mosquito certainly used their advantages in manpower and strategic knowledge to violently acquire captives, new evidence suggests that previous studies have likely overestimated the scale of Mosquito raiding, and more importantly, mischaracterized its purpose. Regarding scale, a 1995 study by Germán Romero Vargas estimated that the Mosquito captured twenty thousand slaves over the course of the eighteenth century—in other words, two hundred slaves per year, every year, over an entire century—and more recent studies have treated this estimate as authoritative.[12] Nonetheless, a closer examination of Romero Vargas's method in the context of wider evidence reveals that this number is likely inflated. Romero Vargas's study derived the estimate by using a single Spanish report written in the 1720s in which the governor of Costa Rica estimated that the Mosquito had captured two thousand slaves in the previous ten years. The study then assumed that this number was not only literally accurate for this period, but that it could be extrapolated without variance for the entire century. Wider archival evidence reveals, however, that both of these assumptions are dubious. In the original report, the number two thousand was essentially a guess rather than a systematic count, and the governor had a motive to put forth the highest estimate possible since the purpose of the report was to request additional resources at the king's expense to deal with the Mosquito threat. In contrast, eyewitness accounts of specific Mosquito slave raids in the same period show that they were usually small-scale events. The captives referenced at the beginning of this chapter who met with the Mosquito king in 1711, for example, had been enslaved in a raid that resulted in less than ten captives, and testimonies from other escaped captives throughout the century indicate that this was the norm, making it unlikely that such small raids would add up to two hundred captives per year.[13] It is also likely that this was an exceptional time in Mosquito slave raiding as a few high profile yet uncommon events occurred during this period, such as a well-documented attack in 1719 that resulted in the capture of eighty-five slaves.[14] Accordingly, even though Mosquito slave raiding had a devastating effect on many real people, the scale of these raids varied at different times over the century, and the overall numbers were probably lower than previous studies estimated.

Even more importantly, however, previous studies have mischaracterized the purpose of Mosquito slave raiding. With limited information about specific instances of Mosquito slave-raiding, most studies have assumed that the purpose was economic, with the Mosquito taking slaves primarily for sale in English markets.[15] Granted, there is clear evidence that the Mosquito did sell many slaves to the English. Yet the assumption that this was overwhelmingly the primary purpose of raiding obscures the bigger picture of Mosquito geopolitics. In fact, when one compiles descriptions of specific events, the archival record is full of examples of slave raiding serving broader imperial purposes, such as intelligence gathering, ransom negotiations, and gunboat diplomacy. Moreover, the Mosquito kept many of these slaves for themselves for physical labor in both agriculture and maritime activities, as well as intellectual labor in wayfinding and translating. Ultimately, while it is impossible to know for sure the precise scale of Mosquito slave raiding, it is certain that the practice was not simply about acquiring trade goods. In fact, the events described throughout the present book illustrate that slave raiding was a calculated component of a broader package of conquest practices facilitating Mosquito expansion through the acquisition of strategic knowledge, manpower, and diplomatic leverage.

In summary, Jeremy I's consolidation of various Zambo and Tawira-Mosquito factions into a single confederation was a major step in securing the military advantage necessary for expansion. No independent village or band could assemble armies of comparable size for defense, and even European colonies in the region were spread far too thin to match concentrated Mosquito forces. The Spanish Matina Valley, for example, rarely had more than fifty soldiers at any given time, and even these men were scattered over several settlements and three ports.[16] The English were similarly spread thin, with the governor of Jamaica estimating in 1707 that the entire island had only between five hundred and six hundred militia members.[17] In contrast, released captives who lived among the Mosquito around the same time estimated that the Mosquito Confederation boasted seven hundred to eight hundred fighting men in a smaller area.[18] Mosquito forces were also highly mobile since they concentrated along coastal settlements, and the confederation's efforts to gather geographic and linguistic knowledge made its fleets even more efficient.

Jeremy I died around the year 1711 and was succeeded by his son, Jeremy II. The precise date of the elder Jeremy's death is unknown, but the testimony of a Spanish-speaking captive of the Mosquito named Andres sheds some light on this question. Escaping sometime in 1711, Andres reported to Spanish authorities that the Mosquito king had died before the escape. What is more, Andres's account mentions that the question of succession remained unsettled, implying that the death had been recent.[19] M. W.'s earlier account corroborates that Jeremy I was alive though somewhat aged in 1699, around the same time as Andres's capture.[20] Thus, it is almost certain that Andres was talking about Jeremy I when he referenced a recently deceased king in 1711.

Andres's mention of the king's death also sheds important light on the ethnic features of the expanding confederation. Accounts of King Jeremy I's visit to Jamaica in 1687, as well as M. W.'s interview in 1699, describe Jeremy I as an Amerindian, yet documents for the rest of the eighteenth century associate the kingship with the Afro-descended Zambo-Mosquito. This has led historians to wonder how this shift came about, with some hypothesizing that some sort of rebellion or ethnic civil war must have taken place. Andres's testimony, however, demonstrates that ethnic lines were not so clearly drawn as to require a regime change for the ascension of a Zambo king: according to Andres, the deceased king's only son was Zambo. Interestingly, this detail from Andres's declaration also helps to clarify which Jeremy began negotiations with the Costa Rican captives. It remains unknown if Jeremy I was still alive, but the captives specifically reported Zambo fisherman picking them up and taking them to their leader, suggesting that there were talking to the Zambo Jeremy II.[21]

Andres went on to explain that this situation was at the center of a succession question, with some preferring to crown the deceased king's Tawira brother in order to prevent the ascension of a Zambo.[22] This tension was at least partially corroborated by Nathaniel Uring, who noted after his 1711 visit to the Mosquito Shore that one small group of Mosquito Amerindians had moved away from the main body in order to avoid being ruled by upstart Zambos.[23] From Uring's description this reaction seem isolated, however, and neither Uring nor Andres mentioned a civil war. Regardless, subsequent events demonstrate that in practice the matter was settled quickly. In 1711 Jeremy II was already negotiating with Costa Rica on behalf of the entire confederation, and at least as early as 1713, he had the visible support of a highly unified group of Zambo and Tawira leaders who worked closely with him during the well-documented negotiations with Costa Rica.[24]

To summarize, these two factors—Indigenous manpower and knowledge—provided the basis of Mosquito power, and while the potential riches of European trade may have motivated the Mosquito to apply these factors into an expansionist geopolitical project, Mosquito capacity for conquest did not depend on this trade. As a caveat, it might be reasonable to argue that the Mosquito Confederation did come to rely on slave-raiding to maintain this system. However, in contrast to previous assumptions, this was not because the Mosquito needed the foreign goods acquired from selling slaves: rather, they relied increasingly on the strategic labor and knowledge that slaves provided.

Ultimately, it was during the tenure of Jeremy II that the Mosquito Confederation began to enact an even grander vision, which included the Spanish as political and economic partners. Even though Spanish ports overall offered fewer commercial opportunities than the lucrative English markets in Jamaica, the Mosquito still had much to gain from these alliances. For example, Costa Rican ports offered access to valuable commodities such as cacao, which the Mosquito did not grow themselves yet could resell to the English. And even more importantly, Costa Rica offered logistical advantages as a potential supply depot for Mosquito fleets traveling further south. It was against this background, then, that Jeremy II met with the Costa Rican captives at his home in 1711. From this point on, Costa Rica became caught up in the broader imperial strategy of the confederation, leading to a lasting peace in the Matina Valley as the Mosquito worked to expand their imperial orbit even farther.

The Ongoing Spanish Conquest and the Emerging Mosquito Threat, 1685–1710

Until the middle of the seventeenth century, Spanish colonizers made little effort to expand the conquest into the Caribbean side of the isthmus. After all, the region was relatively poor in precious metals and Indigenous laborers, the primary objectives sought through the conquest.[25] Of course, it was not a given that the Spanish could have subjugated the region even if they had been highly motivated since the local environment and peoples combined to create a landscape that was highly resistant to the Spanish conquest practices. Covered by thick forests, steep hills, mosquito-infested swamps, and wide rivers, the landscape made overland travel exceedingly difficult, rendering Spanish incursions sluggish and vulnerable. These logistical challenges were then compounded by the fact that local Indigenous peoples were skilled fighters able to mount effective resistance against the invaders. Metal weapons and firearms made little difference: Spanish muskets were prone to misfire in the wet environment, and ambush-style attacks were more common than pitched battles. Spanish invaders also complained that horses were useless on the difficult terrain, negating yet another technology that may have given the Spanish advantages in other conquests.[26]

The Caribbean borderlands, however, began to weigh more heavily on the minds of Spanish officials during the second half of the seventeenth century. The reasons for this were both idealistic and pragmatic. On the one hand, missionary zeal provided a sense of urgency to continue the conquest. Franciscan Recollects Antonio Margil de Jesús and Melchor López, for example, arrived in Guatemala in 1685 to plant missions in frontier territories. To do this, the ambitious Recollects founded the Colegio de Cristo Crucificado in Guatemala to increase the number of trained missionaries in Central America. They also went into the mission field themselves, notably founding new missions in the mountainous Talamanca region of Costa Rica.[27] A more pragmatic motivation for continuing the conquest, however, was security. During the second half of the seventeenth century, the Spanish settlements in Central America began to suffer the increasing wrath of pirates and buccaneers who competed violently for the wealth circulating in the Caribbean. Not only did frontier settlements suffer from pirate raids but even established colonial centers such as Granada suddenly became vulnerable.[28]

On these grounds, Central American colonial officials encouraged new waves of conquest in the final decades of the seventeenth century. In Honduras, for example, missionaries and soldiers worked together to establish control over various Indigenous groups, referred to as *Payas* in Spanish documents, who inhabited the inland territories beyond Comayagua. One report from 1698 claimed that soldiers forcibly removed seven hundred Payas from the mountains, moving them to settlements overseen by missionaries.[29] These specific numbers may be exaggerated, but numerous reports confirm that during this period, Spanish Central Americans revived the conquest by launching occasional raids against the Payas in order to populate new frontier settlements with neophytes.[30] Similar processes occurred in Costa Rica as well, where a combination of missionaries and soldiers under the direction of Fray Antonio Margil de Jesús set out in 1698 to reduce the Indigenous inhabitants of the mountainous Talamanca region.[31]

Despite these efforts, however, converts proved difficult to control, and missions faced the constant threat of Amerindians fleeing into territories beyond Spanish reach. This problem was then compounded by the sudden emergence of an aggressive Indigenous coalition of Amerindian and African-descended groups from the Mosquito Coast. The detrimental impact of Mosquito raiding on missions was already evident in Honduras and Nicaragua in 1705. Mission reports specified that missions near Lean, Mulia, and Comoapa were under enormous stress. Significantly, the contemporary reports indicated that missions were becoming untenable, not because Mosquito attacks razed the missions entirely but rather because the looming threat of Mosquito slave raiding in and around the missions inspired native flight. Concluding that it would be impossible to retrieve these runaways, some officials counseled abandoning the interior mission projects altogether.[32] In rare cases, the Indigenous peoples themselves, not wanting to lose their status as Spanish subjects, petitioned to be allowed to move to safer locations. In 1709, the pueblo of Letegua sent a petition to the governor of Honduras asking for permission to move the entire town to a location where Mosquito attacks would be less likely.[33] Missionaries in the region also frequently requested additional soldiers.[34] These requests were rarely heeded, however, and flight remained the most effective strategy for defense. Moreover, the reach of Mosquito raiding only seemed to be growing, as expeditions reached all the way to Peten, earning the attention of the governor of Campeche.[35]

The situation was similar in Costa Rica. The mountainous Talamanca region to the south of Cartago had been Costa Rica's flagship mission field since the 1690s when the influential Franciscan Recollect Antonio Margil de Jesús revived Spanish presence in the area. However, these missions too began to fall within the rapidly expanding orbit of Mosquito raiding. A report by missionaries Antonio Andrade and Pablo de Rebullida, for example, referenced specific incursions into the Talamanca region in 1708.[36] This claim was later corroborated by interrogations of captured Mosquito sailors in 1710, who explained that the Mosquito occasionally took captives in Talamanca by traveling up the Estrella River and attacking vulnerable Indigenous settlements.[37] These raids intensified an ongoing pattern of native flight, which the missionaries countered with increasingly heavy-handed tactics. This approach proved unsustainable, and in 1709, a coalition of Talamancans drove the missionaries out in a widespread uprising that exposed the fragility of frontier missions and of Costa Rica more generally.[38]

Within these circumstances, Central American authorities began to view the Mosquito as a serious threat to ongoing missionization and conquest efforts, and a growing chorus of officials began calling for the extermination of the Mosquito. By the end of the first decade of the eighteenth century, Spanish authorities in Guatemala, Honduras, and Nicaragua had adopted this view. As early as 1707, officials in Granada were building a case for taking action, and in October of that year, the Nicaraguan governor collected interviews from several Indigenous Nicaraguans and Hondurans who had recently escaped from Mosquito captivity.[39] During the interviews, the officials pressed for information about the size of Mosquito settlements, the geography of the area, the Mosquitos' political organization, and their relationship with the English.[40] They then forwarded the information to the president's office in Guatemala, which assembled a war council in October 1708 to decide on a course of action.[41] Recognizing the difficulty of launching an expedition without more information, Guatemalan officials tried working with a French ship captain who had offered to raid the Mosquito coast and capture slaves for guides, though the effort yielded no tangible results.[42] Officials also sent an expedition of roughly one hundred men from Cobán that attempted to reach Mosquito territory overland. However, the group made little progress over the difficult terrain, and even the guides could not find a viable path.[43]

The urgency to address the Mosquito threat only increased when soldiers stationed at Fort La Inmaculada at the mouth of the San Juan River reported a Mosquito attack in March of 1709.[44] The incident was relatively minor, with the main result being the theft of a Spanish canoe.[45] Still, the incident was alarming given that the same Mosquito contingent had also reportedly skirmished with a militia outpost in the Matina Valley just south of the San Juan River.[46] Moreover, if the fort at the mouth of the river proved ineffective in deterring the Mosquito, then the entire San Juan River, as well as the important Nicaraguan city of Granada, might become vulnerable as well. These fears seemed to be further confirmed in August 1709, when reports indicated that Mosquito explorers had indeed traversed the entire San Juan River and arrived at Lake Granada by working with their own Indigenous guides.[47] In response to these events, officials in the Guatemalan capital assembled again the following year to report the situation to the king and appeal for support.[48] The meeting resulted in a packet of hundreds of pages of documents describing Mosquito attacks over the previous decade, recommending the extermination of the Mosquito, and petitioning for resources to support these efforts.

It was against this background that the Mosquito king opened diplomatic relations with Costa Rica in 1711 by offering a protection alliance in exchange for commercial privileges. Given the difficulties that Mosquito raiding had created for missionaries, as well as reports that the Mosquito traded with Spanish enemies such as the English, hardliners in Nicaragua, Guatemala, and Honduras continued to label the Mosquito unequivocally as enemies. On the other hand, Costa Ricans living at the frontier had no choice but to take the offer seriously. Accordingly, frontier actors in places like the Matina Valley took a different approach to the Mosquito threat and ultimately came to play a key role in shaping Central American geopolitical outcomes for decades to come.

The Ongoing English Conquest and Early Mosquito Ties, 1670–1710

Even though Spanish conquest had a much longer history in Central America compared to the colonization efforts of the English, both these expansionist projects took on new vigor in the late seventeenth century. Following the Royal Navy's occupation of Jamaica and other strategic Caribbean islands, the 1670 Treaty of Madrid attempted to clarify English and Spanish colonial holdings by recognizing the right of each empire to keep the colonies that they possessed at the time.[49] This agreement did clarify the status of visibly occupied sites such as Jamaica, and the island's inhabitants gained a degree of respite from the constant fear that the Spanish would try to reconquer it. On the other hand, the treaty left the status of Central America's Caribbean borderlands somewhat ambiguous, and debates later emerged regarding what it meant to possess territory. From the Spanish perspective, conquistadores had in theory conquered the isthmus back in the sixteenth century. Therefore, even though Spanish institutions were minimal to nonexistent in much of Caribbean Central America, the Spanish argued that the treaty upheld their claims to the entire isthmus. English officials later challenged these claims, however, arguing that the Spanish had never actually conquered these territories in the first place, thus making English expansion to the mainland perfectly legitimate, even within the terms of the Treaty of Madrid.

Against this backdrop, English expansion to the mainland generally followed a pattern of first establishing informal settlements or "pirate nests," which gained logistical support from the English foothold in Jamaica and sometimes gained official recognition from the Crown.[50] Lacking strong state support, however, English colonialism in the Caribbean was long characterized by vulnerability and the need to seek outside protection. Soon after taking Jamaica in 1655, for example, the commanding officer of the English troops, Colonel Doyley, invited the buccaneers of Tortuga to help defend the exposed island from the expected Spanish retaliation. Recent research has questioned to what extent these pirate auxiliaries were intended to provide military services as opposed to logistical support in feeding the island.[51] Nevertheless, the episode illustrates a broader pattern among English settlers in the Caribbean borderlands: they were intensely aware of their vulnerability, and many colonial practices were rooted in fear and reactionism.

The ongoing fear of slave revolts provides another salient example. Even after the Treaty of Madrid in 1670 diminished the threat of a Spanish invasion, Jamaica's incipient plantation economy and heavy reliance on enslaved labor left the island facing the constant specter of revolts. These fears appears frequently in Jamaican colonial documents around the turn of the eighteenth century and were seemingly confirmed by the outbreak of a small-scale slave uprising in 1704.[52] The planters managed to quell the rebellion on this occasion, but fears that the enslaved would soon become unmanageable only increased.[53]

Therefore, as both the formal and informal colonies of the English remained vulnerable, the Mosquito Confederation came to play a central role in the English colonial project. Trade ties, for example, dated at least as far back as the Providence Island venture of the 1630s, where English leaders saw establishing positive relations with the Mosquito as an important step in later expansion to the mainland.[54] The early English settlers of Jamaica also carried on frequent trade with the Mosquito. In fact, it is possible that one of the most powerful Mosquito chiefs even visited London around the same time, an event referenced in the travel writings of an English sailor known only by the initials M. W. who visited the Mosquito Coast in 1699.[55] The exact details of this possible diplomatic visit remain unconfirmed, but multiple sources corroborate that in 1687, the Mosquito king Jeremy I visited Jamaica to meet the newly arrived English governor.[56] The latter was hesitant to sign any formal agreements, yet the English ultimately welcomed Mosquito support, with the same Mosquito king reportedly sending troops to Jamaica to help catch runaway slaves a few years later.[57]

Regarding economic ties, English castaway turned travel writer Nathaniel Uring provided interesting details. For example, Uring's account describes the lucrative trade in tortoiseshell, which was already well established by the time of his 1711 trek through the Mosquito Coast. Mosquito fisherman handled the extractive labor of turtle-hunting, setting out in seasonal hunting voyages all along the coast. Jamaican merchants then sent sloops to the Mosquito Coast to purchase the quantities of shell, which could be sold for a substantial profit in English markets. Uring also observed that Jamaican merchants purchased Amerindian slaves from the Mosquito. The scale of this trade was relatively small, though Mosquito fleets did frequently raid vulnerable Indigenous settlements along the coast, selling many of these slaves to the English.[58]

Uring described these processes in general terms without citing specific events, but a well-documented example of this system occurred in 1719. In that year, a particularly large Mosquito fleet, after hunting for turtles at Bocas del Toro on the coast of present-day Panama, forcibly enslaved an estimated eighty-five captives from an Amerindian village on the nearby Cocle River. The Mosquito fleet then stopped for supplies at Matina Valley, where King Jeremy explained that he already had English buyers lined up, whom the fleet was going directly to meet.[59] Independent reports then confirmed that the rendezvous was successful, with English merchants from Jamaica purchasing the tortoiseshell along with most of the captives.[60]

The Mosquito also proved vital to English legal claims relative to other colonial powers. According to M. W., the Mosquito king Jeremy already considered himself an English subject, proudly displaying a royal commission. M. W. went on to claim that King Jeremy's father had actually traveled to England, and that he had received the royal commission during the visit. M. W. also referenced King Jeremy's visit to Jamaica in 1687 as further evidence of the Mosquito leader's affinity with the English. It is not clear if M. W. intentionally used his account to bolster English claims. Indeed, the stated purpose of the account was entertainment only, hoping to "divert the reader with the very strange manners and customs" of the Amerindians.[61] Nonetheless, the account previewed the arguments of English officials who later defended mainland colonies in the contested Caribbean borderlands by claiming that the Mosquito became English subjects long before the 1713 Treaty of Utrecht, and possibly even before the 1670 Treaty of Madrid.

Courting Mosquito goodwill, therefore, became fundamental to expanding English settler colonialism on the mainland. In addition to providing physical support for English colonial ventures, the Mosquito Confederation also played a key role in the legal arguments that the English used in order to gain recognition of their territorial claims. Moreover, by the same logic, English officials recognized that the Mosquito rather than the Spanish had the right to grant territory to settlers on the Mosquito Coast, though this meant that the English needed the Mosquito to certify the necessary land grants and treaties to justify these claims. Consequently, the English found themselves dependent on the Mosquito Confederation for Central American land claims in both local and global contexts. For the most part, the Mosquito were dependable allies, and the English conquest grew stronger with their support. However, the English understood that these vital allies were beyond their control, and fear of losing Mosquito support became a recurring theme characterizing English colonization efforts in Central America throughout the century.

The Mosquito Confederation and Matina Negotiations, 1711–1713

Against this background of intertwining Mosquito, Spanish, and English conquests, a critical series of events began in April of 1711 when a small group of Mosquito mariners passing by Costa Rica's Matina Valley decided to make an incursion at the Matina port of Suerre. The intruders quickly overpowered the small guard of unsuspecting militia, proceeding to sneak onto a nearby cacao hacienda where they took several captives, including an *ayudante* named Joseph de Chaverria, a laborer named Francisco Jimenez, and a Black slave named Reimundo. The raiders then carried the captives back to Mosquito territory, keeping them as slaves. The fate of these captives changed dramatically when they attempted to escape from the Mosquito village where they were held. The escape did not go well, and the captives soon became lost in the unfamiliar terrain. Desperate to survive, they surrendered to a group of Zambo-Mosquito fishermen who happened to pass by, and the prisoners soon found themselves at the court of King Jeremy.[62]

In June 1711, roughly one month after a meeting between the Costa Rican captives and King Jeremy, a small delegation of one Zambo captain, four soldiers, and a "mestizo" translator carried some of these captives to the Matina Valley where they made port at Suerre. Upon their arrival, the Mosquito released the first captive, Francisco Jimenez, along with an Amerindian woman named Maria who had been captured in the Chontales region.[63] Jimenez's message, delivered on behalf of King Jeremy II, was a simple one: the Mosquito king wanted a peaceful relationship with Costa Rica, and he offered protection in exchange for trading privileges at the coastal ports of the Matina Valley. After dropping off Jimenez, the piragua did not stay long enough to hear the Costa Rican decision, but the Mosquito captain promised to return soon to continue negotiations.[64]

The Mosquito captain kept his word, and in August of 1711, he returned to drop off another delegation of released captives.[65] In this second encounter, Matina authorities once again received the delegations graciously, though they balked at entering into any official treaty agreements. In theory, therefore, the treaty remained pending. In practice, however, the representatives of the Mosquito king had succeeded in establishing a precedent for peaceful interactions at Costa Rican ports. From the Mosquito perspective, this distinction mattered little: from this point on, Mosquito leaders expected that they would be treated as allies in Costa Rican ports.

As a caveat, it is possible Jeremy's 1711 plan to negotiate with the Spanish did not yet have the backing of the entire confederation. Jeremy's messengers implied that the treaty applied to all Mosquito factions, though the messengers specified that the king was the one who initiated the negotiations and that they could not necessarily speak on behalf of other leaders. By 1713, however, the entire confederation council had decided that allying with Costa Rica was a worthwhile endeavor, and in June of that year, a more impressive delegation—six war piraguas filled with reportedly one hundred Zambo and Tawira soldiers—arrived in the Matina Valley. Not only was the size of this delegation intimidating but among the ambassadors were two high-ranking members of the Mosquito council: the Zambo general Peter and the Tawira governor John Hannibal. King Jeremy II was not present at the meeting, though he was still well represented, having personally selected another captive to be released on his behalf: a trusted Spanish-speaking *pardo* named Francisco Corella who had served for years as a translator.[66]

The delegation arrived at the Matina Valley's port of Moin on June 20, 1713, and after exchanging signs of peace, the Mosquito guards left Corella in the custody of the ranking officer of the Matina militia. Corella then traveled to the Costa Rican capital of Cartago to deliver his message. Just as Francisco Jimenez had done two years before, Corella confirmed that the Mosquito leaders were truly committed to establishing friendly relations with the inhabitants of the Matina Valley. After briefly describing the Zambo territory where he had lived for the past five years, Corella mentioned that Jeremy also had a treaty with the English in Jamaica but stated that this treaty was neither permanent nor exclusive. As in 1711, the proposed treaty stressed commerce, yet this time, the Mosquito also suggested a more far-reaching military alliance, offering to use their growing fleet to protect Spanish shipping along the coast from pirate attacks.[67]

After dropping off Corella, the fleet promised to return within forty days and headed further down the coast to spend a few weeks hunting turtles, as well as enslaving additional captives from among the free Indigenous groups. In keeping with the plan, the convoy then returned on July 31, 1713, to hear the Costa Rican response. The Matina militia once again greeted the delegation graciously, bringing both Francisco Corella and Joseph de Chaverria back to the port to facilitate a peaceful discussion. Peter and Hannibal then released even more captives in a show of good faith, including a man from San Pedro de Ulua who like Corella had served as a Mosquito translator.[68] After spending the night at the port, the delegation received word on August 1, 1713, that the Costa Rican governor still did not have an official answer on the treaty and that in the meantime, the convoy should continue its journey.[69] Still, this marked the fourth peaceful Mosquito visit in the last two years, and while the details of the treaty remained unresolved, the Mosquito Confederation had effectively established a diplomatic presence in Matina. Accordingly, the confederation's leaders came to expect that Mosquito convoys could count on being received peacefully in future encounters.

Spanish Reactions to the Matina Negotiations, 1711–1713

From the Spanish perspective, however, the opening negotiations with the Mosquito were less successful: even though local authorities in Costa Rica came to tacitly accept Mosquito overtures of peace, higher authorities in Guatemala exerted pressure on them to reject the peace terms, creating a tension that would characterize Spanish policy toward the Mosquito for decades. When the first Mosquito delegation arrived in the Matina Valley in June 1711, the deputation was unintimidating, described by Costa Rican reports as only a single piragua—one of the large, versatile, oceangoing canoes that the Mosquito used for long-distance travel—carrying a Mosquito captain, four mariners, a "mestizo" interpreter, and a few captives who delivered the peace offer on behalf of the Mosquito king.[70] Unsure how to respond, the Matina lieutenant arranged for the informants to travel with him to Cartago in order to testify before the governor, Lorenzo Antonio de Granada y Balbín. According to the informants, the Mosquito king—called by the Hispanicized name "Bernabe" in Spanish documents—had decided to organize the peace delegation because the Mosquito were interested in trading in Matina. Consequently, the Mosquito offered to cease all raiding in the province if the Costa Ricans would allow Mosquito fleets to trade peacefully in Matina. Reports also framed Jeremy's offer in the language of submission, claiming that the Mosquito were willing to become "vassals" of the Spanish king.[71]

Completely dependent on the released captives for information, Costa Rican officials in Cartago approached the news with cautious optimism. On the one hand, they were not yet sure if the Mosquito offer was sincere. On the other hand, the same officials—with the 1709 Talamanca uprising still fresh on their minds, along with the ongoing possibility of pirate and Mosquito raids—were desperate to reduce the number of threats facing the province and so had to take the proposal seriously. From the Costa Rican perspective, therefore, a Mosquito alliance held the promise of alleviating security pressures that had come to threaten the very existence of the province.

When Governor Granada y Balbín sent a report of the Mosquito visit to Guatemala, however, Central America's higher officials considered the treaty proposal with a different set of priorities. The Costa Rican governor completed his report on July 4, sending it from Cartago to the capital in Santiago de Guatemala. It took over a month for the letter to arrive, with the Guatemalan fiscal Joseph Guthierrez finally opening it on August 8. The matter then remained pending for almost two weeks until the fiscal finally penned a definitive response on August 20: the Mosquito were officially named enemies, and the proposed peace was impermissible.[72] Guthierrez justified the decision in part by citing the history of Mosquito hostilities in other Spanish frontier provinces, yet this was only a minor issue. The main point of contention was trade. Specifically, the fiscal was aware of the reports that the Mosquito traded regularly with the English, which was illegal given Spain's monopolistic commercial laws. Consequently, the fiscal determined that any exchanges with Mosquito traders would, by definition, also be considered contraband. In a legal sense, therefore, the sincerity of the Mosquito commitment to peace was irrelevant. Unless the Mosquito provided proof that they had severed ties with the English in order to become exclusive trading partners with the Spanish, no treaty could be valid.[73] The fiscal went on to specify that this decision applied not only to Costa Rica but also to Nicaragua, Honduras, and any other provinces that might have received similar offers from Mosquito leaders.[74] It is also significant that this was not fiscal Guthierrez's first time addressing the Mosquito issue, as he had participated in the previous efforts calling for Mosquito extermination.[75]

Guthierrez's hardline interpretation of the situation then gained strength as even more impassioned Mosquito detractors joined the debate. In November 1711, Nicaraguan bishop Fray Benito Garret y Arlovi began circulating a series of letters to the Guatemalan captain general, the king, and other provincial leaders that harshly denounced the Mosquito as deplorable savages. Appealing to the religious sensibilities of his readers, Garret y Arlovi claimed the Mosquito were committing horrible sacrileges against the church by attacking missions, murdering converts, and defiling sacred symbols. Garret y Arlovi's sources were unclear and, making the literal veracity of his claims even more questionable, his impassioned descriptions did not match earlier eyewitness reports from frontier missions that had criticized the Mosquito in milder terms, mostly accusing them of inspiring mission flight rather than perpetrating unrestrained violence. Nonetheless, the bishop presented the situation as if it were common practice for the Mosquito to raze entire missions in a bloody campaign to eradicate Christian influence completely. On this basis, the bishop argued that officials should not only deny any Mosquito treaty proposals but should actively work toward Mosquito extermination.[76]

Despite Garret y Arlovi's incendiary rhetoric, Costa Rican officials remained unconvinced that the bishop's extermination plan was either possible or desirable. For his part, Governor Granada y Balbín agreed to at least pay lip service to the fiscal's demand to label Mosquito trade as contraband. At the same time, however, he certainly did not force the Matina guards to attack Mosquito emissaries, despite their being labeled enemies of the church and Spanish Crown. Instead, Costa Rican officials generally allowed the Mosquito peace to go into effect unofficially while they waited for another opportunity to build a legal case for making this a recognized practice.[77]

This opportunity arose in June 1713 when the larger delegation of six piraguas arrived in Matina. Paralleling the 1711 negotiations, the Mosquito released several captives into the custody of the Matina officials, and these former prisoners served as messengers delivering the proposed terms of peace.[78] By this time, a new governor in Costa Rica—a man named José Antonio Lacayo de Briones y Palacios—had replaced Granada de Balbín, so when the captives arrived in Cartago to testify about their experiences, it was the governor's first time addressing any sort of interaction with the Mosquito. The primary captive spokesman of the Mosquito was a Black man—described in official documents as "pardo"—named Francisco Corella. Corella had been born in a pueblo called Atanagua in the jurisdiction of Granada, and after moving to Matina, was kidnapped by Mosquito slave raiders sometime around 1708. After quickly picking up the Mosquito language, Corella became a translator for the Mosquito king. Now entrusted with a diplomatic mission on the part of the king, Corella returned to Matina as a highly influential intermediary.

Perhaps intentionally, Corella's 1713 testimony refuted many of the accusations that had been leveled against the Mosquito by vociferous detractors such as Bishop Garret y Arlovi. For example, Corella countered the bishop's accusation that the Mosquito were savage and cruel, instead testifying that he and his fellow captives had received kind treatment. Moreover, Corella's testimony addressed Fiscal Guthierrez's earlier concerns about trade violations. Corella conceded that the Mosquito had been trading with the English, but he argued that this was not a permanent alliance. In fact, Corella testified that the Mosquito might be willing to cut ties with the English in order to secure an alliance with the Spanish. Finally, he stressed that the Mosquito bore no ill will toward Christians. In fact, they were open to learning about the faith and even receiving Spanish missionaries.[79]

The Costa Rican governor spent several weeks in July working with the Matina lieutenant Francisco Ibarra to prepare a package of documents reporting the new developments to Guatemalan authorities. Still, officials in Guatemala remained stubborn. After a lengthy delay, the captain general's office finally penned a decision November 6, 1713, more than four months after the Mosquito delegation had first arrived in Matina. Once again, Guatemalan officials rejected the proposed treaty, even citing the precedent set by Fiscal Guthierrez's decision two years earlier: since Guatemalan officials could not verify that the Mosquito would stop trading with the English, Mosquito promises to protect Costa Rica and accept Christianity did not matter. Consequently, Guatemala stipulated as a prerequisite for any treaty that the Mosquito agree to abandon their homeland on the Mosquito Coast and resettle in Spanish missions.[80]

Conclusion

As the events and processes described in this chapter illustrate, the period of 1687 to 1713 was critical in developing the economic, political, and social practices that would come to characterize the Mosquito Kingdom. Whereas the Mosquito already had a reputation as skilled hunters, warriors, and mariners, it was during this period that they also forged a novel political system capable of conquest. At the center of these practices was the Mosquito Confederation itself, which united a significant proportion of the dispersed Miskitu-speaking peoples under the leadership of a central council. This council convened regularly to plan commercial, diplomatic, and military activities that required more manpower than any individual Mosquito leader could assemble on his own. Perhaps indicating the growing cosmopolitan nature of Mosquito society, the central council members took titles such as king, governor, and general that were at least translatable to English and Spanish if not full loan words. Nonetheless, early accounts of Mosquito council meetings and decision-making indicate that this system was not a foreign imposition but rather the product of Mosquito thinkers who designed a political program unique to the culture, way of life, and geopolitical vision of the Mosquito themselves.

The most fundamental component of this program was alliance-making. Indeed, whereas King Jeremy I on his own did not command enough support to coordinate long-distance expeditions large enough to overwhelm any village or militia outpost along the way, he began to approximate this power by working closely with other Mosquito headmen such as Hannibal and Peter. And by the time Jeremy II assumed the kingship, these alliances were strong enough to press diplomatic relations with the neighboring province of Costa Rica from a position of strength. As this move indicates, foreign alliances were also a key component of the Mosquito strategy, which even before the formation of the confederation had involved working closely with English settlers and other Indigenous groups not only to trade in goods but, even more importantly, to trade in knowledge. Combining their newfound manpower with geographic and linguistic knowledge gained from these alliances, the Mosquito created the unified fleet system that came to characterize Mosquito power both symbolically and concretely. Indeed, the fleet system expanded Mosquito access to crucial resources such as turtle hunting grounds and, perhaps even more characteristic of imperial powers, sustained the slave system through which the confederation forcibly extracted additional knowledge and labor from unwilling subjects. In this way, the Mosquito Confederation acquired the ability to do what empires do, and by 1713, the Mosquito conquest was in full force.

CHAPTER 2

Consolidating the Mosquito Imperial System, 1713–1729

As Francisco Corella stood on the riverbank to receive the priest's blessing, he understood the importance of his mission. It was the morning of April 9, 1722, and the inhabitants of Costa Rica's remote Matina Valley had gathered for mass before Corella and two companions embarked on a difficult journey up the coast in hopes of reaching Dacora, a settlement deep within the territory of the Indigenous Mosquito Kingdom. Even though Matina had maintained an informal peace with the Mosquito for years, higher officials in Guatemala and Spain had labeled them enemies and were now pressuring the Costa Ricans to cut ties. The governor of Costa Rica—a relatively new arrival to the province—had no direct experience with the Mosquito and therefore was inclined to simply follow orders. Corella, however, argued that this policy would needlessly provoke the Mosquito, leading to dangerous repercussions for the Matina Valley. An experienced diplomat and translator who had led negotiations between Costa Rica and the Mosquito for several years, Corella eventually received permission to visit Mosquito territory in hopes of negotiating a stronger treaty that would satisfy Guatemalan authorities. Now as the expedition set out, Corella found the fate of the Matina Valley in his own hands.[1]

The purpose of this chapter is to evaluate Mosquito history during the period from roughly 1713–1729. As the events described here demonstrate, this period was characterized by the maturing of the Mosquito Confederation's policies into an empire-like program: controlling foreign ports as bases for further expansion, asserting the right to establish norms of trade and legitimate violence, enacting gunboat diplomacy to force recognition of these norms, and carrying out these activities under the careful direction of a closely unified confederation council. Moreover, whereas it is likely that these practices originated through the new thinking of specific Mosquito leaders, the political system did not depend on the personalities of these leaders; rather, the core practices that emerged during this period continued as established norms in subsequent generations of leaders. Accordingly, this chapter argues that this period was crucial for establishing the internal political structures and foreign policy practices that would characterize the confederation until its eventual collapse into civil war at the end of the century.

These processes had numerous implications for the ongoing Spanish conquest as well. Within this context of Mosquito expansion, practices on the ground often remained out of sync with official policy. Costa Rican ports, for example, largely accepted Mosquito norms of trade and diplomacy even while official Guatemalan and Iberian policy declared the Mosquito enemies. Practices also varied over time. Costa Rican officials in the capital of Cartago did eventually try to put the hardline stance against the Mosquito into practice for a brief period in the early 1720s, yet after swift reprisals from Mosquito fleets, the more knowledgeable actors on the ground quickly reverted to treating the Mosquito as allies. Regarding the English conquest, the Mosquito remained valuable allies, providing economic support through trade as well as military protection. Nonetheless, English settlers continued to worry about the growing Mosquito ties with Costa Rica.

In describing these processes, this chapter further highlights how Indigenous and African-descended peoples were the primary actors on the ground shaping "Spanish" relations with the Mosquito. Indigenous peoples living at or just beyond the Spanish frontier had particularly intense contact with the Mosquito Confederation. Moving between Spanish and Mosquito spheres of influence, these peoples frequently became informants, influencing both the policies and practices of the Spanish as well as the Mosquito. Moreover, as exemplified by Francisco Corella, people of African descent were likewise on the front lines of handling Mosquito relations. People bearing the racial labels of "negro," "pardo," or "mulato" formed a significant portion of frontier militias that guarded Caribbean ports, and free blacks frequently served as messengers to the capital. Furthermore, slaves and free blacks were occasionally caught up in Mosquito slave raids, and if they regained their freedom, they became invaluable informants or translators. Consequently, this chapter not only details an important phase in the Mosquito Confederation's solidification as a regional power but also encourages reflection on the extent to which global empires depended on diverse local actors, whose daily activities were necessary for converting imperialism from an idea in the metropole into a tangible reality in the colonies.

Mosquito Southern Expansion and the Matina Truce, 1713–1720

Overall, the Mosquito Confederation's naval expansion of the 1710s was a major success, and by the end of the decade, the Mosquito had come to exert much greater influence in both intensity and geographic range. Toward the south, large expeditions routinely reached Bocas del Toro, using their overwhelming naval power as a basis for extracting tortoiseshell and slaves. And while small Mosquito fishing convoys and raiding parties were probably making this journey even before 1711, the size of these expeditions changed dramatically after the establishment of Matina as a reliable supply depot. Now, the expeditions grew into massive fleets capable of overwhelming free Indigenous settlements and coastal Spanish outposts alike. The large 1713 fleet that dropped off Francisco Corella provided an early indication of this trend. Whereas previous Mosquito encounters this far from Mosquito territory had always been described as comprising smaller groups, this particular convoy included over one hundred fighting men, who continued further down the coast to hunt, scout, negotiate, and raid before returning to Matina almost a month later during the return voyage.[2]

In subsequent years, this military component in long-distance voyages—as opposed to long-distance expeditions for fishing or small raids—became increasingly visible. For example, a Mosquito force attacked the Spanish militia at the mouth of the Cocle River in 1716, taking several captives.[3] Reports suggest that this particular attack was a small-scale affair, but it paved the way for a massive attack in 1719. In March of that year, a massive convoy of nine large war piraguas and other smaller vessels set out for Bocas del Toro carrying over one hundred fifty fighting men, in addition to several slaves and guides. After harvesting a large quantity of turtle shells for sale in Jamaica, the force invaded a Guaymi settlement near Portobelo, taking eighty-five captives—by far the largest documented slave raid up until this point.[4] King Jeremy II led the attack, and after securing the captives, the expedition set out on the long journey home, making two additional stops. First, the convoy stopped on the Island of Tovares, where Jeremy negotiated a truce with the local free Indigenous peoples by offering gifts such as blankets, hatchets, and machetes. This truce was apparently only a ruse, however, and the Mosquito used this opportunity to gain strategic intelligence for future raids—a process later described by escaped captives who witnessed the series of events.[5] Then, to address the logistical difficulties of such a large undertaking, the massive fleet took advantage of the previously established peace with Matina to make port and gather supplies for the return voyage, which now involved well over two hundred people.

The fleet arrived on April 3, 1719, and stayed for three days.[6] Indicating the planning that went into the large expedition, the Mosquito had sent word to Matina back in January to expect a visit from the king, so the Matina guard was not surprised at the fleet's arrival in April.[7] In addition to easing the supply burden of such a large force, Jeremy II used the stop in Matina to formally reaffirm his commitment to the ongoing peace. He even spoke briefly with Francisco Corella, who had continued living in Matina after his 1713 diplomatic mission on the confederation's behalf. For their part, the Costa Ricans still offered no formal acceptance of Jeremy's terms, but in practice, this mattered little: as long as Mosquito fleets could use the valley as a supply depot for long-distance expeditions, the confederation's navy would have a strong presence in the distant south, allowing privileged access to hawksbill turtle for hunting as well as access to vulnerable Indigenous settlements where the Mosquito took slaves for strategic knowledge, labor, and sale in English markets.

From the Mosquito perspective, therefore, the 1719 visit to Matina gave no reason to doubt that the Costa Rican alliance would continue as normal, and confederation leaders planned fleet activities accordingly. Following the expedition of Jeremy's large 1719 fleet, the Mosquito Confederation launched another fleet to the south in 1720. This time, the expedition used Matina as a staging ground before heading further south, arriving at the port of Moin on April 17 in preparation for maneuvers further down the coast. The fleet reportedly consisted of nine large war piraguas, supplemented by smaller vessels and two English cargo ships. King Jeremy II reportedly sailed with this expedition as well, though instead of disembarking to visit the port himself, he left the diplomatic duties to Governor Hannibal, who approached the port guard with a three piragua-escort. Hannibal received the usual welcome, conversing with the Matina officials through the trusted interpreter Francisco Corella. As a show of good faith to his allies, Hannibal reported that English agents had recently attempted to persuade the Mosquito to attack Matina, but that he and Jeremy had flatly refused. Hannibal also told the Matina guard about the fleet's current plan, which was to attack the Indigenous inhabitants of the nearby Island of Tovares. Finally, Hannibal requested that Matina have the customary food and supplies ready for the fleet on its return voyage.[8]

Hannibal then spent the night at the port, and in the morning, the fleet headed south toward the Island of Tovares. While still en route, the Mosquito fleet encountered a large group of Indigenous Tovares traveling by canoe, and rather than making a land invasion, they decided to enslave this group in a rapid naval assault. Furthermore, shortly after the attack, the fleet encountered a small group of French pirates whom the Mosquito arrested, confiscating additional boats to carry the Indigenous captives. The entire venture took roughly two weeks, and on May 2, the fleet arrived at Matina once again to pick up the requested supplies for the return voyage north.[9]

Additionally, the Mosquito naval presence expanded along the northern coast of present-day Honduras. Reports indicated that in this direction, expeditions reached at least as far as Puerto Caballos, where large fleets similarly overwhelmed free Indigenous peoples in slave raids, and here as well, strategic political and economic alliances provided an important complement to military force. For example, just as the Mosquito made routine stops in Matina when traveling south along Costa Rica, they also stopped at Trujillo when traveling north along Honduras.[10] In fact, a massive fleet of thirty piraguas made a show of force in San Pedro de Sula in December 1720, briefly skirmishing with the Honduran coast guard, which did little to slow the fleet.[11]

Moreover, the confederation also used its military prowess to cultivate stronger ties with the English in Jamaica. Even though the Mosquito negotiations with the English predated their more recent overtures to the Spanish by at least two decades, Mosquito leaders had maintained little direct contact with English officials, keeping up the alliance mostly through commerce with English merchants who arrived at the Mosquito Coast. In fact, whereas King Jeremy II had kept up regular contact with Costa Rica since his ascension in 1711, there is no documented evidence of his visiting Jamaica or sending delegates until June 1720. After the southern fleet's May expedition that passed through Costa Rica, King Jeremy II made his way to Jamaica in order to meet the new English governor in person. During the meeting, Jeremy II agreed to send a contingent of fifty Zambo warriors to help catch runaway slaves.[12] As with his promise to protect Matina, Jeremy II stayed true to his word, sending the troops later in November 1720.[13]

Diego De La Haya Fernández and New Tensions in Costa Rica, 1713–1719

Even as the Mosquito Confederation was beginning to count on Costa Rica as an allied province, debates at different levels of Spanish government made the tacit peace increasingly tenuous. At the time of Guatemala's second rejection of Mosquito peace terms in 1713, officials on the Iberian Peninsula still had yet to offer any opinion on the matter. Soon after Fiscal Guthierrez's initial decision in 1711, Guatemalan officials attempted to give a strong voice to Mosquito detractors by forwarding Bishop Garret y Arlovi's passionate condemnations to the Spanish king, along with a few independent reports of Mosquito attacks. These efforts worked, and the Crown did eventually side with the hardline position of the fiscal and the bishop, agreeing that a treaty would be unwise and that the Mosquito deserved extermination. On these grounds, the Crown officially ordered officials in Mexico, Tierra Firme, and Guatemala to help bring this about.[14] However, this decision was not written until April 1714, and it carried little force when it finally arrived in the Americas, now several years removed from the events that it was supposed to address.[15] The governor of Tierra Firme, for example, replied in July 1715 that he simply could not comply with the order to help with the Mosquito extermination because he lacked the resources.[16] And Costa Rica had already established a precedent for peacefully receiving and supplying Mosquito convoys. Interestingly, the king's request for help in exterminating the Mosquito even reached as far as the Philippines, where authorities in Manila finally replied in 1719 to politely decline as well.[17] Accordingly, the Crown's intervention in the debate over Mosquito peace negotiations ultimately had little bearing on how events transpired.

In fact, the only province that took any concrete steps to follow through on the extermination efforts was Honduras, in an extremely limited and ineffective way. In the spring of 1717, authorities in San Pedro de Sula outfitted a small expedition of two piraguas to explore the coast. However, the expedition was attacked by a joint Mosquito and English convoy, and the two piraguas along with their arms and supplies were lost.[18] In response, Honduran authorities spent the summer scraping together resources to build two new piraguas and outfit a new expedition, appealing to Guatemalan authorities for funding as a royal expenditure.[19] The new piraguas were eventually finished, yet the efforts failed to result in a new expedition. According to the Guatemalan fiscal, a series of earthquakes interrupted the preparations, and authorities decided to call off the expedition.[20]

In the meantime, Central American authorities in Guatemala, Honduras, and Nicaragua continued to gather evidence in support of labeling the Mosquito enemies. In 1717, for example, Nicaraguan authorities interviewed a recently escaped captive named Micaela Gomez, a baptized, Spanish-speaking, "free mulata" who had lived among the Mosquito as a slave for about ten years. In this instance, Central American authorities became dependent on the specialized knowledge of a Black woman for information about what was happening at the frontier, and given Micaela's previous status as a married, Christian woman, the testimony contributed to the narrative that the Mosquito were natural enemies of God and the Crown. Accordingly, Guatemalan authorities forwarded the declaration to Madrid along with the documents about the failed Honduran expeditions in order to continue building a case for Mosquito extermination.[21]

In practice, however, no additional efforts to attack the Mosquito manifested for several years, and despite higher authorities labeling the Mosquito enemies, officials in Costa Rica's Matina Valley established a precedent for receiving Mosquito visitors with diplomatic courtesy. At least in the short term, therefore, Francisco Corella's work as an ambassador for the Mosquito king proved more consequential than Spanish royal orders to exterminate the Mosquito, and thus Costa Rica maintained an informal truce with the Mosquito following the first diplomatic encounter in 1711.

This truce became more complicated, however, when Diego de la Haya Fernández became the new governor of Costa Rica in 1718. On the one hand, De la Haya understood how vulnerable Costa Rica was, so like his predecessors, he remained open to the idea of negotiating a peace treaty with the Mosquito. On the other hand, De la Haya prioritized eliminating the legal gray areas that his predecessors had indulged, especially regarding contraband trade. Accordingly, the new governor was not satisfied with the ongoing informal peace and sought to negotiate a formal treaty that would still follow the letter of Spanish commercial laws.

De la Haya's first opportunity to start building this case came in April 1719 when a large delegation headed by King Jeremy II himself arrived in Matina. Indicating that peace was already the norm, the Matina guard was actually expecting the king's arrival, having received advance notice of the visit three months earlier from a passing Mosquito convoy.[22] When Jeremy's delegation finally arrived, the militia guard welcomed the visitors with customary gifts and provisions.[23] The visit lasted three days, and Francisco Corella—who had stayed in Matina after being released from King Jeremy's service in 1713—served as the primary translator, corroborating the peaceful intentions of his former master. The delegation ultimately left the treaty unresolved, though Jeremy promised to return within a year with the rest of his captains to continue the discussion.[24]

As in previous visits, witnesses then had to travel from Matina to Cartago—a journey that took express couriers at least three days and mule carts up to two weeks—to offer official testimonies before the governor. In 1719, however, the tone of the follow-up interviews was somewhat different. Whereas De la Haya did not go as far as to say that the guard should have attacked the Mosquito visitors, he drew a clear distinction between diplomatic and commercial activities. Thus, while he interpreted diplomatic encounters as legal despite the king's extermination orders, De la Haya still considered Mosquito trade as contraband, and he pressured the witnesses to confess if anyone had conducted any trading during the visit. Understanding the danger of contraband accusations, witnesses had to confirm under oath that they had only given food and basic supplies as a diplomatic courtesy, and that no commercial exchanges had taken place.[25] Accordingly, the ongoing peace between the Mosquito Confederation and Costa Rica's Matina still held, though the increased scrutiny from Governor De la Haya made the arrangement increasingly fragile. Over the next few years, the governor's policies would only alienate the Mosquito further, eventually leading to retaliation.

Mosquito Expansion and New Challenges, 1720–1722

At the same time that Costa Rican authorities were placing the tacit alliance with the Mosquito under increased scrutiny, the confederation began to experience a new set of challenges to its rapid expansion. One of these came from the growing threat of piracy. As exemplified by Jeremy's treaty negotiations with Matina, protection agreements were a fundamental part of Mosquito diplomacy. Significantly, the agreement with Costa Rica offered Mosquito protection on two fronts: first, Matina would be off limits to Mosquito raiders themselves; and second, the confederation would use its fleet to defend Matina against non-Mosquito threats. Negotiating in this way, the confederation asserted a degree of imperial influence. Whereas Mosquito expansion did not necessarily conquer territories or incorporate them under the day-to-day administration of Mosquito governance, the Mosquito

Confederation did assert the right to a sort of monopoly on military violence along large swaths of the coast. Significantly, evidence suggests that the council was successful in these efforts as small-scale, independent Mosquito raids such as the one that led to the capture of Jeremy's first Costa Rican ambassadors in 1711 disappeared from the documentary record in Costa Rica at the same time that the large, confederated fleets began appearing in Matina.

However, achieving this monopoly on violence also meant waging an anti-piracy campaign in order to—in the words of one Matina officer—"clean the coasts of pirates."[26] Here the confederation had some early successes, indicated for example by reports of Hannibal's 1720 rout of French pirates near the Island of Tovares.[27] In the following years, however, the anti-piracy campaign became more challenging. For example, a major setback occurred in April 1721 when a failed rendezvous left part of the fleet exposed to attack. The well-documented incident happened near Matina, which is where the rendezvous had been planned. On April 2, 1721, an advanced guard of six piraguas, one cargo ship, and roughly eighty-five armed men neared the Matina port of Moin in full view of the guards. Instead of approaching the port as usual, the fleet camped overnight on the nearby beach until the next morning when Francisco Corella and one of the militia officers took a canoe out to welcome the visitors. None of the confederation's central council members were present, but the fleet captains explained that Governor Hannibal was close behind with another six piraguas. As in the previous year, the plan was to invade the Island of Tovares in another slaving expedition. In the meantime, the captains intended to use Matina as a staging ground, gathering supplies and waiting for the rest of the fleet. The militia ultimately acceded to the request, allowing the fleet to stay and gather food.[28] Unlike previous years, however, the expedition turned out to be a disaster. Before Hannibal arrived to assemble the entire fleet, a group of French corsairs attacked, sinking several of the piraguas. This effectively ended the expedition.[29]

Another challenge facing the Mosquito Confederation in the early 1720s was the increasing unreliability of its Costa Rican allies. An early example of the brewing tension with Matina occurred only a few months after the April 1721 pirate attack. The confederation remained determined to control the southern coast, launching a massive fleet only a few months later composed of ten large war piraguas, sixteen smaller boats, and as many as five hundred people.[30] Hannibal himself led the force, arriving at Matina's port of Suerre on October 10, 1721, expecting to gather the usual supplies before continuing down the coast to hunt a group of French pirates—presumably the same band responsible for the previous attack. However, as Hannibal approached the port with a small guard, rather than greeting the Mosquito governor with diplomatic honors, the Matina militia rejected Hannibal's approach. At one point, the militia even opened fire. A brief standoff ensued, and while no one was injured, Hannibal was furious at this treatment by his longtime allies. Eventually, Francisco Corella and another militia officer arrived to diffuse the situation, setting out in Corella's canoe under a flag of truce to meet with Hannibal offshore. Speaking through Corella, the officer tried to explain that the soldiers who had opened fire were new to Matina, and that they did now know that Hannibal was a friend. This reasoning only partially assuaged Hannibal's anger, who did agree to come ashore to continue the visit as planned, though he sent orders to his fleet to raze the entire valley if he did not return safely.[31]

Combined with the depletion of the fleet at the hands of pirates, the suddenly questionable loyalty of the Costa Ricans represented the second major threat to the confederation's southern strategy in only a few months. Accordingly, Hannibal worked urgently to stabilize the situation, pressing the Costa Ricans to formalize the long-standing truce. No longer satisfied with the informal agreement, Hannibal demanded an official title from the governor of Cartago, as well as a series of gifts such as a silver-tipped cane to signify his official status.[32] These items Hannibal saw as fair recognition of the confederation's ongoing work to defend the Matina Valley from pirates, which Hannibal claimed his fleet had done on several occasions. Moreover, as a further demonstration of good will, Hannibal offered to sell the Costa Ricans weapons in exchange for outfitting his fleet with food and supplies. After outlining these terms, Hannibal rejoined his fleet, promising to return shortly to collect his gifts. The fleet then continued its journey down the coast, leaving the Costa Ricans to consider the demands.[33]

The rest of the expedition went smoothly, reestablishing the Mosquito Confederation as a major power along the southern coast. After cruising a short distance, the fleet encountered a large group of free Talamancan Amerindians near the mouth of the Estrella River. Having been unable to raid the Island of Tovares earlier in the year as planned, Hannibal decided to make up the losses here, reportedly taking over one hundred prisoners. Hannibal claimed later that he had tried to negotiate with the Talamancans, attacking only after they had refused the fleet's demands. Nonetheless, regardless of why Hannibal chose to attack, he ultimately perpetrated the largest Mosquito slave raid on record. Afterward, the fleet decided to start the long return journey without continuing the hunt for pirates, a task made more difficult by the logistics of guarding and transporting so many captives. As previously planned, the fleet stopped again at Matina, arriving on November 10. This time, the port greeted Hannibal graciously, and indicating that Hannibal had succeeded in renegotiating the alliance, the ranking captain of the militia presented Hannibal with all requested gifts, officially naming Hannibal a captain of the Spanish coast guard. This renewed Hannibal's confidence in the Costa Ricans, and he promised to visit again with King Jeremy II and General Peter within the next three to four months.[34]

The follow-up visit did not occur on schedule, however, as the confederation continued to face a series of challenges. To begin, the fleet was simply exhausted, and Mosquito leaders needed time to repair their piraguas before sending another southern expedition. The exact itinerary of the fleet during this period remains unknown, but the confederation navy made at least one other long-distance expedition in January 1722, carrying out a successful slave-raid along the northern coast and stopping in Trujillo on the return voyage. It is also possible that the fleet suffered additional losses from fighting freebooters, particularly a band headed by a pirate referred to as Pitipie. Hannibal later explained that pirate attacks were a major cause of the depletion of the fleet, though sources are unclear if he was referring to the earlier attack in April 1721 or later events. Either way, when the estimated time for Hannibal's return voyage came up, he and the other confederation leaders were still rebuilding the fleet.[35]

Moreover, the Mosquito relationship with the English in Jamaica also became more complicated. English ship captains continued to pressure Mosquito leaders to attack Matina, and when the Mosquito repeatedly refused, the English became incensed.[36] These tensions grew even more complicated, then, when an unexpected Costa Rican delegation—composed of Francisco Corella and two Matina officials—appeared suddenly at Hannibal's primary residence in Dacora. The delegates arrived on April 19, 1722, and while Hannibal greeted them warmly, he was far too busy with other urgent matters to give the visitors his full attention. After explaining the situation with the depleted fleet, as well as the increasing pressure from their English trading partners to cut ties with Matina, Hannibal sent word to Jeremy and Peter in order to arrange a council meeting in Dacora. Hannibal then set out with a guard of soldiers to keep watch over the coast, leaving his son

Briton in charge of the visitors. Jeremy and Peter arrived soon after, echoing Hannibal's explanation that temporary difficulties with the fleet had delayed the usual southern expedition. Still, they reassured their guests that nothing had changed regarding the confederation's ongoing peace with Matina.[37]

The Costa Rican delegates stayed in Dacora for about three weeks, but before they left, they had a chance to witness the tensions with the English firsthand. As the council prepared to send the delegates back to Matina, an English trading vessel unexpectedly arrived, demanding that the Costa Rican delegates be arrested and carried to Jamaica. The Mosquito leaders refused, saying that the Costa Ricans were still friends of the confederation, and that their delegates had to be treated with respect. Furthermore, the Mosquito leaders argued that having a treaty with the Spanish in Costa Rica did not violate their agreement with the English, and they accused the English of hypocrisy since the Jamaican smugglers similarly traded with the Spanish at Havana.[38] Frustrated, the English merchants eventually left, and the Mosquito council prepared an official letter to be carried by Corella to the governor of Costa Rica. The letter reiterated the confederation's commitment to peace, though it explained that the Mosquito intended to continue trading with English Jamaica. All three principal headmen signed the letter, sending the delegates back in a three-piragua convoy led by Hannibal's brother-in-law Yorosel.[39]

The small escort arrived in Matina on May 29, 1722, and the port guard greeted Yorosel with a warm welcome. After immediately dispatching the council's letter to Cartago to be viewed by the governor, the Matina lieutenant invited Yorosel and Corella to stay in his own house, offering food, drink, and gifts to make sure the delegation leader felt welcomed. In return, Yorosel offered information about the confederation's activities, such as a successful attack on Pitipie, which Yorosel himself had led. Ultimately, by the end of the visit, Yorosel and the other Mosquito were once again convinced of the goodwill of the Costa Ricans. As a final request, Yorosel asked that Francisco Corella be sent back to Mosquito territory to deliver the Costa Rican governor's response to the confederation's letter.[40]

In the following year, however, diplomatic relations suddenly soured. The Mosquito council may have suspected that something was amiss when Corella never returned with the governor's response, yet the confederation fleet still decided to stop in Matina for the usual supplies during an expedition in January 1723. On this occasion, one of Jeremy II's most trusted followers, a captain named Yanes, commanded the fleet.[41] The eight-piragua convoy arrived on January 11, yet in a stunning contrast to Yorosel's welcome only a few months earlier, the Costa Rican militia stood poised for defense, refusing to allow Yanes to land. Enraged, Yanes asked to speak with Diego de Bonilla, a trusted translator who, like Francisco Corella, had worked with the Mosquito in the past. After Yanes threatened to raze the valley, Bonilla finally arrived to diffuse the situation, though his explanation was disappointing: after more than a decade of peaceful relations, the Costa Rican governor in Cartago had arbitrarily canceled the treaty, and Matina now had strict orders to reject all communication with the Mosquito.[42]

On this occasion, the fleet decided not to follow through with Yanes's threats, and the fleet continued its journey south without further incident. Nonetheless, the confederation did not take the affront lightly. The first sign of the Mosquito willingness to punish their wayward allies occurred in April 1723. On the twentieth of that month, an intimidating twelve-piragua fleet with as many as two hundred soldiers arrived in the Matina Valley's port of Moin at the same time that a Spanish cargo ship happened to be in the port loading cacao. On King Jeremy's orders, the fleet committed the first act of aggression in Matina since opening negotiations more than ten years earlier. The Mosquito soldiers boarded the Spanish cargo ship, cast the crew onto the beach, and sailed away with the ship and its entire cargo of cacao.[43] The incident was far from an all-out attack, yet the message was clear: reopen the Matina ports to Mosquito fleets, or lose the protected status that Mosquito leaders had enforced for over a decade.

Diego De La Haya Fernández and Rupturing the Mosquito Alliance, 1719–1722

From the Spanish perspective, the alliance with the Mosquito had been weakening since 1719: not because of Mosquito aggression, but rather because of the Costa Rican governor's mistrust of the Mosquito, as well as his increasingly legalistic approach to formalizing the alliance. Of course, the Costa Rican governor depended almost entirely on Black and Amerindian informants for information about the Mosquito. In this, a native Guaymi and former Mosquito slave named Christobal came to play an important role in the deliberations. In the weeks following the 1719 Mosquito visit, Governor De la Haya had the unique opportunity to interview Christobal, who had traveled with the Mosquito convoy as a guide, subsequently escaping during the fleet's lengthy stay in Matina. Adding legal weight to his testimony, Christobal spoke Spanish and had been baptized. He had also served as a member of the Spanish militia at a guard post on the Caribbean coast near the mouth of the Cocle River, which passed by his home village. In contrast to Francisco Corella's praise for the Mosquito, Christobal offered a far more negative image, describing how they had captured him three years earlier from the militia outpost and forced him to serve as a guide for future raids. In fact, just before arriving in Matina, the Mosquito fleet had attacked Christobal's home village, enslaving eighty-five captives, including his wife, who also escaped in Matina, though she left no recorded testimony of her own.[44]

Christobal's harrowing story seemingly made an impression on Governor De La Haya, casting doubts on efforts to normalize relations despite Corella's assurances and the ongoing truce in Matina. Moreover, the negotiations were further frustrated when King Jeremy II did not return for a follow-up visit as he had promised. Another Mosquito fleet did stop in Matina the following year in April 1720, but King Jeremy himself did not make an appearance. Instead, his close ally Hannibal disembarked at the port, conversing with translator Francisco Corella to offer an update on the negotiations. For his part, Hannibal tried to reassure Corella that Jeremy's absence was not an indication that the Mosquito were reconsidering the peace agreement. In fact, according to Hannibal, both he and Jeremy still considered Matina to be under a protection agreement, and they had sent clear messages to the English that Matina was off limits to piracy or raiding.[45]

This report was only partially reassuring for De la Haya, who immediately ordered additional troops to be sent to Matina to prepare for a possible invasion.[46] Then, to make matters worse, the governor of Nicaragua sent a letter to Cartago a few months later in December 1720, describing rumors that the Mosquito were constructing a massive fifty-piragua fleet in order to attack the Spanish.[47] Around the same time, the governor of Honduras also reported that a large fleet of thirty piraguas had menaced San Pedro de Sula, briefly skirmishing with the coast guard.[48] These reports, combined with Christobal's alarming declaration from the year before, made De la Haya even more fearful of the Mosquito and inspired him to send further reinforcements to Matina in January 1721.[49] Consequently, even though the Mosquito Kingdom had not allowed any attacks on Matina since Jeremy II's initial peace offering in 1711, fear mounted in Matina as rumors of an impending attack, and the arrival of new troops from Cartago put the valley on edge.

It was against this background of mounting fear that a force of six Mosquito piraguas and a small French vessel arrived at the port soon after on April 8, 1721. Even though such visits had become routine in the last few years, the Matina guard worried that this was the invasion referenced by the governor of Nicaragua, and the ranking officer of the militia sent a panicked letter to Cartago declaring that Matina was surrounded and defenseless.[50] Despite these fears, however, the Mosquito never attacked, and eventually the Matina guard allowed Francisco Corella to approach the fleet to find out its purpose. Corella confirmed that, as usual, the fleet had no intention of attacking Matina, but rather that the Mosquito were simply using the beach as a rendezvous point to wait for the rest of the fleet. The situation remained tense, but Corella's diplomatic efforts assuaged the militia's fears enough to prevent any escalation.[51]

Spanish fears remained high, however, and the nervous militia almost sparked an all-out war when an even larger Mosquito fleet visited a few months later in October 1721. As in previous encounters, the Mosquito sent a small delegation to approach the port while the rest of the fleet waited. Fearing an ambush, however, the guard at the mouth of the river opened fire on the Mosquito delegates, forcing them to turn back. This act of aggression stunned the Mosquito, who after nearly ten years of informal alliance had become accustomed to peaceful receptions at Matina. Luckily for the Costa Rican guard, the Mosquito decided to try diplomacy one more time, sending another messenger to approach the port in a single canoe to find out why the militia had rejected the original delegation. By this time, word of the altercation had reached the Matina lieutenant, who rushed to the port to diffuse the situation, once again bringing along the skilled negotiator Francisco Corella. Apologizing for the earlier provocation, they arranged a meeting with Hannibal, the leader of the Mosquito fleet. Francisco Corella met with Hannibal face-to-face, and while Hannibal threatened to raze the valley if the militia committed any more perfidy, Corella managed to reassure him that the port was safe, allowing the negotiations to continue peacefully.[52]

Ironically, this near catastrophic visit by Hannibal turned out to be a useful opportunity for Governor De la Haya Fernández to clarify the legal relationship between Costa Rica and the Mosquito. Echoing previous negotiations, Hannibal reaffirmed that he and his people wanted peace with Matina, promising to continue protecting the Matina Valley not only from Mosquito raids but also from pirates. Moreover, recognizing the valley's weak defenses, Hannibal even offered to sell arms to Costa Rica. In return, Hannibal requested an official Spanish title, as well as a series of gifts to confirm his status.[53] Again, the Costa Rican governor had no direct contact with the Mosquito delegates himself, though after receiving word about Hannibal's offer in the capital of Cartago several days later, De la Haya rushed to prepare the requested items. The gifts arrived just in time for Hannibal's return on November 10, 1721, and in a ceremony with important legal significance for De la Haya, the Matina lieutenant officially named "Anibel" a captain of the Spanish coast guard.[54] After the ceremony, Hannibal promised to return with the rest of the Mosquito leaders in order to officially become vassals of the Spanish king.[55]

When Hannibal received his commission as a Spanish captain, the negotiations seemed to be following exactly the path that Governor De la Haya needed in order to legalize a broader treaty with the Mosquito Kingdom. Whereas trading or entering into a treaty with an independent, non-Christian, Indigenous group—especially one that traded with the English and had already been labeled an enemy by the crown—simply raised too many legal problems, negotiating with groups that had formally accepted Spanish vassalage was far more legally promising. De la Haya's plans stalled, however, when Hannibal failed to arrive at the allotted time. As the months passed with no word, the governor began to fear that the negotiations had failed once and for all. Other Central American officials then reinforced these fears, with the governor of Honduras stating emphatically in February 1722 that he believed Hannibal's peace offering to be a ruse.[56]

Still, De la Haya found a spark of hope in March 1722 after interviewing a former Mosquito captive named Antonio. Described as a "negro congo," Antonio explained that he had been a slave on a cacao plantation in Matina twenty years earlier when he had been taken captive by passing Mosquito mariners. Given the timing of the interview, Antonio's interviewers directed their questions toward finding out the status of Hannibal's promised return. Antonio did not disappoint. When asked about Hannibal, he reported that the Mosquito chief did indeed consider the Costa Ricans friends, and that he planned to return soon to offer obedience to the Spanish king. Furthermore, Antonio claimed that two other major chiefs who had appeared in previous negotiations—Jeremy II and Peter—also planned to send delegates, even if they could not attend themselves.[57]

Following Antonio's testimony, the Costa Ricans decided to take the bold step of sending their own delegation to Mosquito territory. Governor De la Haya approved of the plan, though he warned that in the meantime, commercial exchanges with the Mosquito were still illegal.[58] The small delegation was headed by Francisco Corella, and by every indication, he played his part well. The expedition set out on the morning of April 9 after the locals gathered at the shore of the Matina River where the local priest blessed the voyage. Under Corella's guidance, the delegates navigated the route successfully, arriving safely at Hannibal's home ten days later on April 19. Hannibal was surprised, but he greeted the delegates warmly, and after explaining to Corella that he had not been able to return to Matina because the piragua fleet was in need of repair, Hannibal sent word to Jeremy and Peter to arrange a meeting.[59] Throughout the visit, the Mosquito leaders gave Corella and the other delegates every indication that they already considered the Costa Ricans to be allies. The Mosquito treated the delegates with great hospitality, and when an incensed English ship captain who happened to be passing by tried to arrest the delegates, the Mosquito headmen refused, arguing that the Costa Ricans had long been friends of the Mosquito and thus had every right to be there.[60]

Unfortunately for De la Haya, however, Corella was not able to convince the Mosquito to agree to the terms necessary for an ironclad legal case that would be convincing to Guatemalan officials. At a meeting that included Jeremy, Peter, Hannibal's son Britan, and other influential captains, Corella explained De la Haya's terms, which followed the strict stipulations laid out by Fiscal Guthierrez over a decade earlier. Specifically, Corella tried to convince the Mosquito leaders to sign a document clearly stating that they would convert to Catholicism, accept the supremacy of the Spanish king, and cut off all relations with the British. Faced with these terms, the Mosquito leaders answered Corella honestly: they cordially explained that they considered the Costa Ricans friends, but that they had no intention of ending their profitable trade with the English. Accordingly, Corella's mission accomplished mixed results. On the one hand, he carried a letter signed by all three Mosquito headmen promising that peace would continue. On the other hand, this letter admitted that they would not be able to follow the letter of De la Haya's strict legal terms.[61]

The delegation returned to Matina on May 29, 1722, escorted by three Mosquito piraguas captained by Hannibal's brother-in-law Yorosel.[62] When they arrived, Corella traveled to Cartago to deliver the letter to Governor De la Haya, while the Matina lieutenant hosted Yorosel in an informal diplomatic visit. At this point, the policies of Matina and Cartago began to diverge. For his part, the Matina lieutenant treated Yorosel and the rest of the small guard as honored guests, reaffirming the long-standing practice of treating the Mosquito as allies.[63] Accordingly, Matina officials continued to promote the alliance as official policy, preparing gifts for when the other Mosquito leaders finally arrived.[64] On the other hand, Cartago ceased to be a center of Mosquito advocacy, now fully aligning with the hardliners in Guatemala. Despite Corella's testimony about the loyalty of the Mosquito, as well as his insistence of Matina that allying with the Mosquito was still the best policy, Governor Diego de la Haya treated the letter from the Mosquito chiefs as decisive: since they did not accept the necessary legal terms, then they were enemies of the Crown, making any interaction with them illegal.[65]

Significantly, De la Haya not only stated this position in official correspondence—something he could have done only to give the appearance of compliance—but he also took proactive measures to enforce the Mosquito ban. First, he ordered Matina officials to cease preparing gifts for the Mosquito leaders, declaring even diplomatic gift-giving to be illegal.[66] Then, De la Haya took the extra step of sending a trusted officer from Cartago to make sure his orders were followed, as well as to prosecute any accusations of contraband trade. Soon after arriving, the new officer followed through on these threats, arresting the Matina lieutenant who had hosted Yorosel.[67] With these actions, De la Haya finally accepted Guatemala's long-standing anti-Mosquito stance, ending Cartago's ten-year period of advocating for peace.

Interestingly, De la Haya's decision to cut ties with the Mosquito in June 1722 happened to coincide with the arrival of an order from the Spanish Crown likewise declaring the Mosquito enemies, though this intervention by the distant Peninsular authorities was actually unrelated to the recent events. The royal order had been written in August 1721, before the Corella expedition or even Hannibal's title ceremony.[68] Ironically, Crown officials would change their minds years later and support a Mosquito peace when they found out about Hannibal's 1721 vassalage ceremony, yet once again, the decision did not have any real effect on policy or practice in Central America.[69] By the time the Crown's new policy of peace arrived in late 1723, it was simply too late: De la Haya had already brought Costa Rica policies in line with those of hardliners in Guatemala by stopping all communication with the Mosquito, canceling Corella's follow-up meeting with Hannibal, and prosecuting contraband accusations against Matina officials. And even if the Crown's pro-Mosquito letter had arrived in time, it is unlikely that the Guatemalan officials would have complied. They knew that the Crown based the decision solely on reports of Hannibal's first visit in 1721 without the added context of the letter from the Mosquito chiefs in 1722. Indeed, when Crown officials found out about Corella's meeting with the Mosquito chiefs, the Crown returned to the original anti-Mosquito position, though once again the decision was years out of step with events on the ground.[70] Consequently, local actors on the isthmus continued to shape Spanish relations with the Mosquito in practice, and the royal orders that trickled in at random intervals played virtually no role.

Mosquito Reprisals and Gunboat Diplomacy in Matina, 1723–1728

At the same time that Mosquito leaders were facing these new complications with their Costa Rican and English allies, the Mosquito Confederation also faced increased aggression from the Spanish province of Honduras. In August 1723, the Mosquito fleet encountered a Honduran expedition of roughly fifty men approaching Mosquito territory from the mouth of the Ulua River. The much larger Mosquito fleet intercepted the attack, defeating the Spanish force and taking several captives. Nonetheless, the Mosquito suffered significant casualties, and Mosquito leaders now had to consider the possibility of future invasions.[71]

Mosquito leaders understood that the Costa Ricans had nothing to do with the Honduran invasion, though the threat of more attacks from along the northern coast, combined with the ongoing pirate menace, may have given Mosquito leaders increased urgency to reestablish Matina as a reliable external harbor. Regardless of how the Honduran attack may have influenced Mosquito thinking, the bottom line is by 1724, confederation leaders had grown tired of wondering whether Matina could be trusted, and they decided to take decisive action. In the darkness of early morning on April 17, Hannibal and Peter arrived in the Matina Valley with a massive invasion fleet including an estimated five hundred men, twenty-two piraguas, and three additional cargo vessels. An advance force entered Suerre and subdued the small guard in a rapid surprise assault. The rest of the troops then followed, securing the port before swarming the nearest cacao haciendas. With no hope of stopping the overwhelming invasion, the rest of the Matina militia surrendered without a fight.[72]

The occupation lasted three days. During this time, Hannibal set his troops to work expropriating the recent cacao harvest. The invaders took the cacao in bulk to Suerre, where it was loaded onto the three cargo ships. In addition to cacao, the Mosquito soldiers also forced the militia to hand over supplies such as iron weapons and tools, and they took several captives. Moreover, during the occupation, Hannibal met with one of the Matina militia officers along with a translator to write a letter explaining his actions to the ranking captain of the Matina Valley. The letter placed the blame for the invasion entirely on the recent duplicity of the Costa Ricans, who had reneged on their obligations as allies. Hannibal went on to demand that in the future, Mosquito fleets be treated with respect and given whatever supplies they requested. Finally, as a show of good faith, Hannibal said that he would keep the captives safe, asking that Francisco Corella be sent with a ransom payment to signify acceptance of the terms.[73]

As a show of force, the 1724 occupation of Matina was a huge success. Leaving the destitute valley behind, Hannibal's convoy headed north toward the mouth of the San Juan River, where it camped for two weeks awaiting the arrival of three British transport ships from Jamaica. Once the British traders arrived, Hannibal sold the cacao for various goods, such as muskets, powder, iron pots, aguardiente, and clothes, though as promised, he did not sell any of the captives.[74] The success of the attack in reviving the Costa Rican alliance, however, was not immediately apparent. Since Corella never arrived with the ransom payment as requested in Hannibal's letter, the council began to wonder if Costa Rica would remain recalcitrant. Consequently, after sending a large fleet of roughly thirty piraguas along the northern coast in August to patrol against pirates and raid Indigenous settlements near the Ulua River, the confederation decided to send a follow-up voyage along the southern route past Costa Rica in December 1724.[75] After a council meeting that included all three principal headmen, Hannibal and Peter headed south once again with a fleet of ten piraguas. During the journey south, the fleet did not make port in Matina, but Hannibal did drop off a messenger to give one final warning: if the port refused to have the customary supplies ready for the fleet's return journey, then the Mosquito would occupy the valley again.[76]

Reminiscent of previous expeditions, the fleet reportedly continued to the Bocas del Toro region, hunting turtles, plundering French pirates, and taking about forty captives from among the free Indigenous groups. It then returned to Costa Rica in early January 1725, and this time, the port guard heeded Hannibal's warning: as the fleet disembarked on the beach near the port of Moin, the Matina captain complied with Hannibal's request, sending food and supplies.[77] This visit tentatively reestablished the confederation's alliance with Matina, and Hannibal promised that King Jeremy II would return soon to release the captives taken during the previous invasion.[78] Hannibal was true to his word, and King Jeremy arrived in March 1725 with a small four-piragua convoy, carrying with him twenty-six of the thirty captives.[79] The Costa Rican governor still refused to authorize the ransom payment, however, so the fate of the captives remained unresolved. Still, King Jeremy's requests for food and safe passage at the port were indeed fulfilled, indicating that the confederation had tentatively succeeded in pressuring Matina back into submission.

Following these interactions, the Mosquito Confederation launched one final show of force in August of 1726. The conflict began when the Matina guard arrested a small group of English traders earlier that year, in the process seizing two piraguas.[80] This was not a direct attack on the confederation fleet, but Hannibal and other confederation leaders found this behavior offensive and moved once again to assert Mosquito authority in the Matina Valley. Invading with a fleet of roughly thirty piraguas, Hannibal took another group of twenty-four hostages as well as forty bags of cacao.[81] This follow-up show of force was effective, and when another Mosquito fleet of twenty piraguas appeared the following May in 1727, the Matina militia greeted the fleet graciously. In return, the Mosquito expedition commander reiterated the confederation's desire for peace, promising that Hannibal would return by January to deliver the hostages.[82]

The fleet then continued on its usual southern voyage to Talamanca, stopping again in Matina two weeks later to gather supplies for the return trip, as well as to release two captives without ransom as a show of good faith.[83] Hannibal himself did not make it back to Matina within the allotted time, but he did send two additional delegations to reiterate his commitment to peace, the first arriving in August 1727 and the other in January 1728. The second visit, led by Hannibal's nephew, delivered nineteen more of the captives who had been taken in the most recent invasion in 1726.[84] Through this sequence of events, the Mosquito Confederation succeeded in reestablishing a working alliance with the Matina Valley.

Costa Rican Reactions to Mosquito Reprisals, 1723–1728

Even though Governor De la Haya's rejection of Mosquito peace offerings alienated the Mosquito as potential allies, the policy did establish a precedent, at least in official policies, for decades to come. Following De la Haya's decision to cut off diplomatic relations with the Mosquito, Spanish Central America was more united against the Mosquito than it had ever been before. Within this context, the province of Honduras even felt emboldened enough to venture an offensive campaign. Since Bishop Garret y Arlovi began his anti-Mosquito campaign in 1711, various Spanish officials had issued calls to exterminate the Mosquito, though few took tangible steps to put this grandiose vision of conquest into practice. In August 1723, however, the governor of Honduras outfitted a fleet of five small vessels with roughly fifty men to invade Mosquitia by sailing along the Honduran coast from the mouth of the Ulua River. The expedition hoped to catch the Mosquito by surprise, but after only three days of traveling and before reaching Mosquito territory, the small convoy encountered a much larger Mosquito fleet with dozens of crafts and as many as one hundred fifty armed men. A naval skirmish ensued, and the Honduran expedition was soundly defeated, with most of its members taken captive.[85] Nonetheless, the unprecedented attempt to invade Mosquito territory demonstrated the newfound resolve of Central American leaders in the early 1720s to oppose Mosquito expansion.

Costa Rica never attempted to attack Mosquito territory, but De la Haya's decision to cut off diplomatic relations was more than enough to provoke a Mosquito response. The first signs of increased tension occurred in January 1723 when a fleet of eight Mosquito piraguas arrived at the port to ask for the usual supplies. The captain of the fleet was stunned, however, when the port guard refused the request. Offended at this sudden ill-treatment, the Mosquito captain sent an interpreter to issue an ultimatum: if the militia did not send Captain Baraona and Alferez Bonilla—two trusted officers who had negotiated with the Mosquito in previous years—to meet the fleet within three days, then he would raze the entire valley.[86] Matina officials gave in to the pressure, sending Baraona and Bonilla to diffuse the situation, even though this violated De la Haya's ban on communication. They then sent a letter to Cartago explaining how poorly defended Matina was and begging for leniency given the circumstances.[87] The Costa Rican governor remained stubborn, however, reiterating his earlier orders to avoid all communication with the Mosquito.[88]

That the Costa Rican governor's actions would lead to retaliation by the Mosquito became apparent when another fleet of twelve piraguas arrived a few months later, passing close to the mouth of the Matina River on April 22, 1723. At the time, a Spanish cargo ship happened to be docked with a full cargo of cacao. Still on guard after the tense January encounter, the Matina militia sent men to the beach to keep an eye on the fleet's movements. The exact interactions between Mosquito messengers and these militiamen remain obscure, but according to reports, the Mosquito sailors convinced the Costa Ricans that the fleet was simply passing by on its way to Bocas del Toro further south.[89] The next morning, however, the Mosquito fleet suddenly reappeared and seized the cargo ship, subsequently sailing off with the cacao.[90]

This incident sent a new wave of dread through Costa Rica, and this fear only increased when an escaped captive named Martin appeared in Matina a month later, on May 22. Martin testified that he had traveled with the twelve-piragua convoy as a slave and that the assault on the cargo ship had been led by King Jeremy himself. Moreover, Martin claimed that the Mosquito were amassing arms in order to prepare for a massive invasion of Matina later in the year.[91] Martin's prediction was half correct. The rest of the year passed without any more violent encounters in Matina, yet the following year, on the evening of April 20, 1724, a messenger arrived in Cartago carrying a letter from Matina. Three days earlier on April 17, in the darkness of early morning, a massive force of five hundred Mosquito soldiers had overtaken the port of Suerre and then swarmed into the rest of the Matina Valley. A free Black man named Tomas had been the first to notify the Matina authorities, rushing from the port to the lieutenant's house in order to sound the alarm. By this time, however, it was too late. The Mosquito invaders had already occupied the town, and the eight militia members who were with the lieutenant—along with four conscripted slaves—were unable to reach the armory. The only recourse was to send a dispatch to Cartago. After a harrowing three-day journey from the coast to the interior capital, the messenger from Matina finally arrived in Cartago and rushed to find Governor De la Haya to report the news.[92]

De la Haya immediately went to work organizing relief for the valley. After calling an emergency meeting with other officials in the town, the governor sent a small guard of scouts to head toward Matina to gain additional information. This group left the capital at three in the morning on April 21, now almost four days after the attack on Matina had begun with no additional news having yet arrived.[93] The governor also sent messengers out to assemble other military officers in settlements around the valley. It took almost two days to assemble roughly one hundred soldiers in the capital, and finally, at about three in the morning on April 23, the governor set out with the force from Cartago, leading it on a six-hour march to the nearby settlement of Santiago where the expedition made camp.[94] By this time, almost a week had passed since the invasion began back on April 17, and as De la Haya's forces camped at Santiago on the evening of April 23, the governor finally received an update on events in Matina when a militiaman named Juan Solaro arrived with three letters to deliver to the governor: two reports from Matina officers who had witnessed the entire event and one letter from the Mosquito governor Hannibal.[95]

These reports confirmed that despite De la Haya's efforts to move quickly, it was far too late to provide any military assistance to Matina. The Mosquito had already left three days earlier on April 20, ironically around the same time that Cartago was first finding out about the invasion. During the three-day occupation, the invaders had carried off a large portion of the cacao harvest, using Matina's own slaves and mule carts to load the harvest into their piraguas and cargo ships. They also carried off numerous captives, as well as various tools and supplies.[96] The invaders had not followed through on their earlier threats to raze the valley, however, leaving the haciendas and cacao trees intact for future production. Additionally, Hannibal's letter explained that he did not intend to sell the captives into slavery but simply to ransom them, and he requested that Francisco Corella be sent to deliver the ransom payment. The letter also justified the invasion by citing the perfidy of the Costa Ricans themselves, who had violated their obligations as allies by cutting off communication and denying supply requests. Nevertheless, Hannibal hoped that moving forward, the alliance could be restored without additional violence.[97]

After Hannibal's invasion, Costa Rica's relationship with the Mosquito became more complex. In the immediate aftermath, Governor De la Haya attempted to shift the blame to authorities in Guatemala. Taking Hannibal's explanation to heart, De la Haya wrote bitterly that his strict compliance with Guatemalan contraband policies had provoked the Mosquito, who previously had been at peace with Matina.[98] Still, De la Haya remained stubborn about enforcing the letter of the law, and he left the orders in place to avoid all trade or communication with Mosquito vessels. In doing this, De la Haya left the captives to their own fate, denying Hannibal's request to send Corella with the requested ransom payment. For their part, Matina officials took a far more pragmatic approach, returning to the unofficial policy of supplying visiting Mosquito fleets with gifts and supplies. Hannibal himself visited Matina in January 1725 at the head of a ten-piragua fleet, and after he threatened to invade the valley yet again, port officials simply ignored orders from Cartago and fulfilled Hannibal's supply requests.[99]

From the perspective of Matina officials, giving in to Hannibal's demands was simply a necessity to ensure the safety of the valley. From Cartago's perspective, however, the interaction pushed the limits of legality. In follow-up interviews, De la Haya pressed to find out if the Mosquito had brought any goods to trade, reiterating his commitment to prosecuting contraband trade.[100] De la Haya also reiterated his opposition to ransoming captives, clarifying that if the Mosquito did bring the captives back in a later expedition, any form of ransom payment would be prosecuted as contraband.[101] The opportunity to test this policy arrived soon in March 1725, when King Jeremy II arrived in a small four-piragua convoy bringing along the captives from Hannibal's invasion. De la Haya remained stubborn about the ban on ransoming captives, yet his exhortations to cut off communication proved unenforceable, and Jeremy's visit turned into an opportunity for Matina officials to normalize relations.[102]

This pattern remained the norm for the rest of the 1720s, as Matina pragmatically maintained the truce by receiving Mosquito fleets with gifts and supplies, whereas officials in Cartago continued to express indignation at these activities. Within this context, Costa Rica suffered one final outburst of violence before the end of the decade. The episode began in March 1726 when Matina officials arrested a small group of English traders. The original reports from Matina did not clarify if Mosquito traders were also among the party, but regardless, later informants specified that this event is what provoked Mosquito leaders to take vengeance.[103] Accordingly, Hannibal occupied Matina again in August 1726, taking cacao and additional prisoners for ransom.[104]

After the attack, Cartago continued its hardline stance against any friendship with the Mosquito, including ransoming captives. This remained consistent even when a new governor—Balthasar Francisco Valderrama—replaced De la Haya in 1727. When a massive fleet of twenty piraguas appeared in Matina on May 31, 1727, promising to return the prisoners later in the year as a sign of peace, Valderrama issued explicit orders once again not to offer any kind of payment.[105] Matina officials, however, continued to welcome Mosquito fleets graciously, clearly breaking the ban on communication, though arguing emphatically that no contraband trade was taking place. In 1727, Mosquito fleets would visit Matina peacefully on two more occasions—once in June and once in August—dropping off one or two prisoners each time.[106] Then, in January 1728, Hannibal himself visited Matina, releasing the rest of the prisoners from the 1726 invasion.[107] At this point, the unofficial peace of the 1710s was firmly reestablished, and Mosquito fleets visited Matina peacefully at least five more times in the year 1728 alone.[108] For his part, Valderrama tried to reiterate the ban on Mosquito communication, but Matina officials simply ignored his orders.[109]

Conclusion

The events described in this chapter have helped to illustrate how Mosquito leaders during the 1710s and 1720s built on the collective power of the confederation to exert an empire-like influence over neighboring peoples in Caribbean Central America. Far from simply carrying out a series of isolated raids for extracting resources, the Mosquito council coordinated a series of strategic activities aimed at establishing long-term authority in the region. Along with long-distance raids, these activities included robust negotiations with Spanish Costa Rica, campaigns to control piracy along the coast, efforts to protect Mosquito and English trading parties from abuse, and gunboat diplomacy to pressure negotiations with foreign allies. Significantly, the constituent factions of the confederation displayed a notable unity in carrying out all of these activities, and while some studies have hypothesized that this was a period of intensifying ethnic rivalry between Zambo and Tawira factions, the new archival evidence this chapter draws on shows that this was simply not the case.[110] Indeed, the Tawira-Mosquito governor Hannibal worked closely with the Zambo-Mosquitos King Jeremy II and Governor Peter in all of the activities described above.

An even more common misunderstanding addressed by this chapter, however, is the long-standing assumption that the Mosquito negotiations with the Spanish were inconsequential until the end of the eighteenth century.[111] Significantly, misunderstandings regarding Hannibal's 1724 invasion have contributed to this view. Whereas the historiography has long noted Hannibal's acceptance of a Spanish title in 1721, early studies interpreted the 1724 attack on Matina as definitive proof that Hannibal's negotiations were simply a ruse perpetrated by a perfidious savage.[112] A major contribution of this chapter, therefore, has been to explain the true causes of the 1724 invasion for the first time by presenting a close narrative of surrounding events using new archival evidence revealing that the invasion rather than the peace negotiations was the true outlier, and that the Mosquito were not the ones who broke the alliance. Far from using the negotiations as a ruse, Mosquito leaders proved themselves to be serious about the alliance, only to have the terms later rejected by the Costa Rican governor. Within this context, the 1724 attack was not a raid at all but rather a retaliatory measure intended to force Costa Rica back into the alliance.

Ultimately, these approaches to internal politics, as well as to foreign policy, would largely continue under the next generation of Mosquito leaders. In some ways, the geopolitical situation would become more complex as agents of English colonialism increased their efforts to formalize settlements on the mainland—a process that began in earnest in the 1740s and depended heavily on Mosquito support. Indeed, the changing nature of the Mosquito alliance with the English added new variables for Mosquito leaders to consider, such as how to regulate raiding under the authority of the confederation council while still allowing individual Mosquito subjects to participate in private expeditions under English leadership. Nonetheless, even in a shifting geopolitical landscape, the hallmarks of Mosquito imperial practices, including coordinating unified fleets for long-distance expeditions, acquiring strategic knowledge and labor from slaves, and carrying out robust negotiations with foreign allies including Spanish provinces, continued to characterize the confederation's role in Central America's Caribbean borderlands.

CHAPTER 3

New Challenges and the Recovery of the Confederation, 1728–1749

When the fugitives arrived at the Port of Matina in their battered piragua, they hoped that they had finally found a safe haven. It was March of 1736, and the group of five men of Black and Amerindian descent explained that they were part of a larger group, including women and children, who had stayed further down the coast to make camp. Two members of the group spoke Spanish; according to their testimony, they had been slaves of the Mosquito but had managed to steal the piragua and escape, killing several Mosquito guards in the process. They further explained that even though they were armed, they hoped to live peacefully under Spanish protection, using their arms only to attack passing Mosquito bands.[1] Eight months later, however, it became apparent that allowing the fugitives to stay was not an inconsequential decision. In January 1737, the Mosquito king himself arrived in Matina at the head of a large fleet to demand that the Costa Ricans turn over the fugitives. The visit itself was peaceful; however, reminiscent of Hannibal's negotiations in the 1720s, the Mosquito king threatened to return and sack the valley if his demands were not met.[2]

The purpose of this chapter is to examine the practices and wider impacts of the Mosquito Confederation during the period from roughly 1728 to 1749. This period began with a brief lapse in Mosquito power caused by a smallpox epidemic that interrupted confederation activities and resulted in the deaths of Jeremy II and Hannibal. However, the mid-1730s saw a resurgence of the Mosquito as a new confederation council revived the characteristic fleets and continued a familiar pattern of turtle hunting, slave raiding, protection agreements, and gunboat diplomacy. Accordingly, this chapter argues that far from creating factional strife, the disruptions of the late 1720s did little to damage Mosquito political institutions and the confederation emerged from the epidemic just as united as ever. In practice, this meant that Costa Rica continued to be a key site of contact between Mosquito and Spanish conquest efforts, and while Mosquito leaders continued to view the Matina Valley as a potential ally, a renewed stubbornness in Spanish policy to resist Mosquito demands led to increased hostilities in the 1740s.

At the same time, English efforts to expand into the mainland accelerated during this period, as agents worked closely with Mosquito leaders to not only found new settlements on the Mosquito Shore but also have these settlements formally recognized by the British Empire. In describing these parallel processes, this chapter further demonstrates how from its inception, the English conquest of Caribbean Central America was heavily dependent on the Mosquito for both physical support and political legitimacy. While the English did not have any official colonies on the mainland in 1711, adventurers were already expanding English influence in practice by establishing mainland trade contacts and even planting informal settlements. Indeed, throughout the eighteenth century, the English conquest relied heavily on informal actors to first occupy territories that might later be declared formal colonies of England's colonial empire. Significantly, the Mosquito were central to these processes in Central America. For example, English officials used agreements with Mosquito leaders to add legitimacy to their claims when negotiating territorial rights with other European powers. Moreover, the colonists themselves depended on the Mosquito for physical support, such as commerce and military protection. Ultimately, whereas most research has presumed that the Mosquito became economically and culturally dependent on the English, this chapter shows that the English were far more dependent on the Mosquito than the other way around. And while Mosquito power lapsed briefly in the early 1730s following the smallpox outbreak, the confederation reemerged as strong as ever, leaving these power dynamics intact even as English colonizers worked to increase their presence on the mainland.

New Challenges and the Resurgence of the Confederation, 1728–1747

Despite the rapid expansion of Mosquito power during the years of Kings Jeremy I and Jeremy II, the Mosquito Confederation suddenly faced a grave set of challenges in the late 1720s. The first major problem was a deadly smallpox outbreak that led to numerous deaths and interrupted confederation activities. Records of the event are sparse, but escaped captives testified before Costa Rican officials in 1728 confirming that the epidemic was already having visible effects.[3] In addition to causing countless personal tragedies, the plague had a tangible effect on the collective power of the confederation. A fundamental component of the confederation's power was its relatively large population, strategically assembled through political alliances in a region characterized by low population density. The devastating plague diminished this advantage, however, as individual settlements were forced to focus more on their own survival rather than joining with other Mosquito factions for conquest. As late as December of 1728, the confederation was still sending regular fleets of fifteen piraguas to Bocas del Toro in the south, but indicating the effects of the disease outbreak, these large expeditions suddenly stopped arriving in the following years.[4] Further corroborating this link between population loss and a decline in the confederation's power, an escaped captive named Manuel Garcia testified in Cartago in 1733 that after living as a slave among the Mosquito for over thirty years, he had finally managed to escape because, in his words, so many men had died that only widows and children were left to guard the slaves.[5]

The harrowing epidemic also accompanied political transitions that likewise constituted temporary setbacks to the Confederation. The first major political change was the death of Jeremy II, which occurred in either late 1727 or early 1728. Demonstrating the strong unity of the central council, the ascension of the new king—the Zambo-Mosquito Peter, likely the same man who had previously held the title of general—occurred without any problems. Indeed, the influential Tawira governor Hannibal supported Peter's ascension, and both headmen led the southern fleet together in April 1728, stopping in Matina along the way in order to inform their Costa Rican allies of the change.[6] When Hannibal died soon after in 1729, however, the ascension of a new governor went far less smoothly. Whereas Hannibal's son Briton immediately claimed the title, some of Hannibal's Tawira Mosquito followers decided to challenge his claim. Details are sparse, so it remains unclear whether this faction supported a different governor, or if it simply tried to exert more independence from the confederation council in general. Regardless, tensions were apparently high enough that the new confederation council took action to punish the rebellious faction, resulting in civil unrest that may have even put English settlers in danger.[7] In October 1729, King

Peter himself admitted in a letter to the new English governor of Jamaica that the Mosquito Confederation had experienced recent turmoil. Consistent with reports in Costa Rica, Peter gave no indication that his own position as king was in jeopardy, yet he did indicate a temporary breakdown in the intensive power of the central council to assert law and order. Accordingly, he used the letter to apologize for not having been able to fully guarantee the safety of English settlers—a situation that he vowed to swiftly remedy.[8]

Here it is worth noting that some previous studies have hypothesized that the political tensions during this period resulted from ongoing ethnic discord between the Zambo and Tawira factions.[9] New archival evidence from Costa Rican archives, however, demonstrates that this interpretation is incorrect. Ever since the Zambo Jeremy II became king around 1711, constant collaboration among Zambo and Tawira factions had characterized the confederation, demonstrated in the frequent council meetings as well as the large joint fleets composed of Zambo and Tawira men. And this cooperation was still the norm in the late 1720s and early 1730s. When the Zambo-Mosquito Peter became king in 1728, the Tawira governor Hannibal, his son Briton, and other Tawira captains supported the bid. Similarly, Peter supported the Tawira governor Briton's ascension, and as explained above, the faction that rebelled against Briton was not Zambo at all but rather Tawira just like him. Moreover, the same informants who told Costa Rican officials about the rebellion explicitly stated that Zambo and Tawira populations continued to work closely across ethnic lines.[10] In sum, the political tensions of 1729 were the exception rather than the norm, and they had nothing to do with ethnic rivalry. In fact, the crucible of the smallpox outbreak and the transition to a new generation of leaders only proved the resilience of the confederation.

Consequently, even though the power of the Mosquito Confederation visibly shrank during the 1730s, the inner workings of the confederation ultimately withstood the disruptions of the outbreak and the governor's ascension conflict, and the next generation of leaders succeeded in refortifying the confederation's bases of power in the 1730s. Significantly, the new set of leaders who emerged to replace Jeremy II and Hannibal not only had large individual followings but also had enormous experience in confederation affairs. As mentioned, Peter, who took on the title of king after Jeremy II, most likely was the same person who had previously held the title of general, leading the Zambo-Mosquito faction located along the Caribbean coast of Honduras near Black River. In this role, Peter had worked closely with Jeremy II and Hannibal to conduct matters of foreign relations, including the extensive Costa Rica negotiations.[11] The replacement general, then, was a man named Charles Hobby who lived near Black River. As early as 1711, British traveler Nathaniel Uring reported that Hobby was one of the leading captains in the region, indicating that Hobby likewise had extensive leadership experience.[12] Furthermore, the new governor, John Briton, was the son of the previous Governor Hannibal. And even though Briton's bid to replace his father was initially challenged, he worked closely with the other council members to secure his position. He also had direct experience in confederation affairs, having worked closely with his father by leading the southern fleet on occasion and even sitting in council meetings when his father was not available.[13]

The ongoing relationship between the Mosquito Confederation and Costa Rica's Matina Valley—which confederation fleets had become accustomed to using as an external port despite Spanish unwillingness to enter into a formal treaty—helps to illustrate these phases in Mosquito collective power. Whereas large confederation fleets had arrived routinely for over a decade, these visits stopped abruptly after January 1729. The next documented visit of a Mosquito piragua at Matina did not occur until February 1733, and even these visitors were not official representatives of the confederation but rather a passing group of about a dozen Mosquito traders acting independently.[14]

Nonetheless, even in its weakened state, the Mosquito Confederation did not completely shed its geopolitical influence. Long-range displays of power became less frequent, but reports from Spanish frontier missions indicate that the Mosquito continued raiding Indigenous peoples just inland from the confederation's core settled territories, as well as cultivating alliances with other neighboring groups.[15] Additionally, Mosquito leaders worked to strengthen their economic and political ties with the British. Peter led this effort with his letter to the new Jamaican governor in 1729, but other leaders continued this correspondence. General Hobby, for example, in 1731 recovered an impounded English ship after a skirmish with the Spanish coast guard on the Honduran coast. Hobby sent the ship to Jamaica, along with a letter emphasizing his commitment to the alliance.[16] Mosquito leaders also welcomed increasing numbers of English settlers on the mainland. These settlers were largely concentrated in a specific settlement called Black River. Nonetheless, the presence of English settlers gradually became a noticeable characteristic of the region.[17]

King Peter did not live to see the full recovery of the confederation, dying sometime in 1733.[18] Perhaps indicating the continued weakness of the confederation, the Mosquito council did not bother to inform their trading partners in either Matina or in Jamaica about the king's passing. Nonetheless, the confederation continued to regain its strength. As early as April 1734, the southern fleet was at least partially restored, with the confederation sending sixteen piraguas to Talamanca to revive the lucrative turtle-hunting and slave-raiding practices. The fleet did not stop in Matina for the usual negotiations, though Costa Rican scouts did see the fleet passing, and they found evidence that the Mosquito had camped nearby.[19]

As the confederation's naval power revived in the late 1730s, the council began to reclaim its former assertiveness in foreign affairs. In September 1736, for example, the Mosquito King sent a diplomatic envoy to Trujillo on the coast of Honduras in order to propose a formal peace treaty. Echoing the imperial strategy of the previous generation, this treaty stressed that Mosquito fleets should be allowed to gather provisions at Trujillo's port—a practice that was apparently not uncommon during longer voyages of the northern fleet during the 1710s and 1720s.[20] Moreover, only a few months later, the king reopened diplomatic relations with Costa Rica, sailing at the head of the revived southern fleet and making port in Matina on January 16, 1737, to demand that the Costa Ricans turn in a small group of fugitive slaves suspected to be in Matina.[21] Whereas escaped captives often arrived in Matina without drawing much attention from Mosquito leaders, this case was unique given that the fugitives had not only escaped but had apparently killed five Mosquito men and stolen a piragua in the process.[22] Accordingly, the new Mosquito king asserted the right to exact retribution, and even though the confederation had long considered Matina off-limits to raiding, he threatened to sack the valley—much like Hannibal had done back in 1724 and 1726—if Costa Rica interfered by protecting the fugitives.

The Mosquito did not immediately carry out this threat, but it was against this background of revived Mosquito power and diplomatic insults from Costa Rica that an English agent named Robert Hodgson arrived on the Mosquito Coast in March 1740 to renegotiate the English alliance with the confederation. At the time, the long-influential Zambo-Mosquito leader Charles Hobby still held the title of general, which he had taken in 1728, and Hannibal's son Briton remained governor, having held the position since

1729. Peter had died in 1733, however, and a new king named Edward—possibly a son of Jeremy II—had taken his place.[23] Additionally, a fourth position on the central council had emerged in association with new southern settlements in the Pearl Key Lagoon area. This position came with the title of admiral, and the first leader to hold it was a Tawira-Mosquito called Dilly. Upon the arrival of Robert Hodgson to the Mosquito Shore, both King Edward and Governor Briton met with the English visitor in the governor's home of Dacora. During this meeting, they signed a treaty to formalize the long-standing Mosquito alliance with the English.[24]

Soon after the treaty was signed, the confederation organized a massive fleet to cruise the southern coast, bringing Hodgson and a few other Englishmen to participate. The expedition set out in April 1740 with over two hundred Zambo and Tawira men on over twenty piraguas. In keeping with the established practice of using slaves for both labor and strategic knowledge, the expedition used as a guide an Amerindian slave taken as a child from the Island of Tovares, most likely during the raids of Jeremy II and Hannibal twenty years earlier. Hodgson encouraged the fleet to enter the San Juan River and attack a Spanish fort, yet the Mosquito ignored this request, instead continuing the traditional route further south to the turtle-hunting grounds in the Bocas del Toro region.[25]

In addition to accumulating a profitable harvest of tortoiseshell, the fleet also moved to reassert a military presence in the region. Specifically, the piraguas attacked the small Spanish garrison—composed primarily of Amerindian and African-descended militiamen—at the mouth of the Cocle River in present day Panama. The Mosquito fleet took several captives in the attack and then continued upriver to raid the village of Penonome, though by the time the fleet arrived, the villagers had already heard about the invasion and fled.[26] Moreover, on the way back up the coast, the Mosquito decided to follow through with their previous threats to demonstrate the confederation's renewed power in Matina. On July 14, 1740, in the darkness of early morning, Governor John Briton sent an advance force to the port of Suerre to speak with the guards and request a meeting with the lieutenant, only to arrest the guards once the lieutenant arrived.[27] The massive Mosquito force then entered the valley, spending the next two days seizing cacao from Matina haciendas.[28]

In many ways, the southern fleet's 1740 expedition signaled a return to the imperial practices of the previous generation of leaders. The fleet was composed of multiple Mosquito factions, and it facilitated economic and diplomatic activities in addition to warfare. Moreover, paralleling Hannibal's invasions in 1724 and 1726, the 1740 fleet timing suggests that the attack was at least in part a response to specific provocations on the part of Costa Rica in protecting fugitives accused of murder. Moreover, the Mosquito did not enact unrestrained hostilities in Matina. Rather, they took precautions to minimize damages, expropriating cacao and other goods yet doing little actual fighting.[29] It is also significant that Mosquito leaders struck a diplomatic tone, using the invasion to assert their authority while highlighting the culpability of the English in trying to escalate hostilities in the region. In fact, the Mosquito captains explained that they felt no ill will toward Costa Rica, and as a show of good faith, they offered several gifts to the ranking Spanish officer of Matina, as well as intelligence about English plans for future invasions.[30] Consequently, the 1740 invasion was fundamentally a continuation of the norms established under Jeremy II and Hannibal, in which the Confederation viewed Costa Rica as an allied but weaker partner that needed to be reminded of its place on occasion.

In other ways, however, the 1740 expedition signaled important changes in the confederation. For example, even though Mosquito leaders continued to make their own decisions independent from English rule, Mosquito expeditions increasingly included English mariners along with allied Zambo and Tawira soldiers. This presence was miniscule in 1740, but English involvement in joint expeditions became more prevalent in subsequent years. This situation adds a degree of complication to assessing Mosquito foreign policy: whereas in previous decades Mosquito expeditions were tightly organized and executed by the central council, this was not always the case from the 1740s onward. Sometimes the council planned the expeditions, but oftentimes Mosquito seafarers participated in ventures that were planned and enacted by British captains. Accordingly, whereas large fleets such as the 1740 venture can still be traced to the direction of the central council, the origins of smaller raiding parties are more difficult to assess. Significantly, small raiding parties that included both English and Mosquito participants became more common in Costa Rica in the 1740s and 1750s, and while this may have represented at least some degree of the confederation council's increased hostility toward the Mosquitos' Spanish neighbors, it is likely that it also reflected an expansion in private raiding apart from the will of the council. Indeed, future generations of confederation leaders would eventually pass reforms in the 1770s to regulate privatized raiding.[31]

Still, even though they granted their English allies an increased presence in raiding, the Mosquito remained unified during this period, creating a manpower advantage that allowed the confederation to maintain its status as a regional power. Consequently, even while allowing smaller private raiding ventures, the confederation continued its core imperial practices of resource extraction, raiding, and gunboat diplomacy via unified fleets. This was especially evident in relations with Costa Rica. After a show of force in 1740 that resulted in the theft of a large portion of the cacao harvest, the confederation continued to press Costa Rica for commercial privileges similar to those it had enjoyed in the 1710s and 1720s.[32] In April 1745, for example, a Mosquito fleet of as many as twenty-four piraguas, supported by an English brigantine, surrounded a recently constructed Spanish fort at the mouth of the Matina River. Despite its superior force, the fleet decided not to attack, instead making signs of truce in order for the English captain to deliver a letter to the Matina officer requesting that Matina open the port to future Mosquito fleets.[33] Still, the presence of the fleet served as a warning that the trade request was not optional, sending a clear message the confederation would resort to force when necessary to accomplish its economic and political agendas.

The confederation then followed up the 1745 incident with two more shows of force in 1747. The first occurred in April 1747, and after simply bypassing the fort, the invaders raided the plantations closest to the Matina River, seizing captives and carrying off the cacao harvest. After the raid, the Mosquito released several of the captives with a familiar ultimatum: if the Costa Ricans would open their ports to Mosquito trade, then the hostilities would cease. On the other hand, if the port continued to resist Mosquito traders, then the fleet would return to destroy the fort.[34] This was not an idle threat, and the fleet returned in August with an allied force of Mosquito and English soldiers to attack the fort in a surprise offensive. As in previous encounters in Matina, the invasion force limited the damage, allowing the militia to surrender after a brief skirmish that resulted in only two casualties. With the defenders subdued, the fleet burned the fort to the ground; still, before leaving, the Mosquito instructed the captives to reiterate the offer of peace in exchange for commercial privileges.[35] Costa Rican authorities remained resistant, however, and instead of accepting the Mosquito terms, they further provoked the confederation by building a new fort in Matina. Within this context, Mosquito piraguas made another incursion into the Matina Valley in 1748, taking additional captives in yet another bold show of force, though releasing most of them the following year.[36]

Spanish Reactions to Mosquito and English Aggression, 1730–1747

In the 1730s, Spanish Central American officials remained preoccupied with their ongoing conquest. One difference during this period, however, was that from the 1730s onward, the urgency to continue the conquest increasingly stemmed from territorial disputes with England. Spanish Central America bore a longstanding animosity toward the English due to the latter's participation in piracy and contraband, but the context changed in the second half of the eighteenth century when English adventurers increasingly settled on the mainland. What is more, by the 1740s, English officials began to officially recognize these settlements as English, challenging Spain's theoretical claims to the entire isthmus. At stake in the ongoing conquest, then, was not only control of Indigenous peoples but also halting English expansion.

Moreover, Mosquito expansion also remained a major concern, though in the first half of the 1730s, direct contact with the Mosquito became rare. In Honduras, for example, the governor received reports in March 1730 that non-Christianized Amerindians were arriving in Spanish frontier settlements near Matagalpa after fleeing from Mosquito raids. The attacks did not reach Spanish towns, leaving officials to rely on reports from refugees. Nonetheless, the events were alarming, threatening Spanish plans to expand mission settlements.[37]

A similar situation was also occurring in Costa Rica. In the coastal Matina Valley, a steady stream of escaped captives kept officials informed about Mosquito activities, even as the valley itself remained insulated from Mosquito attacks. In February 1730, for example, two escaped Amerindian captives from Chiriqui arrived in Matina. When questioned about Mosquito leaders, they informed the governor of Costa Rica that the powerful Mosquito chief Hannibal had recently died, leaving his son Briton to succeed him.[38] Then in December 1733, another escaped captive reported that the Mosquito king Peter had also died.[39] Overall, these reports suggested that the Mosquito had been weakened by a devastating epidemic. Nonetheless, they remained a threat as they continued to rebuild their strength by attacking Indigenous settlements beyond the Spanish frontier.

Despite this brief lapse, however, diplomatic contacts with Mosquito leaders resumed later in the 1730s, signaling a recovery in the confederation's strength. In September of 1736, for example, the governor of Honduras received word that the Mosquito king wanted to negotiate a formal trade agreement with Trujillo.[40] It remains unclear to what extent the governor considered accepting the offer, but local officials must have at least taken the offer seriously enough to host the Mosquito delegates cordially and forward the offer to the president's office in Guatemala.[41] Nonetheless, Guatemalan officials rejected the terms, unequivocally calling the Mosquito enemies, consistent with official policy during the Costa Rican negotiations of the 1710s and 1720s. As an alternative, they recommended that Honduran officials attempt to isolate the Mosquito by courting other Indigenous groups in the area, such as the Payas, as allies.[42]

Despite Guatemala's tough stance, however, realities on the ground remained more complicated. In Costa Rica, for example, a diplomatic crisis ensued when a group of fugitives fleeing the Mosquito arrived in Matina in March of 1736.[43] Given that the fugitives were avowed enemies of the Mosquito who even professed that they would harass passing Mosquito piraguas if allowed to settle in Matina, granting the fugitive refuge would have been consistent with the ongoing policy of treating the Mosquito themselves as enemies, as well as courting enemies of the Mosquito as possible Spanish allies. Accordingly, Costa Rican officials allowed the fugitives to stay and become Spanish subjects.

The enormous stakes of this decision became clear, however, when the Mosquito king himself visited Matina at the head of a large fleet soon after in January 1737—the first time a major confederation leader had visited Costa Rica since 1728—demanding that the fugitives be returned.[44] Despite official policy calling the Mosquito enemies, the outnumbered Costa Rican guard had little choice but to greet the fleet diplomatically. Thus, the Costa Rican stance toward the Mosquito remained more ambiguous in practice, and Matina officials remained open to placating Mosquito visitors rather than simply declaring them enemies. At the same time, however, the governor of Costa Rica did begin to pay more attention to defense, invoking the memory of Hannibal's 1724 invasion in taking the threats of the Mosquito king seriously.[45] Nonetheless, the Costa Rican governor still resisted giving in to Mosquito demands completely, instead focusing on military solutions such as renewing efforts to construct a fort in the Matina Valley.[46]

Consequently, as the revived Mosquito Confederation became more aggressive in the late 1730s, Spanish policymakers became increasingly recalcitrant in the face of Mosquito demands. As in the past, however, the tactics of the ongoing Spanish conquest proved largely ineffective at preventing Mosquito attacks. In 1738, for example, the Mosquito raided the Honduran settlement of Catacamas, striking within Spanish territory for the first time in years. It remains unclear if the invasion had any relation to the failed negotiations started two years earlier, but reports suggested the invasion turned into a slave raid, with invaders taking dozens of captives. At the start of the 1740s, Spanish authorities in Central America remained acutely aware that the conquest of the Caribbean frontier remained incomplete. Missions had made little progress in subjugating free Amerindian groups, the ability to confront Mosquito expansion with superior force remained illusory, and efforts to dislodge English logwood colonies failed to keep pace. Moreover, with the outbreak of war between Spain and England in 1739, these weaknesses became more urgent, as Central American authorities feared that the English might strike at this vulnerable spot.[47]

It was against this background of heightened tensions and Spanish recalcitrance that the Mosquito invaded Matina with a massive twenty-two-piragua convoy in July of 1740. The fleet assembled off the coast of Matina on the night of July 12. At the time, a "mulato libre" named Juan Matias de Baraona, a Black slave named Manuel Garcia, and another free Black named Eufemio de Moya were fishing near the beach at the port of Suerre where they encountered a small group of Mosquito scouts, who quickly captured the Matineros to prevent them from raising an alarm. After leaving the captives tied up with the main force near the mouth of the Matina, the Mosquito invaded, taking the Matina militia hostage and sacking the cacao haciendas along the river.[48] Matias de Baraona later escaped and gave an account of what he had seen, but it was too late to prevent the raid. These attacks made the looming threats to Spanish Central America more tangible. Whereas Mosquito raids in the previous decade had concentrated on Indigenous peoples in the Spanish periphery, the Mosquito suddenly decided to demonstrate their capacity to attack the Spanish directly. This was especially shocking for Costa Rica, since the Mosquito had not launched an invasion of this kind since Hannibal's retaliatory attack in 1726.

Moreover, adding to the anxiety of Spanish Central America, an English captain had in fact accompanied the Mosquito expedition during the Matina attack. Some witnesses presumed that the governor of Jamaica had ordered the invasion, and adding to this fear of future English incursions, Matias de Baraona—who spoke some Miskitu having been a Mosquito captive before—reported overhearing his captors talking about English plans to attack Spanish forts in Chagres and San Juan River.[49] Ultimately, with its weaknesses exposed and new threats emerging, Spanish Central America braced itself to confront these challenges to the ongoing conquest. And as always, frontier actors in provinces like Costa Rica continued to play a central role in these processes.

After the 1740 invasion of Matina, the governor of Costa Rica, Juan Gemmir y Lleonhart, turned his attention toward strengthening the Caribbean coast by finally fulfilling the long-standing call to build new fortifications in the vulnerable valley. Costa Rican officials had considered building a fort in Matina since as early as 1729, yet the cost of delivering materials to the distant port remained a major obstacle.[50] Moreover, the urgency to build the fort waned in the early 1730s when Mosquito fleets stopped arriving and the threat of invasions temporarily dissipated. Governor Gemmir y Lleonhart's predecessor revived the idea in January 1737, however, when Mosquito fleets began to menace the valley once again.[51] Later in 1737, the governor's office sent surveyors to plan the construction and assess the costs, but the project faced additional delays.[52] It was not until after the invasion in 1740, then, that the Costa Rican government began making serious efforts to construct the fort. Progress was still slow, but by the start of 1744, a wooden fortification named San Fernando de Matina stood near the mouth of the Matina River with a small militia garrison of roughly fifty men.

Ultimately, the fort provided little protection for the valley, and in fact, the fort may have made life in Matina even more dangerous by drawing the ire of the Mosquito. In late 1744, for example, a group of escaped slaves from the English-controlled island of San Andres arrived in Matina and reported overhearing that the Mosquito leaders were planning a joint expedition with the English. According to the informants, the purpose of the invasion was specifically to take the fort.[53] The Matina garrison was terrified, therefore, when a large force of twenty-four Mosquito piraguas and an English brigantine surrounded the defensive structure in a brief siege in April 1745. Luckily, the fleet ultimately decided not to attack, instead raising a flag or truce and delivering a message on behalf of an English merchant. The exact contents of this message remain obscure, but it most likely involved terms of trade, which remained a common feature of Mosquito and English visits for the rest of the decade.[54]

The fleet then sailed on without any hostilities. Nonetheless, the Matina militia remained on high alert, understanding that Matina was a highly visible and highly vulnerable target for Mosquito and English attacks. Fears in

Costa Rica further increased in November 1745 when another small group of supposed fugitives arrived at the fort fleeing from Mosquito territory. Not only did the fugitives report that the Mosquito had plans to support an English attack in the upcoming year, but when the captain of the fort ordered the fugitives to be escorted to Cartago, they attacked the guard while in transit. This series of events alarmed Costa Ricans even more, and Governor Gemmir y Lleonhart concluded that the fugitives were spies sent by the English to gather intelligence for the upcoming attack.[55]

The prediction of a Mosquito attack turned out to be correct, though the invasion was not as imminent as it had seemed in 1745. The next year passed without further incident, but in 1747, the province suffered two incursions. The first occurred in April when a large force of Mosquito soldiers simply bypassed the fort, traveling further upriver and attacking various haciendas in the valley.[56] The fort was useless in inhibiting the invaders, and for days after the incursion, the militia could see campfires in the distant hills indicating that the Mosquito were also exploring land-based entry points into the valley for future attacks.[57] Interestingly, roughly two weeks after the invasion, a released prisoner arrived back at the fort reporting that the Mosquito had offered to cease the hostilities if Matina opened its ports to Mosquito trade. Otherwise, Mosquito soldiers would return within the year to destroy the fort, which remained a visible symbol of Costa Rican recalcitrance.[58]

Cartago officials did not seriously consider accepting the offer, instead dispatching additional soldiers to Matina in preparation for a possible invasion.[59] But this made little difference. On August 14, a joint force of roughly seventy English and Mosquito soldiers attacked the fort directly, arriving from the hills rather than the normal entry point at the mouth of the Matina River. The garrison quickly surrendered after a brief skirmish that left two killed and three more injured.[60] The attackers then held the garrison captive as they carried out the previous threat to burn the fort.[61] When the invaders finally left, they released the captives, with some witnesses reporting once again that the English soldiers threatened to invade again within two months if the valley refused to include them in the cacao trade. The threat may have been exaggerated as no full-scale invasion occurred, but the following year, a passing Mosquito fleet did stop in Matina to impress ten members of the militia on watch at an advanced lookout post. The Mosquito forced the captives to serve on the southern fleet before allowing some to escape and releasing others the following year.[62]

English Competition and the Mosquito Shore Intendency, 1720–1749

At the start of the 1720s, the English relationship with the Mosquito was proving to be both economically and politically beneficial. Along with buying tortoiseshell and slaves from the Mosquito in order to make the colonial venture profitable, the English in Jamaica also continued to contract with the Mosquito Kingdom for defense. The fiscal solvency of the colonial venture was a factor here as well. Whereas Jamaica had risen in economic value as a slave-based plantation economy, the ongoing threat of slave insurrections, as well as attacks by armed groups of runaway slaves often referred to as "maroons," placed the planters in a precarious situation. According to Uring, Jamaican authorities first reached out to the Mosquito for help in catching runaway slaves sometime around 1707.[63] Subsequently, the threat of slave revolt continued to be a major concern when Nicolas Lawes was appointed governor of the island in 1718, especially as runaways continued to join powerful maroon colonies.

Consequently, when the Mosquito king Jeremy II visited Jamaica in 1720 to greet Governor Lawes in person, the governor took the opportunity to solicit help. Governor Lawes and King Jeremy signed a contract in June 1720 in which the English hired Mosquito forces as mercenaries to help catch runaway slaves. The contract agreed to pay soldiers forty shillings, officers three pounds, and chiefs four pounds per month of service.[64] For Lawes, contracting with the Mosquito promised a cost-effective solution to the colony's defense problem, and he bragged to his superiors that the agreement would ultimately save money. He also reported that King Jeremy upheld his end of the deal, arriving promptly with a large contingent of troops in November.[65]

Despite this formal collaboration with the governor's office, however, English colonists feared that the Mosquito might shift their loyalties at any time, with disastrous consequences. An early example of this fear manifested in the recurring complaints by English merchants regarding King Jeremy's diplomatic overtures in Costa Rica. It is not clear exactly when the English became aware of these negotiations, but Jamaican merchants were reportedly grumbling about the situation at least as early as 1720. In April of that year, only two months before Jeremy's visit with Governor Lawes, a Jamaican trading sloop had rendezvoused with the Mosquito governor Hannibal and the rest of the fleet on its way south in hopes of convincing the Mosquito leaders to raid Costa Rica's Matina Valley. Hannibal was staunchly opposed, however, instead visiting Matina at the head of a peaceful delegation and reporting the incident to Costa Rican authorities.[66]

According to Hannibal's own version of events, the response had angered the English traders, and while Hannibal may have exaggerated the details in order to ingratiate himself with his Costa Rican hosts, more evidence of English frustration arose in 1722 when Costa Rica sent emissaries to visit Hannibal at his home in Dacora. During the visit, an English trading sloop happened to arrive at the same time. Shocked to find Spanish agents among the Mosquito, the panicked English captain attempted to arrest the Costa Ricans and deliver them to Jamaica. Further frustrating the English traders, Hannibal defied this request, instead intervening to protect his Costa Rican guests. In this case, the event was not only reported by Hannibal himself as in the 1720 example but corroborated by eyewitnesses in the Costa Rican delegation.[67]

These incidents were relatively minor, and they ultimately passed over quickly without interrupting the established pattern commerce. For example, Jamaican merchants coordinated with Hannibal to purchase stolen cacao after Hannibal's invasion of Matina in 1724 only two years later.[68] Nonetheless, these events represented early examples of English fears of possibly losing Mosquito support. Even though early travel writers such as M. W. and Uring had made bold claims about Mosquito loyalty to the English and hatred of the Spanish, English traders and colonists on the ground understood that the situation was more complicated in practice. Indeed, the Mosquito Confederation made no attempt to hide its negotiations with Costa Rica in the 1720s, and English agents witnessed them firsthand.

Against this background, a major turning point in the English efforts to colonize the mainland occurred around the year 1732 with the founding of Black River. Like other mainland colonies, the outpost was not part of any official English conquest. Black River was originally founded informally by English logwood cutters from Belize where harassment by the Spanish coast guard was making smuggling increasingly difficult. Among the founders was a man named William Pitt, a distant relative of the English prime minister of the same name, and a well-connected merchant who had already amassed significant wealth after first arriving in Belize in 1725.[69] Logwood did not grow in the Black River area, but the site offered the potential to participate in other lucrative trades such as in mahogany, sarsaparilla, and tortoiseshell.[70] Moreover, the site was well within the bounds of Mosquito territory, offering the promise of protection from Spanish harassment. Indeed, the principal Mosquito chief in the region was General Hobby, who had just recently demonstrated his willingness to confront the Spanish coast guard.[71]

Even though Black River was founded as an informal settlement, it soon came to play a central role in English efforts to formalize their expansion into mainland territories. This strategy was not unique to Black River: extending legal recognition to informal settlements and "pirate nests" was a key practice of conquest throughout the English Caribbean.[72] Applying this strategy in Black River, however, was especially important since the colony promised to provide a key foothold on the mainland at a time when the English conquest was still primarily relegated to islands. And of course, this strategy depended on the Mosquito, who not only provided physical support to the colony but also had the capacity to legitimize it. To recall, the 1670 Treaty of Madrid had stated that each colonial power would keep the territory currently occupied, and since the Mosquito had been independent at the time of its signing, the English argued the Mosquito Coast did not legally pertain to the Spanish Crown. From this perspective, the English only needed permission from the Mosquito leaders to acquire territory. This interpretation was contested by the Spanish, so higher authorities in England would eventually have to decide whether supporting the colony would be worth the controversy. Nonetheless, within a few years of the founding of Pitt's Black River colony, local officials in the Caribbean were already promoting the idea that permission from Mosquito leaders was enough to formalize English colonization under the terms of the Treaty of Madrid, regardless of Spanish complaints.

An early proponent of formalizing the Black River settlement was the recently appointed governor of Jamaica, Edward Trelawny. After becoming governor in 1738, Trelawny spent the next decade and a half working closely with William Pitt to turn the Mosquito Shore into a legally recognized English colony. One of Trelawny's first acts as governor in 1738 was to grant Robert Hodgson, an ambitious adventurer with close ties to Pitt, a commission as an officer.[73] Then, when war broke out between the English and Spanish in 1739—a conflict that came to be known as the War of Jenkins's Ear—Trelawny sent Hodgson to meet with the Mosquito headmen to secure their support against the Spanish. Hodgson succeeded in gaining an audience with the principal Mosquito leaders in March of 1740, and they signed an official treaty. The Mosquito likely did not view the treaty as a major turning point, approaching the ceremony as just another symbol of the alliance that they had maintained in various forms for decades. For the English however, the treaty was a vital document providing a legal basis for the colony, and officials would reference it for decades to come. For example, the wording of the treaty specified that English settlers would be allowed to settle, and it even claimed that the Mosquito themselves had agreed to become subjects of the English king. Moreover, English officials later titled the document the "Cession of the Mosquito Kingdom to Great Britain" when they reproduced copies.[74]

After signing the treaty, Hodgson set out on an expedition with the Mosquito southern fleet.[75] Along with legitimizing the English presence on the Mosquito Coast, Hodgson's mission also included short-term military concerns related to the War of Jenkins's Ear. English authorities recognized that Central America was a vulnerable spot in Spain's overseas empire, and the high command in the West Indies made the isthmus a central part of the English strategy.[76] The English lacked military resources in the region, however, so Hodgson hoped to mobilize the powerful Mosquito forces for an early strike.

According to Hodgson's report, he commanded the expedition. The events of the expedition, however, indicate that this was a major exaggeration. The twenty-two-piragua expedition of two hundred Mosquito and nine Englishmen set out on April 16, making the slow journey south to arrive at the Cocle River in late May. For his part, Hodgson encouraged the Mosquito fleet to attack the Spanish Fort Inmaculada near the mouth of the San Juan River, a waterway connecting the Caribbean to the important Spanish colonial center of Granada. Highlighting the limits of Hodgson's influence, however, Mosquito leaders disagreed, and they ultimately settled on attacking the small, vulnerable outpost of Veragua on the Cocle River instead. Frustrated, Hodgson continued pressuring the Mosquito to contribute to the war effort by attacking a Spanish garrison, and while the Mosquito leaders stubbornly refused attacking Fort Inmaculada, they did agree to attack the coastal cacao plantations in Costa Rica's Matina Valley. The invasion resulted in a successful cacao heist, yet the Mosquito leaders frustrated Hodgson once again by making overtures of peace and even informing Costa Rican officials about Hodgson's plans to attack Nicaragua.[77]

Despite their propensity to act freely regardless of English wishes, the Mosquito Confederation remained both impressively powerful and generally friendly to the English. Accordingly, after receiving Hodgson's report on the Mosquito treaty and the subsequent expedition, Jamaican governor Trelawny wrote in March 1741 to the Board of Trade in England suggesting further collaboration with the Mosquito in the war effort. Trelawny described the Mosquito condescendingly, confessing that it may seem "ridiculous" to work with such "poor wretches" as the Mosquito Indians. Nonetheless, the letter was a tacit recognition that the English needed help in furthering their colonial expansion, and that the Mosquito were positioned to be arbiters of English designs on the mainland. Trelawny also sent Hodgson back to the Mosquito Shore in December 1741 while waiting for a response from the Board of Trade. In the meantime, Hodgson had orders to begin organizing the Mosquito, whom Trelawny assumed to live in a "natural" state without government.[78]

Whereas the War of Jenkins's Ear technically continued until a new treaty officially ended the conflict in 1748, the main operations of the war abated much earlier, and ultimately, Trelawny's plans for additional Mosquito expeditions never manifested. Still, he continued to view the Mosquito Shore as an important base for mainland expansion and wrote to the duke of Newcastle in July 1743 asking for recognition of the Mosquito Shore as part of an official "intendency" of the English empire. The presence of Black River provided an important justification for the plan, though again, Trelawny tacitly admitted that the creation of an intendency would ultimately depend on Mosquito support. In fact, he argued that the English government needed to establish a presence on the Mosquito Coast sooner rather than later since he feared the supposedly barbarous Mosquito might join the Spanish if left without English governance.[79] In another letter with the same date, Trelawny went on to explain that a Spanish priest from the port of Trujillo on the Honduran coast had recently written to Black River proposing to open trade between the two frontier outposts in exchange for the English preventing the Mosquito from attacking Spanish missions. It is possible that the letter contributed to the English fear that the Mosquito might be swayed by Spanish overtures, though Trelawny ultimately presented the occurrence as an economic opportunity validating government investment in the colony. Accordingly, he suggested sending English troops to Black River to assist Hodgson in setting up a formal government.[80]

Trelawny took additional steps to formalize English colonization of the Mosquito Shore a few months later in December 1743. Writing again to the duke of Newcastle in England, Trelawny argued that the English already controlled enough islands in the Caribbean and that it was now time to concentrate on the mainland. He further argued that while informal settlements had facilitated some commercial expansion, the lawlessness and lack of government in these settlements had presented barriers to growth. Accordingly, he argued that the Mosquito Shore could be a lucrative colonial venture if only it had more government regulation. As a further incentive to government investment, Trelawny explained that settlers in Black River already had plans to cut an overland road to Guatemala that if managed properly would grow trade even further.[81]

The governor of Jamaica also used his own authority to add some preliminary legitimization to the colony, even while awaiting the response of higher authorities in England. Writing to William Pitt in Black River, Trelawny authorized him to make legal land grants, assuring him that private landholdings on the Mosquito Shore would be officially recognized by the Jamaican government. The purpose of the plan was to entice more settlers to Black River, who would be more motivated to invest with their property rights guaranteed by the government.[82] Trelawny also enlisted the help of Robert Hodgson, who drafted a report on the Mosquito Shore for the Board of Trade the following year in 1744. The report echoed Trelawny's assessment of the shore's commercial potential, describing for example the Mosquito piragua fleets that maintained a steady supply of tortoiseshell.[83]

Despite efforts by Trelawny and Hodgson, the matter of recognizing the Mosquito Shore intendency remained pending for several years. In the meantime, English merchants and contrabandists continued to work with the Mosquito Kingdom to informally expand English influence. This included participating in long-established trades such as tortoiseshell and slaves, as well as providing auxiliary forces in the Mosquito fleet. In May 1747, for example, the Mosquito invaded Matina Valley in order to pressure Spanish authorities to reopen ports to Mosquito trade.[84] The fleet then returned in August to exert additional pressure on the recalcitrant Costa Ricans, this time burning the recently constructed fort that garrisoned the Matina militia.[85] It remains unclear to what extent Hodgson or Trelawny were involved or even aware of these activities, though on both occasions, witnesses reported seeing English auxiliaries working alongside the Mosquito attackers.

It was not until 1749 that authorities in England finally acted on Trelawny's recommendations to officially create the Mosquito Shore Intendency.[86] Along with the reports and recommendations that he had sent over the years, Robert Hodgson traveled to England to meet in person with the influential duke of Bedford, who in October gave his official backing to the plan. Hodgson then began the long return journey, arriving in Jamaica in

February 1750 to deliver the news to Trelawny.[87] Afterward, Hodgson returned to Black River, now officially the first superintendent of the Mosquito Shore.

Conclusion

The events described in this chapter help to highlight the durability of the Mosquito Confederation during the 1730s and 1740s despite the disruptions caused by the epidemic and political tensions of the late 1720s. True, the geopolitical influence of the Mosquito did briefly contract as the outbreak limited the confederation's ability to coordinate manpower for expeditions, yet the Mosquito reemerged as a regional power in the late 1730s with a revived fleet and a reinvigorated geopolitical assertiveness. Significantly, while this revived geopolitical program did include raiding—especially targeting neighboring Indigenous groups—the confederation also continued its long-standing practice of making diplomatic overtures to Spanish provinces. Again, these findings run counter to the bulk of previous research, which has widely presumed that the Mosquito overwhelmingly treated the Spanish as enemies. And even though some studies have noted peace offers during this period such as the 1736 treaty proposal to Honduras, they presumed that these events were either ruses to trick the Spanish or isolated attempts in moments of desperation.[88] A fuller recounting of these events and their contexts, however, shows that negotiation with the Spanish provinces, especially Costa Rica, had actually been the norm since 1711, with bouts of violence occurring irregularly and almost always in response to a specific provocation.

This chapter also adds additional evidence against the broader narrative that the Mosquito became economically and culturally dependent on foreign goods, as well as the corollary assumption that this alleged dependence led them into a vicious cycle of raiding and trading that determined their way of life. For example, one influential version of the raiding and trading hypothesis has stressed the importance of imported firearms for Mosquito military power relative to their neighbors, a situation that in theory required constant use of firearms in raiding in order to acquire goods to trade for more firearms for more raids.[89] Yet descriptions of specific raids show that still as late as the 1740s, firearms played only a minimal role in military activities. According to Hodgson's notes on the 1740 expedition, firearms were present though barely used, with the overwhelming numbers and coordinated surprise assault proving decisive. Moreover, a logical extension of the predominant raid and trade hypothesis has been the assumption that the Mosquito, in order to specialize in raiding, abandoned other traditional subsistence activities.[90] Nevertheless, eyewitness accounts for this period contradict this hypothesis as well. Captive narratives from the 1730s, for example, describe Mosquito agriculture as sufficient to produce everything they needed.[91] And Hodgson himself wrote in the 1750s that the Mosquito still produced their own food and crafts.[92]

Ultimately, this chapter has demonstrated that the Mosquito Confederation's activities were more complex than a vicious cycle of raiding and trading, and confederation leaders entered the fray of Central American conquests from a position of strength rather than desperation or dependence. At the midpoint of the eighteenth century, the Mosquito remained a closely united regional power, and English colonies depended more on Mosquito support to remain viable rather than the other way around.

CHAPTER 4

Mosquito Aggression and Reconciliation with Costa Rica, 1747–1763

When the Mosquito fleet came into view, a sense of dread fell over the Matina Valley. It was June 1763, and Costa Rica's relationship with the powerful Mosquito Kingdom had grown increasingly hostile over the past decade. The vulnerable coastal outpost of Matina had suffered the brunt of these hostilities, and the valley's inhabitants were still recovering from a raid only two days earlier when suddenly, the fleet reappeared. This time, however, it approached making signs of peace. The Mosquito captains then released a captive who carried a diplomatic letter on behalf of the principal Mosquito leaders. The news was hopeful: after years of increasing hostilities between Costa Rica and the Mosquito Kingdom, the Mosquito now wanted to offer a treaty. In return for ceasing hostilities, the letter asked for a series of gifts, as well as assurance that fleets could gather food and supplies in Matina on future expeditions. Matina officials feared that the treaty was possibly a ruse, but they also knew that similar protection agreements had worked in the past. Consequently, as the Matina lieutenant forwarded the letter to Cartago to be reviewed by the governor, the valley finally had hope for a truce.[1]

The purpose of this chapter is to examine Mosquito practices during the period of roughly 1747 to 1763, as well as Spanish and English reactions to these practices, in order to highlight the ongoing role of the confederation in shaping imperial outcomes in the region. In describing these events, the chapter argues that this period was characterized by heightened hostility between the Mosquito and the Spanish, with Costa Rica in particular suffering a barrage of Mosquito attacks that stand out compared to other periods for both their frequency and intensity. Nonetheless, these hostilities were temporary, and the Mosquito Confederation initiated a process of reconciliation in 1763, thus allowing Costa Rica to establish a precedent for negotiating with the Mosquito that would inform wider Spanish policy for the rest of the century. Throughout these processes of hostility and reconciliation, the hallmarks of Mosquito conquest remained visible, with the confederation council remaining closely united in coordinating manpower for large fleets, which carried out diplomatic, commercial, and geopolitical objectives.

Interestingly, there is also some evidence that the council exercised looser control over the confederation during this period as smaller, private raiding ventures—often in conjunction with English allies—became more frequent. Accordingly, this chapter further highlights how English efforts at colonial expansion continued to attach themselves to the knowledge, manpower, and political structures of the Mosquito. At the same time, however, the English remained dependent on the goodwill of Mosquito leaders, and indeed, the council would take steps in later periods to reassert tighter controls by taking measures against the English-led privatization of raiding. Furthermore, English settlers would also become increasingly frustrated with Mosquito negotiations with the Spanish, which remained common after the Costa Rican reconciliation in 1763. Accordingly, this chapter also highlights the extent to which Spanish efforts to woo the Mosquito at the end of the century—most famously in the late 1780s after the English evacuated their Mosquito Shore settlements—were not novel but rather drew from extensive precedents that went back to the first half of the century and were later revived in the 1760s.

The Mosquito Confederation and Reconciliation with the Spanish, 1747–1763

During the mid-1740s at the same time that the confederation was increasing its aggression in Costa Rica, Mosquito fleets were also carrying out violent raids along the northern coast of Honduras and within the interior river systems of Nicaragua. In 1746, for example, the Mosquito launched a raid on the primarily Indigenous pueblo of San Pedro de Lovago, occupying the village during a religious festival and, according to later reports, enslaving "half of the village." Many of the captives were sold to the English, though several were kept as laborers, and at least three—a man named Antonio and two women named Thomasa and Agustina—escaped to Matina six years later to describe the events to Costa Rican authorities.[2] Then, in

1749, the Mosquito attacked a recently founded Franciscan mission of Boaco at the Spanish frontier of Nicaragua, killing the head missionary and taking several captives.[3] The same year, a passing Mosquito band also occupied a small mining operation on the Honduran coast, taking six captives from among the miners.[4]

As in Costa Rica, however, violence was not the only tactic available to the confederation, and indeed, Mosquito leaders were open to negotiating with Spanish officials in Nicaragua and Honduras when the opportunity arose. A salient example occurred in 1751 when a Spanish missionary, Juan Joseph Solis y Miranda, arrived in Black River, a settlement on the northern section of the Mosquito Coast. Solis y Miranda met with several Mosquito leaders, including King Edward, as well as a wealthy English settler in Black River, William Pitt. For the most part, the Mosquito leaders received Father Solis y Miranda kindly, showing interest in Catholicism, though more importantly, negotiating with the priest in order to secure trade contacts.[5] The terms paralleled the peace offer that King Edward had previously made to Trujillo back in 1736, though ultimately the negotiations were cut short when English agents arrested Solis y Miranda and carried him to Jamaica for trial.[6]

In many ways, the 1750s ushered in a new era in Mosquito history. Whereas leaders with close personal ties to Jeremy, Hannibal, and Peter still directed the confederation during the 1740s, the 1750s saw the rise of a new generation of leaders. The long-standing fixture in Mosquito politics, General Charles Hobby, died sometime in the 1740s, leaving a new general named Handyside to take his place. Handyside was probably Hobby's son, and while his age at assuming the title is unknown, he was likely too young to have played any major role in the confederation's early days of expansion since he is never mentioned in any documents from the era of Jeremy II's tenure.[7] By 1755 King Edward had also passed away, and a Zambo-Mosquito named George became the next king. According to English sources, George was the younger brother of King Edward and the son of King Jeremy II.[8] Like Handyside, George was never mentioned in earlier documents, so he was likely too young to have played much of a role in Mosquito politics while his father was directing the confederation's expansion forty years earlier.

By 1757, the confederation also had a new governor: a Tawira leader named William Briton, who was probably the son of the previous governor, John Briton, and the grandson of Hannibal. Governor throughout the

1730s and 1740s, John Briton had participated in the confederation's expansion, with Costa Rican documents reporting that he had even hosted the Costa Rican delegation that visited Hannibal's home in 1722.[9] William Briton, on the other hand, was almost certainly too young to have had similar experiences. Finally, a new position of admiral also developed, and while the lineage of the admiral is a bit more obscure, the title was held by a Tawira-Mosquito named Dilson throughout the 1750s. It is possible that Dilson was the same "Admiral Dilly" who met with Robert Hodgson back in 1740, though he also may have been his son. Regardless, the relative newness of the position, and the absence of any reference to the position of admiral before 1740, suggests that the Dilson of the 1750s was not directly involved in the early exploits of the confederation.

Under this new generation of leaders, the relationship between the Mosquito Confederation and Costa Rica became more hostile than ever before. This was partly due to the new central council taking a different approach to foreign relations, though the official policies of the confederation are difficult to assess since many of the Mosquito incursions during the 1750s were not carried out by massive fleets headed by council members; rather, they increasingly comprised small parties that may have been acting independently. Regardless of the exact cause, the 1750s stands out as a unique period of Mosquito imperial practice, with the frequency and intensity of hostilities in Costa Rica increasing dramatically.

1753 presents a good starting point for analyzing this escalation. In that year, Mosquito convoys invaded the Matina Valley on two separate occasions. The first invasion occurred on May 26 when a large force of over one hundred soldiers surprised the Matina guard in an early-morning assault, subduing the militia and proceeding to loot several cacao plantations. The size of the invasion force suggests that this was the united southern fleet organized by the confederation council. Unlike previous incursions, however, the raiders did not leave any letters asking for trade privileges or justifying their actions. Therefore, in contrast to the invasions of the 1740s, which had still followed a pattern of gunboat diplomacy, this invasion was a more direct act of hostility.[10] Then, less than two weeks later, on June 5, the Mosquito invaded again, traveling further upriver to loot haciendas that had not been attacked in the previous invasion. This time the invasion force comprised only three piraguas, suggesting this may have been an independent venture that was not necessarily planned by the council, though it also could have been an offshoot of the main fleet.[11]

Significantly, these invasions still did not represent all-out warfare: the invaders arrested the port guards rather than killing them, and they did not take any slaves, focusing instead on pilfering cacao and other goods. Additionally, the Mosquito council later allowed the British superintendent stationed on the Mosquito Shore to return some of the cacao in an effort to prevent hostilities from breaking out between England and Spain.[12] However, the rapid succession of these two attacks, as well as the lack of accompanying efforts to negotiate commercial arrangements, signaled the intensification of hostilities.

Indeed, relations took a major turn for the worse in 1756 when a passing group of Mosquito mariners kidnapped and executed the recently appointed governor of Costa Rica, who happened to be visiting Matina at the time. The incident occurred on July 2 as the governor was taking a morning stroll along the beach near the mouth of the Matina River. A group of four Mosquito men that had been hiding in the area suddenly approached the governor when he was too far away from the fort to retreat. The group conversed cordially with the governor for some time, even allowing him to send for the militia lieutenant, a translator, and gifts of tobacco. However, the visitors suddenly grabbed the two Costa Rican officials and carried them off to a canoe just as another twenty-five well-armed Mosquito fighters appeared. These reinforcements provided cover fire to prevent the Matina militia from pursuing, and the entire band escaped with the two high-profile captives.[13] The Mosquito later executed the prisoners under circumstances that remain obscure. Rumors of the assassinations circulated among Mosquito and English settlements over the next few months, and one version that was overheard by a slave on an English settler—and later reported in Costa Rica when the slave escaped—was that after traveling a short ways up the coast just out of sight of the Matina fort, the kidnappers had mocked the captives before maliciously killing them with spears. They then disposed of the bodies into the sea, where they were never found.[14]

The exact motives for the assassinations are difficult to discern, in part because the move was so unprecedented. The confederation had a long history of negotiating with the Matina Valley, and even when violent incursions had occurred in the past, they had typically limited bloodshed, especially when it came to Spanish officials. The assassination of two high-ranking officials was a major deviation from the norm. On the one hand, this may have represented the increasing aggression of the new confederation council. Again, by 1756, all of the leaders who had worked closely with Costa Rica in the past had died. Thus, the new generation of leaders, far removed from the personal ties that previous Mosquito leaders had forged in Costa Rica, may have simply decided to take a different direction in foreign policy. On the other hand, the attack may have had nothing to do with the confederation council at all. By all accounts, it was a small band that captured the officials—not a large fleet—so it is possible that the event simply represented the increasing tendency of Mosquito men participating in private acts of piracy. Either way, the shocking assassinations only bred more resentment between Costa Rica and the Mosquito Confederation, ushering in another half decade of intense hostilities before resolving in a lasting reconciliation.

Tensions further escalated in August 1759, when a large trading party of over fifty Mosquito sailors with six piraguas arrived in Matina escorting three Dutch and English cargo ships. Hoping to get around the restrictions on trading with foreigners, one of the Dutch captains first sent a Spanish sailor to the port to ask for a trading license. The rest of the party then followed, spending an entire week at the port trading with the inhabitants of the valley. On the eighth night, however, Spanish soldiers ambushed the traders while they slept, killing dozens and seizing the rest of the cargo. Most of the Mosquito traders died, but a few escaped, and word of the massacre spread.[15]

In the absence of sources such as letters from confederation leaders or interviews with escaped captives who worked closely with Mosquito leaders, the exact reaction of the confederation council to the Matina ambush remains unknown. However, given the long precedent of confederation forces protecting Mosquito traders, the council members were likely incensed by the callous attack. And indeed, for the next four years, Mosquito incursions into the Matina Valley became more incessant than ever. In fact, as evidence of the council's rage, Mosquito leaders even began exploring the possibility of invading the inland capital of Cartago—something that the Mosquito had never even considered before the ambush. After pressuring Costa Rican captives for information about how to reach the city, Admiral Dilson led a massive allied force of Tawira, Zambo, and English forces in 1761 to the mouth of the Colorado River to see if it might provide a way to get closer to the capital. The expedition ultimately decided that they did not have enough information yet to successfully attack Cartago, and instead followed a better-known route along the San Juan River for a brief siege of Fort Inmaculada. Still, Mosquito leaders did not give up on the idea of sacking the Costa Rican capital, and an extension of Dilson's forces made a brief incursion into

Matina on July 24 to take additional captives. And as before, Mosquito leaders pressured the captives for geographical information that would facilitate an attack on Cartago.[16]

Hostilities increased even more the following year, with Mosquito forces making at least three additional incursions into Costa Rica. The first invasion occurred in June, and while only a small force of three piraguas entered the Matina River, the invaders reportedly managed to carry away roughly twenty captives.[17] The next invasion occurred in August when another small group of two or three piraguas carried off a few captives from a hacienda near the Matina River while a larger force of fifteen piraguas hunted turtles off the coast. These invaders may have been part of the larger fleet, though they also may have been contracted by an English merchant who purchased the captives.[18]

The largest invasion, however, occurred in September 1762 when the Mosquito made their first serious attempt at raiding Cartago. The expedition was ultimately a joint operation composed of several hundred Zambo, Tawira, and English fighters, along with additional Black and Amerindian slaves. Descriptions of the event do not clarify which if any of the confederation council members accompanied the expedition, though the attack certainly had the council's approval, with King George sending one of his personal translators to serve as a guide along with the captives that Admiral Dilson had taken and interrogated for geographic knowledge. The ambitious expedition met several challenges as soon as it reached Costa Rica, however, with one the commanders allegedly being eaten by a "tiger" as the force camped in preparation for the inland trek. The invasion force then spent the next two to three weeks searching for a chimerical hidden path to the Costa Rican capital in hopes of launching a surprise assault. Accustomed to rapid water-based attacks, the Mosquito were used to fighting with the element of surprise, and they did not want to risk sacrificing this advantage by disembarking in Matina and taking the main road to Cartago. Nonetheless, the inland corridor remained elusive, and while an advance scouting party did happen upon a Spanish outpost within a day's march of Cartago—far closer than Mosquito forces had ever reached before—the invaders were ultimately forced to give up on assaulting the capital.[19] Instead, the expedition eventually retreated back to the coast in order to raid the more familiar Matina Valley.[20]

Mosquito forces participated in at least one more invasion of Matina in February of 1763 before the confederation council finally decided to intervene to promote a reconciliation. This final invasion was small, consisting of only three piraguas, yet they again managed to subdue the small guard at the mouth of the Matina River and spend several days looting and carrying off captives.[21] When an even larger force of almost two hundred Zambo and Tawira soldiers arrived a few months later on June 7, however, Mosquito policy toward Matina began to take a different course. This was not obvious at first since the menacing force looted the cacao of the valley once again, yet after this initial demonstration of power, the Mosquito fleet decided to finally reopen diplomatic relations with the Costa Ricans. Selecting three delegates from among their prisoners and releasing the rest, the Mosquito traveled north to the mouth of the San Juan River to spend the next day discussing terms. Then, on June 8, the leader of the fleet—probably Admiral Dilson, though the presence of Zambo Mosquito soldiers, as well as mention of the Mosquito king and governor, suggest other council members were also involved—composed an official peace treaty, which one of the captives delivered to Matina the next day on June 9 when the fleet returned.[22] In the short term, the delegation demanded that the Costa Rican governor pay a tribute that included three silver-handled canes for different Mosquito leaders and several articles of clothing. Additionally, the treaty echoed previous arrangements by requiring that Mosquito fleets be allowed to peacefully gather supplies. In return, the Mosquito promised to prevent future invasions.[23]

New Challenges to the Spanish Conquest, 1748–1763

In the years leading up to Costa Rica's acceptance of the Mosquito treaty offer in 1763, the ongoing Spanish conquest of Central America had been facing numerous challenges, both in expanding Spanish governance on the ground as well as in gaining recognition of its territorial claims. With the conclusion of the War of Jenkins's Ear in 1748, hostilities between the English and Spanish formally ended. The problem for Central America, however, was that the treaty did not settle any of the territorial disputes on the isthmus: while the treaty stated that neither side would gain new territories as a result of the war, it failed to clarify what the rightful holdings before the war actually were. From the Spanish perspective, the English still needed to evacuate their settlements on the Mosquito Shore since the Spanish had claimed the lands in the original conquest, thus making English settlements such as Black River unlawful, particularly since no subsequent treaty had ever taken this territory away. On the other hand, English officials argued that the Spanish had never controlled these territories in the first place. From this perspective, the status quo treaty meant leaving the English settlements in place as they had been immediately before the war, and some English officials even felt emboldened to try to get Black River recognized as a formal colony for the first time.[24]

For both the Spanish and the English, the Mosquito Kingdom played a central role in these debates, and both sides began to shape their imperial claims around interpretations of Mosquito history. To support their side of the argument, Spanish officials dubiously claimed that the Mosquito had once been conquered by the early conquistadores, only to later rebel under the influence of English pirates. In this view, the Mosquito were rightly Spanish subjects who simply needed to be brought to order: a process that the English were unlawfully inhibiting. Conversely, English officials argued that the Mosquito were free people who had never been conquered by the Spanish in the first place. This first part of the English claim was historically accurate, though just as dubious as the Spanish counterclaims, the English argument added that the Mosquito had become English subjects after the 1740 treaty in which the Mosquito King Edward had supposedly ceded his territory to the English.[25]

Both of these viewpoints drew from a significant amount of historical invention, yet these perceptions of the past were real enough to influence royal orders emanating from Europe. In 1749, for example, the Spanish Crown sent orders to the viceroy in Mexico and the president in Guatemala to organize military expeditions to force the English to abandon their settlements on the Mosquito Shore.[26] These orders responded generally to the contested treaty terms, though the matter gained even more urgency for local actors when the Mosquito raided the recently founded Spanish mission of Boaco the same year.[27] After the attack, Spanish officials saw removing the English not only as the rightful conclusion of the war but also as an important first step in subduing the Mosquito, who remained close allies of the English.

Within this context, Governor Alonso Fernández y Heredia of Nicaragua emerged as an advocate of plans to attack the English and reduce the Mosquito by force, using the 1749 Boaco attack as evidence of English perfidy and Mosquito savagery.[28] The Nicaraguan governor then became even more incensed in 1750 at finding out that the English governor of Jamaica had designated Robert Hodgson superintendent of the Mosquito Shore in an effort to have the English mainland settlement formally recognized. Ironically, Fernández y Heredia did not find out about Hodgson's presence in Black River through any aggressive military posturing on the part of the English; rather, he discovered it through Hodgson's failed attempt to establish trade contacts with the Spanish. Hodgson had sent a messenger from Black River carrying a letter addressed to the president of Guatemala, but Spanish officials in Honduras redirected the messenger to Nicaragua to meet with Fernández y Heredia.[29] In a performance of strict loyalty to the Crown's recent orders, Fernández y Heredia refused to entertain the idea of trading with the English at Black River, instead demanding that the English evacuate the allegedly illegal settlement.[30]

Hodgson was not the first to suggest a trade agreement between Spanish Central America and Black River. In fact, his plan was largely in response to the efforts of the Spanish missionary Father Juan Solis y Miranda, who had already been in contact with the English settlers at Black River several years earlier. Solis y Miranda had first proposed the idea in 1743 while living in Trujillo, a port town of the Honduran coast that was relatively close to the English outpost at Black River. Writing directly to William Pitt, Father Miranda y Solis proposed the establishment of a mission in Black River that would promote the conversion of the Mosquito as well as facilitate trade.[31] Miranda y Solis then returned to Spain and eventually gained the king's permission for his plan to open peaceful relations with Black River, ironically around the same time that the king issued his 1749 orders to remove the English from the coast by force.[32] Solis y Miranda subsequently returned to Central America, finally arriving at the settlement of Black River on the Mosquito Coast in April 1751.[33]

The divergent approaches of the Governor Fernández y Heredia and Father Solis y Miranda illustrate important trends in Spanish policy at the time. To begin, they reveal how efforts to expand the conquest into the Mosquito Coast were driven by local actors. Royal orders were slow to arrive, vague, and even contradictory, ultimately leaving local officials to decide how to promote Spain's imperial agenda in Central America. Second, Spanish policy was intensely debated, and not even Central American officials always agreed on policies. Whereas Fernández y Heredia favored a more hardline approach based on a strict interpretation of contraband laws, Solis y Miranda promoted a looser interpretation in which the priority of expanding the mission field justified easing trade restrictions. Third, it is significant that both approaches centered on the Mosquito themselves in justifying Spanish claims. Fernández y Heredia wanted to punish the Mosquito while Solis y Miranda wanted to convert them, but in both cases, perceptions of the Mosquito were central to how Spanish officials presented their rights to extend their own influence relative to the English.

Moreover, both approaches to Spanish policy ultimately had limited implementation, indicating the continued weakness of Spanish Central America in practice. Solis y Miranda reported some early success, such as the alleged conversion of the Mosquito king Edward.[34] Nonetheless, English agents arrested Solis y Miranda in November 1751, taking him to Jamaica where he died in prison without having established any missions or lasting trade ties.[35] Moreover, despite his tough rhetoric, Fernández y Heredia never tried to organize any expedition to forcefully remove the English, making his approach to conquest far more rhetorical than practical. This rhetoric did allow him to perform fierce loyalty to the king, perhaps improving his own position within the Spanish colonial system, but it had little impact on day-to-day practices. As an excuse, he blamed the president of Guatemala for not providing enough resources.[36]

Throughout the 1750s, local actors at the frontier continued to shape Spanish policy on the ground, and during this time, relations between the Spanish and the Mosquito became even more strained. This was especially evident in Costa Rica, where Mosquito attacks became far more common than in any other period. This escalation at least partially derived from the increased aggression of Mosquito leaders, though Costa Rican leaders also provoked it by remaining recalcitrant in the face of Mosquito trade requests. Indeed, Mosquito attacks throughout the 1740s largely constituted a pattern of gunboat diplomacy, with invasions frequently accompanying demands to open Matina ports. Juan Gemmir y Lleonhart, the governor during the destruction of the Matina fort in 1747, consistently treated such trade as illegal contraband, which was consistent with monopolistic trade policies emanating from Guatemala and Spain. Furthermore, Gemmir y Lleonhart's successor—a Peninsular Spaniard named Luis Diez Navarro who had close ties to Guatemalan elites—continued these policies with even more vigor.[37]

Of course, just like previous governors, Luis Diez Navarro had no direct experience with the Mosquito and depended entirely on the knowledge of local actors. In September 1752, for example, three recently escaped captives arrived in Cartago to describe how their mostly Indigenous village in Honduras had suffered a Mosquito raid in 1746, and how they had worked among the Mosquito as slaves until escaping a few months earlier and surviving the trek to Matina. While captivity narratives of this type were not uncommon in Costa Rica, these declarations stand out as two of the informants—Tomasa Gutierrez and Agustina Morales—were women, whereas in other cases declarants were almost always men.[38]

Hostilities in Costa Rica reignited in 1753 as the Mosquito launched two separate invasions: first in May, and then again in June. Reports claimed that the invasion force numbered over one hundred Mosquito soldiers, and that the invading forces carried off most of the cacao harvest, along with tools and clothes taken from the haciendas.[39] In contrast to the invasions of the 1740s, however, witnesses of the 1753 attacks did not report seeing any English soldiers or captains. Nonetheless, since the Spanish still considered the Mosquito to be English allies, there was reason for Spanish officials to blame the English, so the invasion threatened the delicate peace that had followed the War of Jenkins's Ear. Because of this, the English superintendent of the Mosquito Shore rushed to make amends. Apologizing to the Costa Ricans for the infraction, Hodgson arranged to have the stolen cacao returned, and it did in fact arrive in Matina in early 1754.[40] The Costa Ricans appreciated the gesture, though they remained suspicious, accusing the English of keeping much of the cacao for themselves.[41]

Tensions escalated even more in July 1756, however, when a passing band of Mosquito sailors kidnapped the new governor of Costa Rica, Francisco Fernández de Pastora, while he was away from the capital on a rare visit to Matina. The incident occurred amid renewed efforts to fortify the valley against Mosquito invasions, as well as against English contrabandists.[42] By 1756 the Costa Ricans had rebuilt Fort San Fernando de Matina, though arms and munitions were still in short supply. To help with this problem, authorities in Spain sent a shipment of arms, which arrived at Matina on June 11. Since reports had been circulating that a large Mosquito fleet was also in the area, protecting the shipment was a high priority, and the governor traveled to Matina himself to oversee the delivery of the arms.[43] The port's remote location, however, threatened to frustrate the process. The governor sent word to Cartago asking for a mule train to be sent to Matina to help carry the cargo, only to have the ranking military officer in Cartago repeatedly deny this request, claiming that there simply were not enough healthy mules available.[44]

It was during this delay, then, that a group of Mosquito mariners surprised the governor during his morning walk along the beach, cornering him so that he could not return to the fort. After a long discussion, Fernández de Pastora sent a slave to bring the lieutenant to join the conversation, as well as gifts of Tabaco. The fort's small guard anxiously waited for orders, but by the time the kidnapping was in effect, it was too late: the four Mosquito visitors carried off the captives while another group of twenty-five armed men arrived to provide cover fire, preventing the militia from following. The group then disappeared with the two captives, never to return.[45]

Costa Rica did not receive news about the fate of the captives until almost three months later at the end of September, and this news arrived by sheer coincidence when seven Black and Amerindian slaves arrived in Matina after having escaped from an English master living on the Mosquito Coast. The escaped slaves reported that Mosquito traders frequently visited the small ranch that their English master owned, and that before escaping, they had overheard an older Mosquito trader talking about the kidnapping. Though not a witness of the event, the visitor reported having heard that the kidnappers had taken the captives only a short distance up the coast before executing them with lances. From these reports, the exact motivations remained unclear, but the old Mosquito trader suggested that the aggressors felt provoked by the shipment of arms meant to fortify Matina.[46]

For the most part, the inland capital of Cartago continued to align with Iberian and Guatemalan policies to treat the Mosquito as enemies, and Governor Fernández de Pastora's replacement likewise worked to reinforce the province against contraband. Nonetheless, despite previous incidents of Mosquito aggression, officials in the Matina Valley showed more flexibility. An example of this complication occurred in August 1759 when a large party of English, Dutch, and Mosquito merchants arrived in the Matina Valley hoping to trade. In total, the party included one English and two Dutch cargo ships, as well as several Mosquito piraguas. The Matina lieutenant allowed the group to make port on August 22, and they spent the next week trading openly, with the merchants providing much-needed supplies, including weapons and munitions.[47] In the meantime, however, the Matina lieutenant sent a letter to Cartago reporting the proceedings, which arrived roughly three days later while the trade fair was still going on. Even though the Matina lieutenant had given at least tacit permission to the traders, the governor of Costa Rica took swift action to stop the exchange, sending a captain with thirty additional soldiers to intervene. On the night of August 30, the soldiers ambushed the traders as they slept, killing dozens and seizing the remaining cargo.[48]

Cartago's harsh intervention in the trade fair had serious repercussions, and Mosquito incursions into the Matina Valley proliferated in subsequent years. Mosquito raiders attacked Matina in October 1760, for example, and then again in July 1761, carrying off dozens of prisoners as well as large quantities of cacao.[49] These invasions were small, but soon after, rumors began to spread that the Mosquito were also planning a massive attack. In December 1761 an escaped captive named Pedro Marselo reported that a Mosquito chief referred to as "Almar" was planning to attack Cartago.[50] No Mosquito invasion had ever reached this far inland, but the captive asserted that the Mosquito chief had been interrogating captives about routes to the capital. Even more frightening for Costa Rica, Marselo reported that the Mosquito had actually tried to invade Cartago a few months earlier, though they called off the attack at the last minute because of logistical difficulties.[51]

After two additional small incursions along the Matina coast in June and August to take additional slaves, Mosquito forces did in fact attempt an inland invasion in September.[52] On the night of September 18, Cartago received an urgent report from a militia outpost within a day's march of the capital that earlier the same morning the guard had spotted a group of Mosquito scouts.[53] The governor immediately dispatched a small detachment of soldiers to investigate, and while these scouts never encountered the Mosquito troops again, they found evidence that a large force had recently camped nearby before retreating.[54] Costa Rican officials did not grasp the true danger of the situation until a few months later in November when an escaped prisoner named Juan de Dios Iglesias arrived in Matina. Dios Iglesias confirmed that a large force of Mosquito, allied with English soldiers and allegedly headed by an English captain, had left Mosquito territory in August with the intention of capturing Cartago. In fact, Dios Iglesias himself had traveled with the expedition, sent by the Mosquito king to serve as a translator. Luckily for the Costa Ricans, however, the expedition was fraught with troubles. For example, the informant claimed that one night while the expedition was camping near the beach in preparation for the inland march, a "tiger" snuck into camp and killed one of the expedition's commanders. Even more devastating, however, the invaders never found a viable path to Cartago, wandering over the mountainous terrain for three weeks before finally giving up.[55]

In the short term, therefore, the invasion was anticlimactic, and Cartago remained safe from attack yet again. Nonetheless, having arrived within a day's march, the expedition demonstrated that the Costa Rican capital might soon fall within the orbit of Mosquito raiding. This realization, combined with the increasing frequency of Mosquito attacks, placed Costa Rica in a precarious position paralleling the situation back in 1711, when the province faced threats on multiple fronts from pirates, Mosquito raiding, and the Talamanca uprising. And as in 1711, Costa Rican leaders decided that the situation called for at least tacitly making peace with the Mosquito, regardless of how this would be interpreted by higher officials.

Against this background of increasing Costa Rican vulnerability, the year 1763 represented a major turning point, setting important precedents for how the rest of Spanish Central America would approach the Mosquito in subsequent years. In the first half of the year, violence continued unabated with at least two more incursions affecting the Matina Valley. On February 10, for example, a combined force of Mosquito and English raiders occupied Matina for five days, carrying off a large quantity of cacao.[56] Then, on June 7, a large Mosquito fleet—this time without any recorded English participants—attacked Matina again, taking several captives and leaving the same day. During the June attack, however, relations began to take a different course. Two days after the attack, the Mosquito piraguas returned, releasing a captive who carried a letter in Spanish signed by a Mosquito captain. The names on the document are difficult to decipher, but the Mosquito "captain" was most likely Admiral Dilson, given that the document mentions an "Alomar" and that Dilson was also seen soon after with the same gifts requested in this letter.[57] The letter also mentions the "rei" and "gobernador," indicating that Dilson acted on behalf of the entire Mosquito Confederation, as had always been the practice with Costa Rican negotiations. Regardless of who wrote the document, future events would demonstrate that the treaty was sincere. The letter explained that the Mosquito wanted to end the hostilities with Costa Rica and instead pursue a policy of peace. Negotiating from a position of strength, the Mosquito demanded a series of gifts, including clothing and a silver-handled cane, as well as a guarantee that Mosquito fleets would receive supplies in Matina. If the terms were met, the Mosquito Kingdom would bring the Matina Valley back under its protection.[58]

For his part, the governor of Costa Rica, Joseph Antonio de Oriamuno, doubted the sincerity of the peace offering, fearing that the Mosquito would simply return to raiding after the treaty was signed. As evidence, he cited Governor Diego de la Haya Fernández's treaty with Hannibal in the 1720s, which had not prevented future hostilities such as the massive invasion of 1724. Still, Governor Oriamuno concluded that accepting the peace was the only option: since Matina had proven virtually defenseless, accepting the Mosquito terms was the only rational choice, even if there was only a small chance that it would work. This was a major change in the policy of Cartago, which had officially opposed any trade or communication with the Mosquito since Diego de la Haya Fernández had cut off diplomatic relations in 1722. And so, in a display of Cartago's newfound willingness to act independently, Oriamuno moved to accept the treaty even before receiving permission from higher authorities.[59] With this action, Costa Rican officials accepted a subservient position by giving in to Mosquito demands. Still, the treaty worked, and the Mosquito attacks—which had become increasingly common in the last four years following Cartago's unprovoked attack on the trade fair—rapidly abated.

English Legal Challenges and Mosquito Unpredictability, 1749–1759

Just as Spanish approaches to conquest proved complex and even contradictory during the 1740s and 1750s, balancing the views and interests of diverse local and metropolitan actors, English practices were likewise varied. Overall, English policy shifted toward formalizing English settlements on the mainland, contesting Spanish claims to the right to conquer all of Central America. At the end of the 1740s, when Robert Hodgson was in England securing recognition of the Mosquito Shore, tensions with the Spanish were already increasing. As explained above from the Spanish perspective, much of the trouble derived from the disputed conclusion of the War of Jenkins's Ear. More specifically, the treaty had left the status of the Mosquito Shore ambiguous by failing to define the limits of Honduras. On the one hand, the treaty recognized Spanish authority of Honduras, which Central American officials interpreted as including Black River and the Mosquito Shore. On the other hand, English officials such as Hodgson and Trelawny continued to assert that the Mosquito Shore was independent from Honduras and had never been administered by the Spanish. As each side pressed its claims, the wealthy Black River resident William Pitt wrote a panicked letter to Governor Trelawny in July 1749 claiming that a Spanish attack was imminent and begging for a contingent of Jamaican troops to protect the colony.[60]

Trelawny was already aware of these new tensions, therefore, when Hodgson returned from England in 1750 with the title of superintendent and the duke of Bedford's letter supporting colonization efforts on the Mosquito

Shore. According to Trelawny's orders, Hodgson had three main objectives as superintendent: to establish a formal government, to facilitate commerce, and most importantly, to keep control over the Mosquito. Trelawny sent Hodgson with a small contingent of troops, but Black River remained highly vulnerable, depending on the Mosquito for protection. Maintaining this system, however, required a tricky balance. On the one hand, the English worried that the Mosquito might be swayed by Spanish treaty offers, so the superintendent needed to make sure that Mosquito leaders remained loyal to the English over the Spanish. In fact, authorities in England had authorized a budget specifically for giving gifts to Mosquito leaders to court their favor. On the other hand, the English also feared that Mosquito raids on Spanish settlements might upset the delicate peace and lead to Spanish reprisals against the English. Accordingly, even while actively trying to prevent any peace agreements between the Mosquito and the Spanish, the superintendent also needed to prevent Mosquito raids.[61]

The difficulty of trying to control both Mosquito raiding and Mosquito peacemaking was apparent from the intendency's inception. In December 1749, only a few months before Hodgson arrived to take up his post on the shore as superintendent, a group of Mosquito raiders attacked the recently founded Spanish mission of Boaco at the Nicaraguan frontier.[62] Witnesses of the attack did not report seeing Englishmen among the attackers, but Spanish officials blamed English settlers at Black River for inciting the attack, reviving calls to remove the English.[63]

Mosquito raiding, therefore, added a complication to England's contested claims to the Mosquito Shore, and Hodgson arrived with orders to prevent future incidents. In fact, Hodgson and Trelawny hoped to use their alleged influence over the Mosquito as leverage in the negotiations with the Spanish, promising to control Mosquito raiding if the Spanish recognized the shore as English territory.[64] Of course, this leverage would disappear if the English in practice proved incapable of stopping Mosquito raids, creating pressure on the English superintendent to make these claims of Mosquito control into a reality.

This leverage would also disappear, however, if the Mosquito allied with the Spanish, thus making English intercession moot. Indeed, as the years progressed, English agents arguably had more trouble controlling Mosquito peace negotiations than Mosquito raiding. English observers typically attributed Mosquito raiding to their alleged natural savagery, as well as to their supposed long-standing animosity toward the Spanish. At the same time,

English actions belied an underlying fear that the Mosquito might turn on them and join the Spanish. Indeed, soon after Hodgson's 1750 arrival, Father Solis y Miranda visited Black River to propose the founding of a Catholic mission among the Mosquito. Solis y Miranda had written to William Pitt back in 1743, and after allegedly gaining permission from Iberian and Guatemala officials to offer trade terms to Black River, he was now visiting in person to promote the plan.[65] In some ways, the visit was a relief for the vulnerable English settlers, indicating that not all Spanish officials in Central America agreed that the English should be removed from the shore. Moreover, Solis y Miranda's offer to open trade suggested new commercial potential for Black River. Nonetheless, English officials worried that if allowed to have a Catholic mission on the Mosquito Shore, the Spanish might successfully court the Mosquito as allies, making Solis y Miranda's presence arguably more dangerous than beneficial.

It was against this background of delicate negotiations and competing interests, therefore, that Hodgson arrived on the mainland in 1750 with his new commission of superintendent. Upon taking his post, Hodgson decided to send a letter to the president of Guatemala attempting to justify the English presence among the Mosquito and negotiate trading privileges. Father Solis y Miranda likely influenced Hodgson's decision to write to Guatemala specifically, since the priest allegedly had the support of the Guatemalan captain general, even though other Spanish Central American leaders were less open to negotiating with the English. Hodgson sent the letter on June 10, 1750, via a merchant and translator named Pablo Ruiz, who though Spanish by birth had grown up among the English. Unfortunately for Hodgson, however, Ruiz never arrived in Guatemala but was arrested by authorities in Honduras and taken to the city of Granada, where he faced interrogation by Brigadier General Alonso Fernández y Heredia, the current governor of Nicaragua and vocal opponent of the Black River colony.[66]

As recently as January 1750, the brigadier general had written to the governor of Yucatán to ask for material support in removing the English by force.[67] And in June of 1750—ironically around the same time that Hodgson was sending Ruiz on a mission to open trade with Spanish Central America—the brigadier general sent a scathing letter to Jamaican governor Edward Trelawny threatening military intervention unless Trelawny ordered the evacuation of Black River.[68] Within this context, Hodgson's efforts to bypass Nicaragua and write directly to higher authorities in Guatemala seemed all the more treacherous to the brigadier general, who responded by writing to Hodgson in September 1750 rejecting the possibility of any trade agreement and reiterating his demands that the English evacuate the Mosquito Shore.[69]

Indicating that they took the threat of a Spanish attack seriously, both Trelawny and Hodgson struck a conciliatory tone in responding to the Nicaraguan governor. Nevertheless, both officials defended English claims to the Mosquito coast by outlining the legal case that the English would use for the next decades to justify mainland colonization. Again, this legal defense revolved around the Mosquito themselves. Writing in October 1750, Trelawny claimed that the Mosquito were longtime subjects of the English and that the Mosquito king had legally ceded the territory to the English even before the 1670 Treaty of Madrid, which theoretically would have made the cession permanent just as the treaty also recognized English possession of Jamaica. On these grounds, Trelawny concluded that the land and inhabitants legally pertained to the English Crown. Furthermore, Trelawny argued that allowing the English to stay was also in the best interest of the Spanish, claiming that English governance would help to keep Mosquito raiding in check.[70] Hodgson then wrote his own letter to the Nicaraguan brigadier general in December 1750, echoing both of these arguments.[71]

In February 1751, Hodgson sent Pablo Ruiz, the same messenger who had previously been detained in Nicaragua, to deliver the messages. This time, however, rather than traveling overland through Honduras, Ruiz traveled directly to Costa Rica's Matina Valley.[72] Ruiz arrived in March and subsequently traveled to Cartago where he penned his own letter to be sent to Granada along with the other messages. In this letter, Ruiz dubiously claimed that the English had already negotiated a general peace with the Mosquito leaders on behalf of the Spanish. According to Ruiz, the Mosquito leaders had consented to the peace, hoping now to be allowed to trade peacefully with the Spanish.[73]

Despite these diplomatic overtures, however, English settlers at Black River continued to fear that a Spanish attack was imminent. In April 1751, William Pitt wrote to Trelawny reporting that the brigadier general remained committed to removing the English and that he was stockpiling arms in Comayagua in preparation for an attack. According to Pitt, this intelligence came from Father Solis y Miranda himself, who had just returned to Black River and was staying as Pitt's guest.[74] Two other leading settlers—a captain named James Lawrie and an engineer named Richard Jones—then echoed these fears. This report likewise cited Father Solis y Miranda, as well as another "gentleman" from Comayagua who reported that Spanish ships had taken up an aggressive position nearby.[75] Hodgson then traveled to Jamaica to deliver these reports, adding his assessment that the situation was indeed dire. According to Hodgson, Black River was almost completely lacking in military supplies, and the settlement's only hope for defense against a Spanish invasion lay with the Mosquito.[76]

Over the next few months, while Hodgson remained in Jamaica, the fear of a Spanish invasion became unbearable, and the settlers decided to act. In July 1751, even at the risk of further escalating tensions, they attacked a Spanish packet boat that was passing near the shore on its way to deliver correspondence. The attackers then forwarded the confiscated Spanish correspondence, which included several letters mentioning vague plans to take Black River by force, to Governor Trelawny as evidence of the imminent threat.[77] Trelawny took advantage of the intelligence, forwarding the letters to England in order to appeal for greater material support from higher authorities.[78] Trelawny also ordered the arrest of Solis y Miranda, who was still staying in Black River. Now accused of trying to "pervert" the Indians with his teachings, the priest was taken to Jamaica to be tried.[79]

Unsurprisingly, the attack on the packet boat and the arrest of Father Solis y Miranda escalated tensions between the English and Spanish even further. The following year, the president of Guatemala joined the brigadier general in writing directly to Trelawny to demand the English evacuation of Black River. According to Father Solis y Miranda, the president had previously been open to the idea of allowing the English to stay and facilitate trade with the frontier provinces. This may have been exaggerated, but by 1752, the president took a clear stance against the English colony, citing the arrest of Solis y Miranda as evidence of English perfidy.[80] Any hope of salvaging the negotiations then disappeared when Solis y Miranda suddenly died while still incarcerated in Jamaica. The series of events terrified Hodgson, who feared that Spanish authorities would accuse him of murdering the priest, and that they would try to take revenge.[81] The early optimism of Hodgson and Trelawny in creating the Mosquito Shore intendency, therefore, had availed little. Whereas Hodgson had arrived on the shore in February 1750 confident that he could work with the Guatemalan president to open trade, by January of 1753, the negotiations had failed miserably, and Hodgson now found himself fearing for his own life.

At the same time that Hodgson was becoming a newfound object of hatred for the Spanish, he also faced increasing scrutiny from English authorities. This was due in large part to the arrival of a new governor in Jamaica, a man named Charles Knowles, who by the start of 1753 had replaced Trelawny in the day-to-day administration of the island. This created new challenges for Hodgson, as well as for the Mosquito Shore intendency more generally. Whereas Trelawny had worked with Hodgson in championing the Mosquito Shore project since the early 1740s, Knowles was skeptical of this mainland colonization scheme. Specifically, Knowles scrutinized the project as a budgetary item, questioning whether the benefits of administering the Mosquito Shore as an official intendency were worth the costs. Furthermore, Knowles questioned whether Hodgson himself was a good steward of these funds.[82] Hodgson was not unaware of these developments. In fact, Knowles even wrote to Hodgson in January 1753 to express concerns regarding expenditures that, from the perspective of the new governor, seemed "extravagant as well as unnecessary." The letter stopped short of accusing Hodgson of outright corruption, though the implication was that the governor suspected Hodgson to be using public funds for his own personal gain.[83]

An even more serious allegation against Hodgson, however, was that his actions might be alienating Mosquito leaders. Indeed, when Knowles wrote to authorities in England two months later in March 1753 to escalate his accusations against Hodgson, the Mosquito themselves played a central role in the complaint. According to Knowles, Hodgson's alleged misuse of public funds had resulted in Mosquito leaders not receiving the appropriate gifts and tributes, jeopardizing the crucial alliance. Knowles went on to explain that this situation, if ignored, could have dire consequences since the Mosquito Kingdom might simply abandon the alliance and side with the Spanish.[84] As evidence of the unstable situation on the Mosquito Shore, Knowles even included an excerpt from Hodgson's own reports that the Mosquito leaders were easily riled up by petty "jealousies and fears."[85] The extent to which Hodgson was actually to blame for these problems is questionable, yet Knowles's accusations are certainly revealing in assessing the policies and practices of English colonial expansion in the region. In the 1750s, the Mosquito were still central to the colonial project, and the fledgling English colonies remained both physically and politically dependent on Mosquito support.

It was against this background that reports began arriving in Jamaica in October 1753 of a Mosquito attack on Costa Rica. Since the Mosquito Shore superintendent was tasked with both maintaining the Mosquito alliance and preventing Mosquito raids on Spanish settlements, the attack further suggested to Knowles that Hodgson was failing at his duties. What is more, Hodgson had failed to even report the incident, leaving Governor Knowles to find out about it from a ship captain named Isaac Tarbor who traveled frequently between Jamaica and the Mosquito Shore.[86] In response, Knowles took the initiative to send his own representative, a trusted military official named Captain Galbraith, to investigate the situation instead of waiting for Hodgson.[87]

Documents leave unclear whether Hodgson already knew about the incident and had failed to report to Jamaica, or if he was still unaware in October 1753 when Governor Knowles sent Captain Galbraith to the Mosquito Coast. Regardless, Hodgson rushed to save face, meeting with Mosquito leaders in hopes of recovering the goods taken from Costa Rica in the raid. Hodgson managed to secure at least a portion of the stolen cacao, which he subsequently sent back to Costa Rica via another English settler named Henry Corrin. In theory, the move demonstrated Hodgson's influence with Mosquito leaders in convincing them to return the stolen goods, though it is possible that he simply purchased the cacao from the Mosquito since the English were the only available buyers for the cacao anyway. The Costa Ricans also complained that only a small portion of the cacao was actually returned and demanded further restitution.[88] Nonetheless, by the end of the year, Hodgson was able to report to Jamaica that he had taken action, making a case to the skeptical governor for keeping his post.

Unfortunately for Hodgson, Governor Knowles was unimpressed with these efforts, only finding new reasons to criticize the embattled superintendent. In January 1754, Knowles wrote to authorities in England to give an update on the situation on the Mosquito Shore. In the report, Knowles praised the professionalism of Galbraith, who gave a thorough account of the incident following his investigation. On the other hand, Knowles criticized Hodgson's handling of the incident, citing the missing cacao, as well as Hodgson's "insolence" as evidence of his being unfit for the position. Knowles went on to explain that he planned to issue a court martial against Hodgson on these grounds.[89] Despite this censure, Knowles did not have Hodgson recalled, and Hodgson continued in his official capacity as the superintendent of the Mosquito Shore. Nonetheless, Hodgson's work remained under scrutiny, creating even more pressure on him to demonstrate control over the Mosquito leaders. This pressure was reflected in Hodgson's writing. In March 1755, for example, amid fears that Spanish coast guard ships might provoke another Mosquito attack, Hodgson dubiously claimed that he was able to diffuse the tension by simply ordering Mosquito leaders "not to stir"—a claim that if true would have been radically unprecedented given the complexity and independence of Mosquito geopolitical decision-making. Indeed, Hodgson himself did not try to corroborate the claim with witnesses but rather relied on stereotypes of Amerindians as childlike savages to make the boast believable.[90]

The illusory nature of Hodgson's control came into sharp relief the following year, however, when a group of Mosquito attackers kidnapped and assassinated the governor of Costa Rica.[91] As explained above, it remains unknown to what extent the attack was sanctioned by Mosquito leaders, or if it was a rogue act carried out by Mosquito pirates. Regardless, witnesses of the encounter left no doubt that the perpetrators were Mosquito, and word of the assassination spread through both the English and Mosquito worlds.[92]

Whereas numerous events over the past decade and a half had already indicated that Hodgson was exaggerating his influence over the Mosquito, the assassination of the Costa Rican governor at the hands of Mosquito sailors made Hodgson's lack of control more evident than ever before. Luckily for Hodgson, the repercussions of the incident were not immediate since it occurred during a period of transition between governors in Jamaica, with the critical Knowles having already stepped down earlier in the year. Nevertheless, the new governor of Jamaica, George Haldane, likewise was skeptical of Hodgson's work as superintendent. By July 1759, Haldane was actively seeking Hodgson's dismissal and wrote to the Board of Trade in England to accuse Hodgson of failing his duties. Echoing Knowles before him, Haldane accused Hodgson of failing to properly disseminate gifts to Mosquito leaders. The accusation once again hinted at corruption on Hodgson's part, though Haldane argued even more explicitly that Hodgson's negative rapport with Mosquito leaders jeopardized the critical alliance.[93]

By November 1759, Haldane's letter had arrived in England, and the Board of Trade took seriously the governor's recommendation for disciplinary action against Hodgson.[94] These events also coincided with the Costa Rican attack on the Matina trade fair in August 1759, which resulted in the deaths of several Mosquito and English traders, including contrabandist and informant to the Jamaican governor Isaac Tarbor. Interpreted as an act of revenge for the assassination of the previous Costa Rican governor, this massacre yet again revealed how little power he actually had in controlling Spanish relations with the Mosquito. Hodgson himself passed away soon after the attack, however, making any disciplinary action against him moot.[95]

Hodgson died a controversial figure among English officials, yet the Mosquito Shore Intendency that he and former governor Trelawny had worked so hard to create remained central to English imperial practices in Central America. In this way, Hodgson had a lasting impact on the English colonial strategy in the region, with the Board of Trade continuing to recognize Black River and other settlements on the Mosquito Shore against Spanish objections. Of course, keeping to the patterns established by Trelawny and Hodgson also meant that English colonialism in Central America continued to rely heavily on the Mosquito Confederation for physical support, as well as for legal legitimacy. Accordingly, future superintendents would face similar pressure to try and keep Mosquito leaders under control, even as the Mosquito continued to pursue their own diplomatic initiatives as they had always done.

Conclusion

The events described in this chapter provide key insights into the activities of the Mosquito Confederation, as well as the Spanish and English reactions, during this period of heightened hostility in the middle of the century. Most significantly, this chapter has demonstrated that even in this period of increasing hostility with Spanish Central America, the Mosquito were not in a default state of constant raiding, nor were the Mosquito following the cycles of war and peace of the Anglo–Spanish wars. True, the Mosquito did raid, and the English did have a more visible presence in joint expeditions than in previous decades. Nonetheless, a close examination of events and new archival documents shows that Mosquito foreign policy continued to follow its own geopolitical logic. And much to the chagrin of the English, the logic of Mosquito geopolitics led to increased hostilities at a time when the English were trying to placate the Spanish to prevent their joining the Seven Years' War. Moreover, as subsequent chapters will demonstrate, Mosquito peacemaking with the Spanish after the 1763 reconciliation would likewise frustrate English plans.

In highlighting this geopolitical logic of the confederation, it is also worth reiterating that Mosquito hostilities against Spanish Costa Rica during the 1750s and early 1760s were major deviations from the norm of peace that characterized earlier and later periods. Still, these acts of aggression were not only raids. Indeed, the escalation of these hostilities followed clear provocations, including the ongoing refusal to allow Mosquito fleets to make port, the construction of the Matina fort in 1747, the buildup of arms in Matina in 1756, and most importantly, the surprise attack on the unarmed traders in 1759. Moreover, this chapter has demonstrated that this period of increased hostilities did in fact culminate in a reconciliation. Much to the frustration of the English who hoped to isolate the Mosquito from the Spanish, the Mosquito Confederation continued in its pursuit to convert key Spanish outposts such as Matina into allies. As subsequent chapters will show, this reconciliation with Costa Rica was not only durable but provided a model for other Spanish provinces to follow in negotiation with the Mosquito long before the English evacuation.

CHAPTER 5

The Mosquito Confederation and New Internal Tensions, 1763–1775

As Joseph Otway watched the Spanish delegation approach the beach at Black River, he already knew the reason for the visit. Serving as the English superintendent of the Mosquito Shore, Otway understood that Spanish officials still considered the territory legally Spanish. It was April of 1764, and whereas the English had agreed one year earlier to destroy fortifications in British Honduras, Otway was prepared to argue emphatically that the Mosquito Shore was not actually part of Honduras. And regardless of the logic of these debates, Otway also had the luxury of arguing from a position of strength given that the immediate arbiters of power on the coast—the leaders of the Mosquito Kingdom—had given the English permission to settle in Black River. Accordingly, after receiving the delegation cordially, Otway flatly denied the Spanish demands for an English evacuation of the mainland, citing orders from his superiors in England, as well as boasting the support of the Mosquito Kingdom, support that remained palpable as Mosquito soldiers watched the Spanish visitors' every move.[1] Of course, in the absence of Mosquito support, the situation would have been completely different. And indeed, when Otway later realized that the Mosquito had been carrying on separate negotiations with the Spanish, his confidence in the English position began to wane.

The purpose of this chapter is to examine the history of the Mosquito Confederation during the period from roughly 1763 to 1775. As the events described here demonstrate, this period was characterized by increasing peace negotiations between the Mosquito Confederation and Spanish Central America. After initiating a reconciliation with Costa Rica in 1763, Mosquito leaders continued negotiating with other provinces as well, even while maintaining close diplomatic and economic ties with the English. For their part, Spanish officials proved more open to negotiations than in previous years, and for the first time, Costa Rican treaties with the Mosquito even gained the approval of higher authorities in Guatemala.

On the other hand, English settlers on the Mosquito Shore viewed these processes with dread—despite the fact that Great Britain was also officially at peace with the Spanish following the 1763 Treaty of Paris—and rumors frequently circulated that the Mosquito council was plotting with the Spanish to attack the English. These rumors turned out to be unfounded, though significantly, in addressing them, confederation leaders during this period demonstrated an unprecedented tendency to criticize each other, whereas previous generations had always shown a united front when talking to foreign allies. Accordingly, this chapter further argues that this period was characterized by growing dissension within the Mosquito Confederation itself, and while it would still be decades before the confederation would erupt in civil war, the distinctive unity that had long characterized Mosquito practices was starting to show signs of wear.

Mosquito Negotiations and Internal Tensions, 1763–1775

In many ways, the Mosquito Confederation's activities of the 1760s showed a continuation of the practices that had characterized the Mosquito conquest during the first decades of the eighteenth century. Indeed, opening diplomatic relations with the Spanish had been a key component of Jeremy II's strategy, and controlling Matina as a source of supplies and tributes was central to enacting this vision. The first test of the renewed peace in Costa Rica occurred in June 1765, when a fourteen-piragua fleet visited Matina. The fleet arrived making signs of peace, sending the unnamed captain of the expedition to talk with the Matina lieutenant. As stipulated by the treaty, the Mosquito requested food such as plantains to help the fleet with the rest of its journey. Generating additional tension, however, the leader of the fleet allegedly provoked the Costa Ricans by demanding an additional payment of two hundred pesos. According to reports, Matina officials balked at this request, but after additional threats from the Mosquito captain, they eventually complied. Having then received the requested supplies and tribute, the fleet sailed away without further incident.[2] In this way, the reconciliation went into effect, though with the Costa Ricans clearly as subordinates rather than equal allies.

A breach of the new peace occurred the following year in 1766, however, when a joint Zambo-English expedition invaded Matina in August. The incursion was more of a heist than an attack since the invaders did not inflict any casualties or take any captives, instead disarming the militia and impressing various inhabitants into loading their piraguas with cacao.[3] Questions remain as to precisely why this seeming breach of the new treaty occurred. One explanation is that confederation leaders thought one more show of force would be necessary to guarantee Costa Rican compliance with the tribute demands. For example, the Costa Rican governor who had negotiated the 1763 reconciliation no longer held the position in 1766, so it is possible that the new governor may have provoked the Mosquito by failing to fulfill the obligation. Indeed, Admiral Dilson later complained about Costa Rica's failure to make proper payments when discussing the situation with the English superintendent.[4] Moreover, it is also possible that the 1766 attack was not sanctioned by the Mosquito Confederation at all, representing instead a private venture more akin to piracy than an official action. Providing evidence to this interpretation, the Zambo captain who led the 1766 incursion did not attribute his actions to any of the Mosquito headmen, instead telling Matina officials that he was working for an English captain named Enrique, who was allegedly the one who ordered the invasion.[5] While the Zambo captain may have been lying in order to exculpate himself and shift the blame for the incursion onto the English, wider evidence does suggest that English ship captains using debt to coerce Mosquito sailors into going on unofficial raids was a growing problem, and one that the confederation council would in fact address with new regulations a few years later.[6] In either case, this incident was the only breach of the 1763 protection treaty. For the next decade and a half, the Mosquito Confederation made good on its agreement to protect Matina from confederation fleets as well as private raiders, mirroring Mosquito foreign policy of earlier in the century.

Regarding the internal politics of the confederation, however, the 1760s was actually a period of significant change. At the same time that the Mosquito were strengthening diplomatic relations with Costa Rica, the unity that had long characterized the central council was starting to wear thin. Whereas earlier generations of Mosquito leaders had always shown a united front when meeting with representatives of foreign powers, members of the central council increasingly began to negotiate individually, and to even criticize their fellow council members. That the members of the central council would eventually turn on each other was still far from inevitable, and it would be the next generation of leaders who would ultimately preside over the 1791 Mosquito civil war. Nonetheless, early signs of disunity were already present in the late 1760s.

A salient example of the brewing tensions within the confederation occurred in 1768. In that year, King George and Admiral Dilson still held their positions, though by this time, Governor William Briton had already died, leaving his son, Timothy Briton, as the new governor. General Handyside had also recently passed away, leaving a new general named Tempest.[7] The trouble began when General Tempest left the Mosquito Coast for an extended diplomatic visit to England. In Tempest's absence, a rumor began to circulate that Tempest was plotting with the English settlers to overthrow and kill King George. Such a move would have been highly unprecedented. While the ascension of new leaders had on occasion generated rivalries within specific Mosquito factions, there is no evidence that the leaders of different factions had ever fought against each other. Nonetheless, King George took the rumors seriously enough to meet with Governor Timothy Briton to discuss General Tempest's supposed plot. King George and Governor Briton agreed that if such a plot did exist, then it might be necessary to arrest the English conspirators allegedly working with Tempest, and they sent word to Admiral Dilson to secure his support if tensions erupted. After this meeting, however, additional rumors began to spread that King George was plotting with Timothy Briton to assassinate all the English settlers on the shore, creating a wave of panic among the English colonists that reached all the way to the Jamaican governor.[8]

An English agent named Richard Jones arrived from Jamaica in June 1768 to investigate the rumors. Tellingly, the Mosquito council did not assemble for a general meeting, but rather each leader gave a separate interview. The governor gave the first statement, explaining that the king had only wanted to arrest the English settlers plotting with Tempest—not kill anyone, much less all the Whites. Still, Timothy Briton made sure to separate himself from the plot, saying that immediately after hearing these plans, he had informed the English settlers about the king's scheming. According to Jones's report of the interview, the Mosquito governor even complained that he did not receive more credit for his own loyalty in exposing the plot. Moreover, Admiral Dilson allegedly made similar claims, saying that he too had informed the English settlers when he heard about the king and the governor's meeting. Indeed, rather than standing up for his fellow confederation council members, Dilson took advantage of the situation to stress his own superior loyalty to the English. For his part, King George denied the charges of disloyalty, saying that he was simply taking precautions against Tempest's alleged conspiracy.[9]

In the end, the episode was anticlimactic: Tempest never tried to lead an uprising against George, and George never tried to kill—or even arrest—any of the White settlers. Still, the event offers an important window into how Mosquito politics developed under this generation of leaders. Despite offering profitable trade opportunities, the English were turning out to be high-maintenance allies requiring constant reassurance. This was certainly not the first time that English settlers had expressed fears that their Mosquito protectors would suddenly turn on them, but after 1768, Mosquito leaders increasingly handled these tricky diplomatic encounters individually rather than as a council. Moreover, reports suggested that they increasingly used these conversations to cast suspicions on each other.

Here it is worth highlighting again that there is no evidence that this ongoing discord was rooted in ethnic tensions between the Zambo and Tawira. The original 1768 dispute discussed above, for example, began as a conflict between the Zambo leaders General Tempest and King George based on rumors of an assassination plot that had nothing to do with ethnic rivalries. Moreover, the king immediately turned to the Tawira governor Timothy Briton for support. In sum, ethnic divisions simply had no bearing on the conflict, and this pattern continued in disputes over the next two decades.

The growing disunity within the Mosquito Confederation manifested again the following year during yet another outburst of English fear of Mosquito perfidy. This time, however, the controversy did not center on King George, but rather on Admiral Dilson. The episode began early in 1769 when Dilson sent a messenger to Matina in order to remind the new Costa Rican governor of the tribute demands and to open a trade in specialty goods such as cattle. Along with the messenger, Admiral Dilson sent his silver-tipped cane—a symbol of the ongoing alliance with Costa Rica that had been part of the tribute demands during the reconciliation—to be repaired. In response, the governor of Costa Rica sent the cane back as requested, along with a letter inviting Admiral Dilson to come to the capital of Cartago to update the negotiations in person.[10] Dilson accepted, but rather than visiting himself, he sent a delegation of captains, including his brother. The ambassadors arrived in July, and after staying in Cartago as honored guests of the Costa Rican governor, they negotiated a formal treaty that granted Mosquito trading rights in the Matina Valley and the San Juan River.[11]

Whereas evidence suggests that the 1763 reconciliation with Costa Rica had applied to the entire confederation—specifically, the mention of the king and governor along with "Almoral," the request for multiple canes that later reports corroborated that both Dilson and George received, the presence of both Tawira and Zambo soldiers in the fleet, and the rapid cessation of hostilities—it is possible that Dilson took advantage of the 1769 renegotiation to secure advantages for his followers only. For example, the treaty mentioned only the "indios moscos," and while the text never says that the Zambo Mosquito factions were excluded, the Costa Rican governor's initial communication did express fear of Zambo raiding, suggesting a distinction between Dilson's Tawira followers and the Zambo Mosquito. The treaty also named Dilson the governor of the Mosquito, even though his title was admiral and Timothy Briton was still governor.

On the other hand, one should be cautious about drawing too many conclusions regarding Dilson's intentions from this document in isolation. Though it indicates in some ways that Dilson may have been negotiating for his own faction only, it remains unclear to what extent these aspects of the treaty were Dilson's intention as opposed to a reflection of Spanish misunderstandings. Indeed, the word "gobernador" could have simply been a general term rather than a claim to a specific role in the confederation, and the negative reference to "Zambos" could have been to pirates participating in private raids under the English as opposed to the Zambo followers of the Mosquito king. Lending credence to this interpretation, the Costa Rican governor's reference to Zambos invoked the 1766 invasion directly, which the Spanish attributed to an English captain as opposed to Mosquito leaders.[12] Moreover, surrounding documents such as former Costa Rican governor Luis Diez Navarro's analysis of the treaty demonstrate that even the Spanish read the treaty as applying to the entire confederation rather than just Dilson's faction. For example, Diez Navarro specifically questioned the validity of the treaty on the grounds that Dilson could not actually speak for the Zambo factions, thus presupposing that the goal was to include the entire confederation.[13]

Accordingly, the evidence remains inconclusive as to what, if any, extent Dilson broke from the long-held tradition of negotiating on behalf of the entire confederation and used the renegotiation of the Costa Rican treaty to secure advantages for his followers only. Nonetheless, what is certain is that the diplomatic visit generated enormous controversy among the English, and Mosquito leaders once again demonstrated a degree of disunity in addressing the conflict. When English settlers found out about the visit, rumors once again began to spread that the Mosquito were conspiring to attack them, this time with the help of the Spanish.[14] Feeling that he had done nothing wrong, Dilson did not try to hide his actions and even sent a letter to English officials in September 1769 explaining the routine nature of the ongoing negotiations with Costa Rica in hopes of clearing his name. The letter did mention, however, that the Costa Rican governor had tried unsuccessfully to convince Dilson to abandon the alliance with the English; it further suggested that the Spanish were indeed planning to attack an English settlement on the Mosquito Shore.[15]

Unsurprisingly, the letter failed to assuage English fears, and the governor of Jamaica sent agents to investigate the rumors. As in the previous year during the alleged General Tempest conspiracy, the Mosquito council did not demonstrate a unified front in addressing the allegations. In fact, not only did King George and Governor Timothy Briton offer individual interviews but they refused to support Dilson's claim that he had rejected the Spanish offer to help attack the English, suggesting that Dilson could actually be involved in such a plot. For his part, Dilson defended his actions, meeting with two different English agents in December 1769 and March 1770 to try and clear his name. Dilson argued emphatically that the meeting was only about trade and had nothing to do with attacking the English. Moreover, Dilson even accused the English of hypocrisy since they were also trying to open trade with the Spanish.[16]

Ultimately, English officials did not have any power to punish Dilson directly, but the admiral remained suspect in the eyes of this important ally. And even worse for the confederation, the fallout alienated Dilson from the other principal leaders of the Mosquito who seemingly encouraged these suspicions rather than rushing to Dilson's defense. Here it is worth noting again, however, that these tensions did not pit Tawira factions against Zambo factions, demonstrating that ethnic rivalry was not a source of these burgeoning hostilities. The Tawira governor Timothy Briton and the Zambo king George both criticized Dilson equally, and there is no evidence that Dilson used the Costa Rican negotiations to diminish the power of the Zambo factions. If anything, the biggest possible insult that the treaty included was to name Dilson the governor, and while it remains unclear if this was Dilson's intention, even if it was, this tactic would not have subverted the Zambo leaders but rather his fellow Tawira governor.

The immediate tensions from the 1769 controversy subsided quickly, in part because Admiral Dilson died only a few months later in March 1770, succeeded by his son, Dilson II. Nonetheless, opportunities for Mosquito leaders to criticize each other continued to emerge in the early 1770s in conjunction with English fears. Ironically, English reactionism was activated not only by rumors of Mosquito treaties with the Spanish but also by rumors of Mosquito attacks on the Spanish, which had the potential to threaten the delicate peace between the English and Spanish Crowns. In 1774, for example, a rumor circulated that Governor Timothy Briton was preparing a retaliatory attack on Matina to avenge the activities of the Spanish coast guard, and an English agent visited the governor's home to confront him in April. Once again, nothing had actually happened: no attack occurred, and Timothy Briton had never even taken steps to assemble a fleet. Nonetheless, the Mosquito governor still used the interview to perform his loyalty, saying that he had refused to carry out the attack solely out of consideration for English interests. Moreover, the Mosquito governor allegedly went a step further to cast doubt on the intentions of King George, hinting that the king was less likely to show such restraint.[17]

Despite these internal conflicts, however, the confederation was far from reaching the point of civil war, and the council members continued to work together on various geopolitical initiatives. For example, in 1775, both King George and Governor Timothy Briton worked with Irish settler Colville Cairns to send a delegation to the Spanish governor in Portobelo.[18] Mosquito leaders also showed unity in their growing disdain for the newest English superintendent on the Mosquito Shore: Robert Hodgson Jr., the son of the first superintendent who had likewise struggled to court Mosquito goodwill. As early as 1769, Admiral Dilson had complained that the younger Hodgson's behavior while investigating the admiral's negotiations with Costa Rica was deeply offensive.[19] In 1773, the Mosquito governor Timothy Briton echoed these complaints, writing his own letter to Jamaica to welcome the newly appointed English governor, in which he complained that Hodgson was stealing the diplomatic gifts that were supposed to be allocated to Mosquito leaders to maintain the alliance.[20] Furthermore, the son and crown prince of King George visited England on a diplomatic journey in 1775 to bring his complaints directly to authorities in London.[21] And when the voyage of the crown prince took longer than expected, King George suspected Hodgson of foul play, allegedly threatening to take Hodgson's own family hostage until the crown prince returned.[22]

Timothy Briton's 1773 letter is also interesting as it provides a window into the daily life of the Mosquito, specifically in relation to food production. In the final paragraph, after congratulating the new Jamaican governor and criticizing Hodgson, the letter concluded by asking for small supplies of flour and rice to help offset food shortages caused by a hurricane three months earlier.[23] At first glance, it may be tempting to read this document as evidence of the hypothesis that the Mosquito had become dependent on foreign trade for subsistence goods. However, wider evidence shows that the opposite was actually the case: that the Mosquito maintained their traditional subsistence practices, and that trade emphasized luxury goods—usually for diplomatic rather than economic purposes—with little bearing on their core productive systems. To begin, the document itself states clearly that the Mosquito governor was only asking for food in this case because of an extreme circumstance caused by a natural disaster—by definition a deviation from the norm of producing their own food. Moreover, multiple eyewitness accounts throughout the century describe agricultural and productive systems as operating independently. For example, escaped Mosquito captives testifying in Costa Rica in the 1720s stated explicitly that the Mosquito produced their own food, supplementing their own labor with that of slaves.[24] Furthermore, English travel writers later in the century, such as Robert Hodgson Sr. who wrote an account of Mosquito life in 1757, corroborate these observations that the Mosquito still produced their own food and traditional handicrafts.[25] Moreover, even after the governor's 1773 appeal for hurricane relief, there is no evidence that food became a common trade good. For example, a 1778 invoice of English gifts included only luxury items and no food or other subsistence goods.[26]

After uniting in their disapproval for Robert Hodgson Jr. in the mid-1770s, however, both the Mosquito king and governor soon passed away, and tensions among the next generation of leaders increased dramatically. Timothy Briton died first, leaving his brother, Colville Briton, to take his place in 1776.[27] Then, in 1777, King George passed away, leaving his son George II to succeed him.[28] Ultimately, Colville Briton and George II, along with Admiral Dilson II and General Tempest, would eventually allow the confederation to descend into civil war, presiding over the destruction of the Mosquito imperial project.

Costa Rica and Spanish Reconciliation with the Mosquito, 1763-1774

At the same time the Mosquito Confederation was starting to show signs of internal disputes, Spanish policy toward the Mosquito was starting to become more consistent. By accepting the Mosquito peace offering in 1763 after years of increasing hostilities, Costa Rica emerged as a leading voice in promoting a new policy of reconciliation, and while higher authorities in either Guatemala or Spain did not immediately recognize the Costa Rican treaty, officials in Guatemala did make their own attempt at negotiating with the Mosquito the following year. In 1764, an envoy led by former governor of Costa Rica Luis Diez Navarro visited the Mosquito Coast to meet with English and Mosquito leaders in Black River. In contrast to the Costa Rican approach, however, the Guatemalans were far more interested in leveling demands than in negotiating, so it was far less effective in alleviating tensions. Following the conclusion of the Seven Years' War, Spanish authorities in Central America hoped to revive the argument that the Mosquito Shore belonged to the Spanish. On these grounds, the Guatemalan delegation demanded that the English evacuate, and that the Mosquito submit to Spanish rule. The Mosquito leaders found this presumptuous attitude offensive, however, allegedly threatening to kill Diez Navarro.[29] Consequently, relations remained fraught from the Guatemalan standpoint, even as Costa Rica was already on the path toward a long-term reconciliation. At the very least, however, Guatemalan officials seemed to be moving away from the earlier hardline stance of pressuring provincial governors to treat the Mosquito unequivocally as enemies. Within this context, Costa Rica served as a test case for whether peace with the Mosquito would hold in practice, and whether Spanish policy would come around to recognizing the treaty as official policy.

The first test of the Mosquito peace treaty in Costa Rica came in 1765 when a fourteen-piragua fleet arrived in Matina. By this time, the Costa Rican governor Oriamuno who had negotiated the reconciliation no longer held the post. In his place, a new governor named Joseph Joachin de Nava had recently arrived. The fleet approached the valley peacefully at first, and the Matina guard let the piraguas make port. According to reports, however, the Mosquito captain struck an aggressive stance, demanding supplies as well as an additional tribute of two hundred pesos. Matina officials informed the visitors that the impoverished valley did not have the money, at which point allegedly the Mosquito captain became so incensed that he began beating one Matina soldier with a saber. Eventually the Matina lieutenant was able to secure a loan from a local hacienda owner, diffusing the tension and securing the safety of the valley. The fleet then sailed away without further incident, demonstrating that at least tentatively, the treaty was working.[30] Perhaps indicating that the new governor did not fully approve of the Mosquito treaty, documents surrounding the event struck a defensive tone, focusing primarily on proving that no contraband trade had taken place. Still, in comparison to the years leading up to 1763 when Mosquito attacks were near constant, the reconciliation was starting to take effect in practice.

In 1766, however, the tentative peace in Costa Rica faced a major setback with the Mosquito breaking the peace for the first time. The incident occurred on August 29 when another fleet of fourteen piraguas arrived. This time the fleet did attack, arresting the port guard and looting plantations for tools and cacao. Follow-up interviews with witnesses of the attack tried to find out why the Mosquito had broken the peace, and reports suggested that English influence had been a factor. Several hostages testified, for example, that an Englishman named Henrique had in fact ordered the attack.[31] Interestingly, Governor De Nava came away from the event with the impression that not only was the attack planned by the English but English merchants were using coercive tactics such as debt peonage to force Mosquito mariners to participate in raids against their will—a point he included in future communications with the Mosquito. Accordingly, Governor De Nava remained hopeful that the breach was an isolated event, and that an opportunity to revive the negotiations would soon arise.

This opportunity came in 1769 when a messenger representing the Mosquito Admiral Dilson arrived in Matina carrying Dilson's silver-handled cane. After reiterating Dilson's commitment to the earlier treaty, the messenger requested that the cane be repaired and sent back to the admiral. In response, Governor De Nava fulfilled the request, sending the repaired cane along with an invitation for Dilson to visit Cartago to talk in person. De Nava also took the opportunity to criticize the English, arguing that their exploitative trade practices made them more enemies than allies to the Mosquito.[32] Admiral Dilson declined to visit Cartago himself, but he did send three captains, including one named Yasparral who claimed to be the admiral's brother. The delegates arrived in July, and working with the Costa Rican governor, they agreed to a series of propositions stipulating terms for trade licenses for Mosquito convoys.[33] Dilson's 1769 negotiations were important for reaffirming the tentative peace, though placed in the context of previous encounters, this was not a major policy shift for either the Costa Ricans or the Mosquito: over the previous six years since the reconciliation began in 1763, peaceful relations had largely held firm with the 1766 invasion representing the only exception. Moreover, Costa Rican officials had openly recognized that even the 1763 agreement was not novel but rather a return to policies from earlier in the century.[34]

In the context of Guatemalan policy, however, 1769 indeed represented a significant turning point. Officials in Guatemala debated for some time whether to approve the treaty, and some leaders including a former governor of Costa Rica, Luis Diez Navarro—the same Spanish ambassador who had visited the Mosquito Coast in 1764—expressed doubt that the treaty would hold. In addition to distrusting the "savage" Mosquito, Diez Navarro also feared that Admiral Dilson did not have the authority to speak for all the Mosquito factions, especially the reputedly more powerful Zambo-Mosquito.[35] Nonetheless, in a major deviation from previous years, the president's office in Guatemala ultimately approved the treaty, even sending a letter in December 1769 to inform the Crown of the new policy.[36] The Crown also approved the decision, though officials did not issue a response until September 1770.[37] This response then arrived back in Guatemala in February 1771, almost eight years after the peace treaty had tentatively gone into practice in Costa Rica.[38]

While Guatemalan officials were still waiting for the king's response, however, the geopolitical repercussions of Dilson's most recent negotiations in Costa Rica became more complicated. In January of 1770, the younger Robert Hodgson arrived in Matina to confront the Costa Ricans about the Dilson negotiations.[39] Hodgson explained that he had intercepted Joachin de Nava's letter, and interpreting it as a plot to turn the Mosquito against the English, forwarded the letter to London as evidence of Spanish peacetime aggression. Hodgson then gave the Matina lieutenant a letter to be sent to Cartago outlining the accusations.[40] For his part, Governor Joachin de Nava defended his actions, forwarding Hodgson's letters to Guatemala, along with his own explanation arguing that the contents of his original letter to Dilson had never encouraged violence against the English.[41] Crown officials also tried to investigate the conflict after receiving complaints from England, though this intervention was too late to be of much importance. The Crown composed a letter to Central American officials in October 1770, though it did not arrive in Cartago until September 1771. When the inquiry arrived,

Governor Nava redundantly defended his actions, though he explained that the tension had already abated since the Mosquito admiral Dilson was now dead.[42]

In the short term, therefore, the Dilson controversy was anticlimactic. Still, it signaled a major turning point in Spanish policy toward the Mosquito: moving forward, Guatemalan and Peninsular officials remained open to Mosquito treaties, empowering provincial officials to negotiate more openly than ever before. In part, these changing policies signaled a broader shift in priorities away from stopping the contraband trade and more toward military defense. Whereas Mosquito trade ties with the English had long served as a justification for legally banning communication, the approval of Dilson's treaty with Costa Rica demonstrated a newfound flexibility in prosecuting contraband when it served for defense.

Significantly, this shift did not only apply to Costa Rica. Another illustrative example of this trend appeared in the contraband trial of a Honduran hacienda owner named Joseph Antonio de Vargas. Vargas's accusers provided substantial evidence that he had participated in illegal trade with the Mosquito throughout the 1760s.[43] Rather than denying the accusations, however, Vargas defended himself by arguing that his interactions with the Mosquito had helped to prevent Mosquito attacks. This defense worked, and Vargas was acquitted by royal order in 1774.[44] This did not mean, of course, that all contraband laws were suddenly void, and Central American officials continued to investigate accusations of illicit trade. Nevertheless, more legal gray areas began to appear as Guatemala and Spain followed Costa Rica's lead in recognizing diplomacy as a legitimate approach to dealing with the Mosquito Confederation.

English Reactions to Mosquito "Conspiracies," 1759–1776

At the same time that the ongoing Spanish conquest was becoming more stable as the Mosquito negotiations reduced the number of imminent threats, English efforts to colonize the mainland suddenly became more precarious as settlers realized that they did not have a monopoly on Mosquito support. After the 1759 death of Robert Hodgson Sr., the first superintendent of the Mosquito Shore, the engineer and longtime Black River resident Richard Jones held the position for the next three years. In 1762, however, the acting governor of Jamaica decided that it would be better to have a military officer in the Mosquito Shore, and he sent Joseph Otway to take over the position.[45] It did not take long for Otway to realize that the fate of the colonial project was inextricably linked to the activities of the Mosquito Kingdom. For example, if Mosquito troops attacked Spanish ships or settlements, the English colony at Black River stood to suffer repercussions. At the very least, the geopolitical fallout could delegitimize the colony in the eyes of other colonial powers, adding fuel to Spanish calls for an English evacuation and possibly risking direct retaliation. At the same time, however, the English needed to be the ones interceding to reduce this violence. Indeed, the idea of Mosquito leaders negotiating peace agreements with the Spanish on their own was even more terrifying than thoughts of the Mosquito raiding the Spanish. Accordingly, Otway found himself in a similar position as Robert Hodgson had when the intendency was first founded: the superintendent needed to prevent Mosquito hostilities against the Spanish, though at the same time, he could not allow Mosquito leaders to conduct peace negotiations either.

When he first arrived on the Mosquito Shore, Otway was primarily concerned with the former of these two problems, which he considered to be the more pressing issue. After describing Spanish troop movements around Trujillo in a 1763 report, for example, Otway went on to explain that the Spanish activities had placed the Mosquito on edge. He went on to lament that the Mosquito were beyond his control, and that he was not sure if he could prevent them from escalating hostilities by launching their own preemptive attack.[46] Otway was more optimistic, however, when reporting on Diez Navarro's visit the following year in 1764. He did note that the Mosquito were still suspicious of the Spanish and would not let them come ashore "until their business was known." Nonetheless, the Mosquito guard was satisfied with the explanation and ultimately helped in facilitating the visit.[47]

Otway's optimism was short-lived, however, and he presented a grimmer picture the following year. In describing numerous problems with the colony, he now hinted that the worst-case scenario was a possibility: that the Mosquito might abandon their alliance with the English and side with the Spanish. Otway explained that he had received reports that the Mosquito king had been negotiating with the Spanish on his own, and that the king had even hosted Spanish visitors at his residence in Sandy Bay. Otway then visited Sandy Bay himself to follow up on the report and found disturbing evidence in the form of diplomatic gifts of Spanish origin, ranging from various "trifles" to silver crosses to a gold-tipped cane.[48] After hearing reassurances from Mosquito leaders that they remained committed to the English alliance, Otway concluded that the Mosquito would likely stay loyal, and that the problem of preventing the Mosquito from raiding the Spanish was still the greater concern. Regardless, the report provides vital insight into the thinking of English colonists at the time: specifically, that they saw their alliance with the Mosquito as weak and that Mosquito disloyalty was a serious threat requiring proactive intervention. In the following years, this fear continued to grow, leading to a colonial policy characterized by panic and reactionary practices.

A notable manifestation of this growing fear occurred in 1768. In March rumors began to spread that the Mosquito king and governor were plotting an uprising against the English that included killing the White settlers. The rumors originated in Bluefields, an English settlement in the southern part of the Mosquito Coast that was still smaller than the principal colony of Black River yet had attracted the attention of colonial authorities as a potential base for further expanding England's formal holdings. In fact, the governor of Jamaica had already sent agents to form a local government, including a justice of the peace named Henry Corrin. Corrin was alarmed by the rumors, allegedly hearing a corroborating report from one of the principal leaders of the Mosquito, the admiral, who also believed that the other Mosquito leaders were plotting. Corrin then traveled to Jamaica in May to give testimony about the happenings, and the governor of Jamaica quickly ordered former superintendent Richard Jones to investigate.[49]

Jones's subsequent interviews with Mosquito leaders revealed that the alleged conspiracy was in reality a misunderstanding that spilled over from tensions among Mosquito leaders themselves. In fact, the issue had almost nothing to do with the English at all. After hearing reports that the Mosquito general was plotting against him, the Mosquito king met with both the governor and the admiral to secure their support just in case the rumors turned out to be true. Thus, the dispute did not directly involve the English, though naturally the king was prepared to arrest any White settlers who were found to be plotting against him.[50] Ultimately, nothing came of the rumors: no hostilities broke out among Mosquito leaders, no White settlers were either killed or arrested, and life on the Shore continued as normal. The incident was telling, however, regarding the status of the English. Their panicked responses to the rumors was a tacit recognition of just how much they needed Mosquito support for the colonial project to survive, as well indicating how little control they had over Mosquito leaders.

Another outbreak of panic occurred in May 1769 after another Mosquito leader, Admiral Dilson, received an invitation from the Spanish governor of Costa Rica to visit Cartago as an honored guest.[51] Dilson did not travel to Costa Rica himself, but he did send a delegation composed of some of his closest advisers, arriving in Cartago in July.[52] Soon after the visit, rumors began to circulate among the English settlers at Bluefields—the English colony closest to Admiral Dilson's residence in the Pearl Key Lagoon—that the Mosquito admiral was plotting with the Spanish to facilitate an attack on the English settlers. Admiral Dilson himself was aware of the rumors, and hoping to assuage the tensions even wrote to the governor of Jamaica in September to address the accusations directly.[53] The effort was in vain, however, and fears continued to mount. In early October, the English settlers of Bluefields decided to send a formal petition to the governor of Jamaica asking for protection.[54] By the end of the month, the panic had spread to Black River, where settlers likewise petitioned Jamaica to intervene on their behalf.[55] What is more, the Mosquito king himself seemingly corroborated the rumors by sending his own letter to the governor of Jamaica distancing himself from Dilson's actions and suggesting that the Mosquito admiral was indeed plotting with the Spanish.[56]

This panic surrounding Dilson's negotiations with Costa Rica, occurring only one year after the king's alleged conspiracy to kill all Whites, revealed yet again the extent to which English colonists saw losing Mosquito support as a very real possibility. Moreover, the response of colonial authorities to this new round of panic revealed an additional weakness of the colonial project: internal divisions. After Joseph Otway's death in 1767, Robert Hodgson the younger—the son of the Mosquito Shore's first superintendent of the same name—replaced Otway as superintendent. Like his father, however, the younger Hodgson was a controversial figure, and his opponents rushed to criticize his handling of this new Mosquito conspiracy. For example, the governor of Jamaica complained that Hodgson had failed to report about the Dilson incident himself, leaving the governor to suspect that Hodgson was shirking his duties and spending too much time away from his post. In response, the governor undercut Hodgson's authority by sending former Mosquito Shore superintendent Richard Jones to investigate the rumors of Dilson's alleged conspiracy.[57] Word of the governor's disdain toward Hodgson soon spread, and the embattled superintendent rushed to defend his position by conducting his own investigation.

It was against this background of panic and internal tensions that both Jones and Hodgson conducted a series of interviews with Mosquito leaders over the next few months regarding the alleged Dilson conspiracy. With Hodgson's job on the line, a complicated tension influenced his report. On the one hand, he was motivated to exaggerate the danger of the situation in order to show that a Shore superintendent was needed in order to manage relations with the Mosquito. On the other hand, he did not want to admit that things had gotten out of hand on his watch. To handle these tensions, Hodgson both exculpated himself and asserted his own influence by playing into racist tropes of Indian simplicity, characterizing Dilson as a wayward child who was easily led astray yet was just as easily brought back under control when firmly chastised. Indeed, in Hodgson's version of events, the childlike Dilson had been tricked by the Spanish who manipulated the simple-minded Mosquito admiral with gifts and shallow praise. Within this interpretation, the episode was not really Hodgson's fault, though neither was it a major problem since Hodgson could allegedly rectify the situation with a simple scolding. According to the report, Dilson had even cried in embarrassment after Hodgson confronted him with the evidence of the alleged betrayal: a copy of the letter that Dilson had received from the Costa Rica governor.[58]

There is much reason to doubt Hodgson's characterization of this meeting. In addition to depending on blatantly racist tropes of Amerindian inferiority and childishness, the report includes various inconsistencies that do not accord with broader evidence. For example, the narrative logic of Hodgson's report revolved around Dilson's supposed embarrassment at having his secret negotiations exposed, yet the negotiations had never been secret. In fact, Dilson himself had written openly about them to the governor of Jamaica months earlier.[59] Moreover, Hodgson's own report presents a contradictory picture of Dilson. For example, the report admits in passing that Dilson defended his actions logically and defiantly by arguing that if the English could trade with the Spanish, why shouldn't he as well? This bolder version of Dilson stands in stark contrast to the embarrassed child described later, and in fact the more defiant version of Dilson matches the characterization presented in Richard Jones's findings.

For his part, Jones included similar racist tropes in his report, ultimately concluding that the Spanish had taken advantage of the simple Dilson by playing to his "vanity." Nonetheless, Jones's recorded interview with Dilson was far more extensive than Hodgson's, recording Dilson's full explanation of the background and context of Costa Rican negotiations. Specifically, Dilson explained to Jones that the 1769 negotiations with Costa Rica were not new, nor were they even initiated by the Costa Rican governor. In fact, the Mosquito had pressured the Spanish province into making tribute payments several years earlier, and the recent visit of Dilson's captains to Costa Rica had been simply to renegotiate the terms of the agreement with Costa Rica's new governor. Jones also cast doubt on Hodgson's work more directly by reporting that Dilson disliked the superintendent and complained bitterly about Hodgson's rudeness.[60] It is possible that Jones exaggerated this complaint in order to make his rival look bad, though future events seemed to corroborate the claim as Mosquito leaders would continue to submit grievances against Hodgson over the next few years. In fact, Mosquito complaints against Hodgson would be an important factor in the later decision to remove him from the superintendent position in 1775.

Following the interviews, the actions of Jones and Hodgson further reveal the extent to which the English considered Mosquito defection to the Spanish a real threat. Whereas both Hodgson and Jones in 1769 tried to impress their superiors by lauding their own influence over Mosquito leaders, in practice neither actually trusted that this influence was enough, and both attempted to cut all Mosquito ties to the Spanish by contacting Costa Rican officials directly. Hodgson, for example, kept his visit with Dilson exceedingly brief, leaving the same day that he arrived in order to continue south toward Matina. Here Hodgson spent several days in the residence of the Matina lieutenant after sending letters to Cartago accusing the Costa Rica governor of trying to incite the Mosquito against the English and demanding that the communication cease.[61] Jones did not visit the Spanish himself, but he did write a letter to Costa Rica on behalf of Dilson, disavowing the allegedly conspiratorial negotiations.[62]

The interventions of Jones and Hodgson did little to assuage English fears, either among English settlers on the Mosquito Shore or among authorities across the Atlantic. Rumors continued to circulate that a Spanish attack was imminent and that Dilson was implicated in the plot.[63] Moreover, when the Spanish coast guard seized an English ship leaving the Mosquito Shore and bound for Curacao in early 1770, authorities in England presumed that the event was related to Dilson's alleged conspiracy.[64] The tensions between the younger Hodgson and his opponents also continued to grow. In addition to reporting Dilson's complaints about Hodgson, Jones also claimed that Hodgson had frequently abandoned his official duties in order to pursue private trading ventures. Jones also hinted at corruption by reporting rumors that Hodgson had used his position to accumulate landholdings of eighty thousand acres.[65]

Meanwhile, Hodgson launched his own accusations against Jones, blaming the former superintendent when Admiral Dilson again became the center of controversy in March 1770. After hearing rumors that Dilson had outfitted a fleet for the purpose of invading Matina, thus risking Spanish retaliation that might affect English settlers, Hodgson set out once again to confront Dilson directly.[66] Hodgson's report of this new incident drew from similar tropes as the previous, characterizing Dilson as an impulsive child. According to Hodgson's version of events, the superintendent arrived just as Dilson's fully armed fleet was about to disembark, allowing Hodgson to intervene just in time. During the encounter, the captains of the fleet allegedly confessed to Hodgson that their purpose was to attack the Spanish, yet the superintendent masterfully talked them out of the foolish endeavor. Hodgson then went on to claim that Jones had used gifts and flattery to manipulate the gullible Dilson into outfitting the fleet. Hodgson then concluded the report by claiming to have prevented another proposed invasion in May, this time allegedly organized by the Mosquito king.[67]

Again, there are reasons to question specific details of Hodgson's account. Perhaps most obviously, the racially charged depiction of Mosquito leaders as gullible fools whose actions were simply determined by their own savage passions contradicts the well-documented history of the Mosquito Confederation implementing foreign policy initiatives based on long-term strategic initiatives. Indeed, as already shown, the confederation had been at peace with Costa Rica since 1763 when Dilson had helped to renegotiate a long-standing alliance from earlier in the century that had lapsed due to Costa Rican recalcitrance rather than Mosquito aggression. Hodgson's claim, therefore, that Mosquito leaders would so easily be duped into deviating from these patterns—especially so soon after Dilson's successful negotiations the year before—does not fit well with wider evidence. Historical context suggests that it was far more likely that the fleet had no intention of attacking Costa Rica in the first place, and then naturally when no attack occurred, Hodgson tried to take credit for maintaining the peace himself.

Moreover, there is no evidence beyond Hodgson's own word to corroborate that either Admiral Dilson or the Mosquito king had in reality attempted the attack that Hodgson supposedly stopped. Admiral Dilson, for example, died soon after without giving any additional interviews or writing his own version of events. Evidence also suggests that Hodgson did not trust the Mosquito king to corroborate the reports. Since February 1770, Hodgson had been trying to prevent the king from visiting Jamaica, and their relationship remained tense over the next few years.[68] Ultimately, this wider evidence suggests that Hodgson likely fabricated the details of the encounter—or at the very least greatly exaggerated—once again in an effort to impress his superiors.

In the years following Dilson's alleged conspiracy, English colonists continued to face similar troubles. Mosquito leaders still negotiated openly with Spanish officials, leading to additional rumors of Mosquito conspiracies against the English. Mosquito fleets also continued to make their own itineraries, leading to ongoing fears that the Mosquito raids might lead to Spanish reprisals against the poorly defended English settlements of Black River or Bluefields. At stake in Mosquito foreign policy, therefore, was the very viability of the English colonial project itself, which ironically found itself simultaneously threatened by both Mosquito peacemaking and raiding. Accordingly, keeping Mosquito foreign policy in check remained the most important duty of the superintendent, whose purpose was to gain a strong enough rapport with Mosquito leaders to influence Mosquito decision-making in ways that would protect English colonization.

Unfortunately for Hodgson, however, Mosquito leaders remained difficult to control. And English settlers themselves recognized this lack of control, with fear continuing to proliferate. After a few years of relative quiet, a new cycle of rumors, conspiracies, and reactionary tactics began in March 1774 when a Mosquito convoy on a routine southern voyage got into a skirmish with a Spanish coast guard vessel near the mouth of the San Juan River, resulting in the death of a Spanish officer. The altercation was an isolated incident, but Mosquito leaders understood that the event might cause panic among the English and rushed to address the issue before it grew into a scandal. The Mosquito governor, for example, immediately wrote to Hodgson to inform him of the skirmish and to reassure him that the Mosquito leaders would investigate the situation in order to keep things under control.[69]

Rather than trusting the Mosquito governor to handle the issue, however, Hodgson treated the situation as an emergency, and immediately upon receiving the news of the skirmish, he wrote to the governor of Jamaica calling the encounter a "rupture" of the peace that was bound to have dire consequences. For example, even though the Mosquito governor's report only talked about setting out to investigate and said nothing about retaliation, Hodgson assumed that the governor was in reality plotting a major punitive expedition against the Spanish that would escalate hostilities further. Hodgson then claimed that he needed to intervene to prevent the Mosquito from enacting depredations all along the coast—depredations that would invite Spanish retaliation negatively affecting English interests.[70]

It is impossible to know precisely why Hodgson's interpretation of events made the situation seem so much more dire than indicated in the initial report that he received from the Mosquito governor. Hodgson briefly referenced word-of-mouth reports in addition to the governor's letter, so it is possible that the spread of rumors contributed to a climate of fear that shaped how Hodgson interpreted the report. But context suggests that it is also possible that Hodgson sought to take advantage of the situation to exaggerate his importance and justify his position as superintendent, which was still under scrutiny. Regardless, Hodgson presented the situation as an emergency, setting out to confront the Mosquito governor directly and prevent his supposed savage impulses toward revenge from leading to further violence.

Despite the dire rhetoric, the resolution of the situation was anticlimactic. Upon visiting with the governor, Hodgson found out that the Mosquito fleet had never even assembled—neither for a punitive expedition nor even to investigate the incident with the Spanish coast guard. Nonetheless, Hodgson still claimed credit for talking the Mosquito out of future expeditions, though even he admitted after his interview that "the rupture appears somewhat less formidable." Hodgson's report then claims that he proposed what he presumed to be a novel idea: that the Mosquito governor should collect tribute from the Spanish in Costa Rica instead of raiding.[71] Ironically, the Mosquito council had maintained such an agreement with Costa Rica for over a decade, a fact that the late admiral Dilson had openly reported to other English agents.[72] Nonetheless, Hodgson reported the ideas as his own, promptly setting out from his interview with the governor to visit Matina.

It is unclear to what extent Hodgson truly believed the arrangement to be novel, or if he merely presented it as such in correspondence with his superiors. Regardless, Hodgson tried to capitalize on the incident to ingratiate himself to Costa Rican officials. For example, Hodgson wrote to the governor of Costa Rica taking credit for preventing any further Mosquito depredations and promising to return the confiscated coast guard ship.[73] The superintendent hoped that the gesture would demonstrate his alleged control over Mosquito leaders, legitimizing his presence on the shore in the eyes of Spanish and English officials alike. He also likely saw the visit as an opportunity to establish contacts for his own personal trading ventures. In any event, Hodgson followed through with the promise to make amends for the skirmish, arriving in Matina in early May to return the vessel and to discuss the tribute arrangement on behalf of the Mosquito governor.[74]

To Hodgson's surprise, however, the gesture backfired, and Costa Rican officials refused to meet with him, demanding instead that he take the vessel somewhere else. Hodgson apparently had assumed that any province would be happy to see the vessel returned. He later found out, however, that the vessel not only had no connection to Costa Rica but was a royal coast guard ship that policed contraband trade—an activity that Costa Rican merchants participated in heavily. Costa Rican officials worried, therefore, that the presence of the vessel would attract attention from higher authorities and interrupt the benign neglect that was currently allowing clandestine trade to thrive.[75] Unsurprisingly, Hodgson's attempted diplomatic gesture to return the coast guard vessel only created panic.

Moreover, just as Hodgson's actions failed to garner favor with the Costa Ricans, the controversial superintendent continued to face skepticism from English authorities as well. At the center of the criticism was his relationship with the Mosquito leaders. Only months before the incident with the Spanish coast guard ship, the Mosquito governor had already written to his "brother governor" in Jamaica specifically to complain about Hodgson. The letter claimed that Hodgson had been keeping the tribute gifts that were supposed to be distributed to the Mosquito and spending most of his time on private trading ventures rather than carrying out his official duties.[76] Combined with Admiral Dilson's earlier complaints about Hodgson in 1770, the letter indicated that Hodgson's relationship with the Mosquito continued to sour. Significantly, the reaction to these complaints in Jamaica demonstrated how much importance English authorities placed on maintaining Mosquito support. The governor of Jamaica took the accusations seriously enough to forward them to London where they appeared in a broader review of Hodgson's performance.[77]

Making matters worse for Hodgson, he also faced criticism from the Mosquito king. In fact, when the king's son and heir went on a diplomatic visit to London in 1775, presenting complaints about Hodgson was one of the primary purposes of the visit.[78] Named George after his father, the Mosquito crown prince traveled with an American merchant named Jeremiah Terry who had settled on the Mosquito Shore some time earlier.[79] The visit lasted several months, and in November, the prince presented a formal complaint about Hodgson to the earl of Dartmouth, who had influence in

American policy. Echoing the letter from the Mosquito governor two years earlier, the prince's complaints focused on Hodgson's alleged neglect of diplomatic duties in order to conduct private trade, including trafficking Amerindian slaves.[80]

It is possible that the specific accusations leveled against Hodgson were exaggerated, and that non-Mosquito opportunists hoping to oust Hodgson for their own gain had a hand in crafting these complaints attributed to Mosquito leaders. Jeremiah Terry, for example, was hoping to become the next superintendent of the Mosquito Shore and therefore had a motive to make Hodgson look bad in front of higher authorities.[81] Nonetheless, regardless of the extent to which the details of these accusations were literally true, independent evidence shows Hodgson had failed to ingratiate himself to Mosquito leaders, who expressed their disdain for Hodgson on numerous occasions.

It is also significant that the complaints against Hodgson specifically implicated him in the trafficking of Amerindian captives as slaves. Again, whether or not these accusations were literally true, the fact that they were made offers important insights into the ideas and practices shaping English colonialism in Central America's Caribbean borderlands. By the time the Mosquito crown prince visited England in 1775, English officials already had expressed concern about the slave trade for years. This concern, however, did not derive from a desire to abolish slavery entirely so much as from the fear that this particular iteration of the slave trade—based on unregulated, privately planned raiding ventures that targeted free Indigenous villages—generated too many dangers for the English colonists and ultimately outweighed the economic benefits. When the Mosquito Shore intendency was first established in 1750, for example, Jamaican governor Edward Trelawny recommended banning the Amerindian slave trade using logic that the market for slaves encouraged raiding, which in turn would alienate neighboring Indigenous groups from the English. Trelawny went on to reason that these groups would likely turn to the Spanish for protection, further weakening the English position on the coast.[82]

Joseph Otway then echoed these arguments in 1765 during his tenure as superintendent on the shore, also fearing that the slave trade was making the already tenuous position of the English colony even more precarious by alienating potential allies. Significantly, Otway's description of the slave trade also helps to clarify why Mosquito leaders likewise came to oppose this trade, even though it was on the surface a valuable market. Otway explained that English merchants had begun to contract directly with Mosquito slave-raiders, encouraging private raiding ventures that Mosquito and English leaders alike struggled to regulate.[83] Accordingly, when the Mosquito crown prince George II met with English officials to complain about Hodgson in 1775, he also asked for English authorities to take legal measures against these practices. Of course, this did not mean that either the Mosquito or English leaders opposed the practice of slavery. Rather, at stake in these negotiations over the slave trade was the respective Mosquito and English governments' ability to regulate violence, which private slave raiding had come to threaten.

Ultimately, the prince's visit to London was productive, and both Mosquito and English leaders took steps the following year to address these issues. In November 1776, the recently ascended Mosquito governor Colville Briton issued new laws targeting the unregulated trade in Amerindian slaves. The new laws did not necessarily bring an end to the slave trade altogether, but they did put the Mosquito central council back in charge of regulation. For example, the new guidelines prohibited Mosquito sailors from contracting directly with English merchants for private ventures, and they banned credit, which English merchants had used to obligate indebted Mosquito men to repay their debts in slaves.[84] English authorities in London also took the complaints against Hodgson seriously. After an investigation, officials agreed that Mosquito support was simply too important for the colonial project to allow the controversial Hodgson to remain as superintendent. In 1776, he was officially removed from his post.[85]

Conclusion

As the events in this chapter have demonstrated, Mosquito negotiation with the Spanish was indeed extensive following the 1763 reconciliation with Costa Rica, and while some tensions remained, the negotiations proved meaningful with the hostilities of previous decades rapidly abating. During this process, Spanish policy adapted considerably. Whereas local actors in frontier provinces had long negotiated varying degrees of pragmatic peace agreements with the Mosquito in practice, Guatemalan and Iberian authorities had usually pressured against making this official policy. In the 1760s, however, the reconciliation in Costa Rica set the stage for further negotiations, which even gained the approval of higher authorities. This created serious challenges for English agents, who recognized that the success of the

English colonial project in the region depended heavily on Mosquito support, yet found Mosquito leaders beyond their control.

Significantly, this chapter sets the stage for more critical understandings of the events leading up to the Mosquito civil war in 1791. For example, the presumption that the Mosquito never seriously negotiated with the Spanish prior to the 1780s has figured heavily in explanations of the civil war, with one influential hypothesis being that the supposed sudden shift from being allied with the English to being allied with the Spanish created unsustainable tensions among Mosquito leaders. As Offen's seminal 2002 article explained, "I would suggest that the rapid transition of Spanish as foe to Spaniard as friend intruded on an incipient Miskitu ethnic space, which many Sambo and Tawira Miskitu were unwilling to accept."[86] As this chapter has demonstrated, however, negotiations with the Spanish were already so extensive that no such rapid transition could have taken place. Moreover, this chapter has provided evidence against the hypothesis that the Mosquito were economically and culturally dependent on English. This hypothesis has led some studies to presume that the British cessation of their Mosquito Shore settlements in 1786 created material pressures that played a direct role in causing the civil war.[87] However, given the lack of evidence for this material dependence in the first place, there is little reason to conclude that subsistence pressures were a major factor in the factional conflict within the Mosquito Confederation.

Ultimately, this chapter has provided important context for evaluating the series of events leading to the unraveling of the Mosquito Confederation, and along with it, the end of the Mosquito conquest. This unraveling was still far from inevitable in the 1770s, yet weaknesses were already visible in the core alliances that gave the confederation its strength. When these alliances finally ruptured, the Mosquito Kingdom would never regain the expansive influence that it had maintained throughout the eighteenth century.

CHAPTER 6

The Mosquito Confederation and Civil War, 1776–1791

When the Mosquito duke Isaac arrived in Matina on a diplomatic mission for his nephew, King George II, he left no doubt that the king wanted to distance himself from the other principal leaders of the Mosquito Confederation. It was October 1784, and while the Mosquito had a long history of negotiating in Costa Rica as a unified confederation, Isaac strategically arranged this visit to make the other Mosquito factions look bad. The key to this diplomatic subversion was to release several prisoners from the Matina Valley who had been captured three years earlier. Testifying in Spanish, the captives stated explicitly that the attackers had acted under the leadership of the Mosquito admiral Dilson II. Furthermore, they stated under oath that the Mosquito king George II and his followers had not participated in this raid, instead maintaining a peaceful stance toward Costa Rica. Moreover, the testimonies painted Dilson as exceptionally cruel, in contrast to Isaac and George, who had ransomed the captives immediately after finding out about their deplorable living conditions. These stories may have been exaggerated, but one thing was clear: the unity that had characterized the confederation's rise to power was rapidly dissipating.[1]

The purpose of this chapter is to describe the period from roughly 1776 to 1791, examining the processes that culminated in the breakdown of the internal alliances of the confederation. In evaluating these events, this chapter argues that, just as the rise of the Mosquito Confederation had less to do with European support and more to do with internal alliances, so too did its decline. Even though the Mosquito Confederation remained a regional power at the time of Duke Isaac's visit to Costa Rica in 1784, personal disagreements among confederation leaders had become more prevalent since the late 1760s. This was evident in how Mosquito leaders interacted with foreign allies as they increasingly negotiated individually rather than collectively—a stark contrast to previous generations. These disputes were manageable as long as the factions continued to work within the established norms of the confederation, and indeed, as shown in the previous chapter, Mosquito leaders in the 1770s continued to collaborate on important issues such as maintaining the fleet system and passing legal reforms to regulate slave raiding more strictly. Nonetheless, conflicts intensified in the 1780s until eventually one of the council members took the unforgivable step of inviting foreign troops into Mosquito territory to support his own efforts to dominate the confederation, thus causing a civil war to erupt in 1791.

This is not to say, of course, that the broader context of Spanish and English relations played no role in this process. The descent of the Mosquito Confederation into civil war played out over a dynamic geopolitical landscape as the Spanish and English renegotiated their own territorial claims, resulting in English authorities agreeing to evacuate their settlements on the Mosquito Coast in 1786. This context shaped how Mosquito leaders chose to strike at each other, though these events were not the primary cause of Mosquito disunity since personal rivalries long predated these events. Indeed, Duke Isaac's diplomatic mission to Costa Rica to undercut Admiral Dilson II preceded the English evacuation by two full years. Moreover, contradicting the hypotheses of some researchers, the sources examined in this chapter provide no evidence that Anglo–Spanish wars created new economic pressures that forced Mosquito leaders to compete with each other for scarce resources.[2] Rather, evidence suggests that a more important effect of this new geopolitical context was to create new possibilities for Mosquito leaders as Spanish officials proved more willing than ever to make concessions. Ultimately, the Mosquito were arbiters of their own fate: Mosquito decision-making was the key to the confederation's rise and fall, and European colonial powers played only tangential roles in these processes.

The Mosquito Confederation and Strained Alliances, 1776–1791

When Colville Briton became the new Mosquito governor in 1776, there were early signs that he might work well with the recently ascended George II. In fact, both of the new leaders started their tenures by presenting a united front on pending issues that affected the English alliance. For example, even though Jamaica was an important market for the purchase of Amerindian slaves throughout the eighteenth century, since the 1740s, several English officials had worked to ban the practice.[3] The Mosquito had continued selling captives to English merchants, but in the mid-1770s, both Colville Briton and George II expressed interest in helping English authorities enforce new restrictions on the Amerindian slave trade. George II discussed the issue with English officials during a diplomatic visit to London in 1775 while still the crown prince, expressing his support for new restrictions on the slave trade.[4] When Colville Briton became governor in 1776, then, one of his first acts was to issue a proclamation fulfilling this promise.[5]

Significantly, the motivations of George II and Colville Briton in supporting English efforts to restrict the Amerindian slave trade were more complex than simply giving in to English demands. Mosquito politics were also at stake. While both leaders did use this issue as an opportunity to reassure their English allies of their loyalty, these efforts also fit within a larger project of increasing the individual power of confederation leaders. For example, Colville Briton's proclamation did not ban the Mosquito themselves from conducting slave-raids; rather, these restrictions applied only to the English settlers. Moreover, in order to prevent English merchants from coercing Mosquito individuals to participate in slave raids, the declaration banned English merchants from extending credit to the Mosquito. It also prohibited any Mosquito subjects from working on English-owned ships. Accordingly, the move had the dual effects of reassuring the Mosquitos' English allies of the Mosquito Confederation's goodwill toward English authorities, while at the same time establishing tighter controls over slave raiding practices that had become increasingly privatized.

This had notable implications for internal politics, as well as the confederation's geopolitical strategy. In previous years, Mosquito raiders participating in independent or English-led attacks had complicated peace treaties since private raiding beyond the direct control of Mosquito leaders made it more difficult for the Mosquito council to offer potential allies a guarantee that raids would stop. Protection treaties depended on the confederation council actually being able to offer protection: as raiding became less centrally directed, this promise became harder and harder to keep. Accordingly, by intervening in the slave trade in 1776, Mosquito leaders positioned themselves to not only assert more direct authority over the confederation's manpower but also to negotiate more effectively in foreign diplomacy.

Nonetheless, despite these auspicious efforts to unify the confederation council and strengthen its authority, divisions among the Mosquito continued to grow. Indeed, only months after issuing his 1776 proclamation, Colville Briton found himself embroiled in new controversy, and the fallout of the scandal pitted the new king and governor against each other. The problem began in March 1777 when Colville Briton hosted a group of Spanish ambassadors from Portobello in his residence in the Mosquito settlement of Tebuppy. Word of the visit quickly spread, sparking another round of English fear, which only intensified when the Spanish coast guard attacked two English ships off the coast of Bluefields shortly after. In the context of this attack, rumors soon spread that during the visit Colville Briton had made an agreement with the Spanish to help them remove the English from the coast.[6]

In reality, Colville Briton had not been plotting against the English: as usual, the negotiations were more about maintaining peace, and he was not even the one who had initiated the encounter. The Spanish envoy was actually responding to the Portobelo negotiations that the previous governor and king had begun back in 1775.[7] Still, the timing of the events looked suspicious, and the recently ascended King George II took advantage of the situation to criticize his peer. Writing to the Jamaican governor in May, George II informed the English about the March meeting and used the occasion as a basis to question Colville Briton's reliability. Ironically, one of George II's advisers had traveled to Colville Briton's residence to participate in the meeting with the Spanish envoy, implicating the king in the same negotiations.[8] Nonetheless, despite knowing that diplomatic visits with the Spanish were simply a routine part of Mosquito foreign policy in which he also participated, the king chose to indulge English fears and question Colville Briton's loyalty in the eyes of a key ally.

Of course, it is important to stress that despite this subtle subversion, the confederation was still a long way from reaching the point of civil war. Indeed, in the aftermath of the Spanish coast guard incident, Governor Briton reportedly met with King George II and General Tempest in order to address the issue with a more united front.[9] It is also important to stress that this strategy of manipulating perceptions and performing loyalty to the English did not interrupt the long-standing practice of negotiating with allied Spanish provinces such as Costa Rica. In February 1778, for example, Admiral Dilson II took charge of updating the confederation's ongoing agreements with Costa Rica, which his father had led during the reconciliation in 1763 and the signing of a formal treaty in 1769. Rather than sending ambassadors to Costa Rica as his father had, however, Dilson II headed the delegation himself. Arriving in Cartago on February 10, the young admiral stayed for almost two weeks.[10] In many ways, Dilson II simply picked up where previous negotiations had left off. Reaffirming the goodwill between the confederation and Costa Rica, the admiral promised that the Matina Valley would remain protected from Mosquito attacks, just as it had been since the last invasion in 1766. In exchange, he asked to be allowed to continue trading in Costa Rica, as well as to receive an official Spanish commission like his father's. Moreover, leaving no doubt that he represented the entire confederation, Dilson also said that other Mosquito leaders, including the king and governor, would soon visit Costa Rica as well in order to reaffirm their own support for the alliance.[11]

Unfortunately for Dilson, however, the visit started another round of English complaints as rumors spread that Dilson had pledged to help the Costa Ricans remove the English settlers from the Mosquito Shore.[12] The rest of the council may have launched new accusations against Dilson in order to distance themselves from the controversy as they had done in previous situations, though this cannot conclusively be proven. What is certain is that following this new round of English accusations, the confederation council chose not to send the follow-up delegation immediately, perhaps indicating that the other Mosquito leaders sought to distance themselves from Dilson rather than coming to his defense.

The Mosquito Confederation's ongoing negotiations with the Spanish then became even more complicated when the American merchant Jeremiah Terry arrived to negotiate a treaty on behalf of the Spanish Crown. Terry had previously lived among the English settlers on the Mosquito Shore, so he already had some rapport with Mosquito leaders. In fact, as already discussed in chapter 5, he had traveled along with King George II, at the time still the crown prince, during his trip to England in 1774.[13] Now working for the Spanish, Terry arrived at the mouth of the San Juan River in the summer of 1778 to negotiate a peace accord with the Mosquito.[14] Terry invited the principal Mosquito headmen to convene a council meeting at his temporary residence at the San Juan River, and when they arrived, he explained his terms. Admiral Dilson II, Governor Briton, and King George II all attended the meeting, and after listening to Terry's explanation, the council signed an accord allowing him to settle in the region for the purpose of facilitating Spanish trade. By all evidence, the Mosquito council did not see this as a particularly novel agreement since they had already been negotiating and trading in Spanish provinces for several years. For example, indicating that the Mosquito leaders saw the Terry treaty as part of a broader set of ongoing negotiations with the Spanish, they explicitly asked for the governors of Costa Rica and Nicaragua to immediately receive copies of the new agreement.[15]

The politics of the Terry accord became complicated, however, when rumors spread that the Mosquito leaders had signed a treaty with Terry to help remove the English settlers from the shore.[16] Within this context, the divisions within the confederation showed more than ever. To begin, General Tempest had never signed the accord in the first place, signaling that his faction may not have fully supported the agreement. Then, when the English superintendent arrived to investigate the allegations and level charges of treason against Terry, Governor Colville Briton seized the opportunity to demonstrate his loyalty. Within this context of heightened English scrutiny, Colville Briton distanced himself from the other council members by alleging that he had never actually signed the agreement, and that his name had been forged, whereas the other Mosquito headmen signed willingly.[17] Regardless of the veracity of this claim, the Mosquito governor went on to lead a contingent of his own followers in ambushing Terry's ship on October 29, which was still anchored at the mouth of the San Juan River.[18]

Colville Briton's letter describing these actions provides an interesting window into how Mosquito leaders worked to manipulate appearances. For example, the letter included extreme claims of exclusive loyalty to the English, even proclaiming that peace between the Mosquito and the Spanish "can never be admitted."[19] Of course, wider evidence shows that these words did not match the governor's actions since Colville Briton openly participated in negotiations with the Spanish both before and after the Terry episode. Not only had Colville Briton hosted delegates from Portobelo the previous year, but he also sent a delegation to Costa Rica after the Terry affair in order to maintain peaceful relations there as well.[20] Accordingly, the most accurate way to interpret these proclamations of loyalty to the English is not as literal truth so much as hyperboles with a persuasive purpose.

It is unclear exactly how this event impacted the relationship between King George II and Colville Briton, but it was the king who took the lead in reassuring Costa Rica that Terry's arrest was not meant to undermine the ongoing peace. In June 1779 King George II sent his nephew, along with his uncle and long-time adviser Duke Isaac, on a visit to Matina to explain their side of the story. The delegation arrived June 23, receiving a warm welcome.

The ambassadors then stayed at the port, discussing the matter with the lieutenant, who reported to the governor in Cartago. At this point, disputes among Mosquito leaders still had not reached a point where they actively subverted each other in front of Spanish allies. Indeed, the Mosquito king's ambassadors traveled alongside a captain representing Governor Colville Briton, so it seems that the governor's decision to arrest Terry and criticize the other Mosquito headmen for signing the treaty had not completely alienated him from the rest of the council, nor even from Spanish Costa Rica. King George's son also visited Matina in a follow-up visit shortly after, receiving letters from the governor of Costa Rica directed toward both the Mosquito king and governor.[21] Moreover, Admiral Dilson II decided to make sure that his own faction continued to be represented in these negotiations, visiting Cartago himself in November 1779 for the second time in less than two years.[22]

As the year 1779 ended, however, the geopolitical context changed with the outbreak of new hostilities between England and Spain. The Mosquito council joined the fray in support of their English allies. In October 1779, for example, General Tempest provided soldiers to help the English take the Spanish Fort of Omoa.[23] Then, in November 1779, King George II sent representatives to Black River to pledge loyalty to Britain in future campaigns, a promise that he fulfilled the following year during an expedition against the Nicaraguan Fort Inmaculada on the San Juan River.[24] Preparations for the attack began in February 1780 when an English officer arrived in Sandy Bay to ask for Mosquito military support. King George II agreed to join the invasion himself, leading a group of Zambo-Mosquito soldiers. General Tempest also agreed to help, though he was too old to go himself, sending his son to represent his faction. The fleet left Sandy Bay in early March, arriving at the governor's home in Tebuppy on March 8 to ask for Governor Colville Briton's help, which he granted in theory, though he delayed the invasion by stalling the preparation of his own fleet. The English officer eventually sailed on without him, stopping at the Pearl Key Lagoon to meet with Admiral Dilson II as well. Dilson was not present, so he did not participate in the invasion.[25] Governor Colville Briton, however, did catch up with the invasion force, and after a brief siege, the united fleet took control of the fort on April 29.[26]

On the one hand, the attack allowed the council to show a certain degree of unity, with almost the entire confederation rallying in response to the English request for assistance. On the other hand, this assistance was limited. Rather than declaring all-out war against the Spanish, the Mosquito provided mostly logistical backup for isolated expeditions targeting specific frontier forts that the Mosquito likely did not view as falling under their protection agreements anyway. Indeed, even after these expeditions, the confederation could still claim to have been loyal to the protection agreement with Costa Rica.

Moreover, the invasion revealed tensions that had built up between the Mosquito and the English, and in October 1780, the entire council—with the exception of the aging General Tempest—gathered at the governor's residence in Tebuppy to formally express their grievances. Significantly, the Mosquito stipulated that while they remained allies of the English, they would not participate in any more joint military expeditions. The main justifications were economic. The Mosquito complained that English efforts to take strategic military sites did not leave room for plunder or other economic activities such as turtle-hunting, thus making long-term expeditions far too costly to be worth the meager benefits. This was especially problematic when Mosquito soldiers died in such campaigns since they produced no compensation for their families, even if the campaign was successful. Ultimately, the confederation promised to continue helping the English, but they would organize their own expeditions.[27]

It was against this background that Mosquito forces invaded the Matina Valley—a major derivation from the norm since the Mosquito Confederation had maintained an ongoing peace with Costa Rica for the past fifteen years. Paralleling Hannibal's famous attack on Matina in 1724, it seems that Costa Rica actually broke the treaty first when a Spanish offensive left Cartago in August 1780. The invasion force did not reach Mosquito territory, but it did skirmish with a handful of English and Mosquito scouts scattered along the coast between Matina and the San Juan River.[28] Seemingly in retaliation for this transgression, a large force of Tawira-Mosquito led by Admiral Dilson II overwhelmed the Matina Valley in a surprise raid on October 1, 1781. As usual, the incident was more a show of force than all-out warfare, but at least four people were killed and as many as twenty-five taken captive.[29] These captives were subsequently taken to the Pearl Key Lagoon, the location of the admiral's primary residence.[30]

Militarily, Admiral Dilson II's 1781 invasion of Matina was a resounding victory for Mosquito forces. The political fallout, however, rendered the success of the operation more dubious. Whereas Dilson II had fostered strong ties with Costa Rica through his recent negotiations in 1778 and 1779, his invasion of 1781 opened a window for King George II to subvert the admiral, positioning himself as the steward of the Costa Rican alliance. King George II did not move against Dilson II immediately, but in the following years, his agents began gathering information about the 1781 attack. The most important step in this process occurred when the king's uncle and long-time adviser, Duke Isaac, visited the Pearl Key Lagoon in 1782. While he was there, the duke came across at least three captives who had been taken from the guard of the Matina port. The duke immediately purchased these captives on the pretext that they were being treated poorly, though he must have also understood their potential power as ambassadors for King George II: these captives were verifiable eyewitnesses of Dilson's 1781 raid and could testify in fluent Spanish.[31]

King George II kept the captives for a time before finally releasing them back to Costa Rica as part of a delegation seemingly designed to destroy Dilson II's reputation in Costa Rica. The king did not visit Costa Rica himself but entrusted Duke Isaac to lead the diplomatic mission, which arrived in October 1784. The duke already had some rapport with Costa Rica, having visited in 1779 in the aftermath of the Terry affair, and as expected, he found a cordial reception in Matina. He then released the captives, along with a translator named Antonio Esguerra, into the custody of the port guard to give their testimonies.[32] In the short term, the visit was a diplomatic victory for King George II. The testimonies painted Dilson and his followers as utter villains while at the same time demonstrating the loyalty of the king's faction. However, the visit had sinister implications for the future of the confederation: moving forward, Mosquito leaders no longer viewed foreign policy as a way to strengthen the confederation as a whole. Instead, each sought foreign allies to help him dominate the other factions.

The ultimate destruction of the Mosquito Confederation played out over a shifting geopolitical landscape. In 1786, English leaders on the Mosquito Shore agreed to evacuate the mainland in compliance with a treaty signed with Spain.[33] On the one hand, this change did not have a major impact on the daily activities of the Mosquito: the English presence on the shore had always been relatively small, and while these settlers had been useful commercial contacts, the Mosquito still had access to English markets via smugglers operating out of Caribbean islands.[34] On the other hand, the shift opened up new opportunities to assert factional interests in foreign policy. With the English officially renouncing their claims to the Mosquito Shore, Spanish leaders in Central America increased their efforts to actively court the loyalty of the Mosquito leaders. Again, it was nothing new for Mosquito leaders to negotiate with the Spanish, and in many ways, this new wave of negotiations mirrored previous diplomatic encounters. Nonetheless, ambitious leaders saw in this changing geopolitical landscape new opportunities to strike against the other factions.

The primary players in this political drama were King George II, Governor Colville Briton, and Admiral Dilson II. These leaders hosted numerous Spanish agents who toured the Mosquito districts, and as Spanish officials showed themselves more desperate than ever to solidify Mosquito alliances, negotiations moved for the first time to colonial centers. Accordingly, all three of these leaders accepted invitations to meet with the viceroy at the port of Cartagena, and at least two of the leaders—George II and Colville Briton—visited the Nicaraguan city of Granada. Through these interactions, George II quickly developed a reputation for driving a hard bargain. Understanding that the Spanish were too weak to dictate terms, George II performed his superior status by setting high standards for tribute.[35]

Colville Briton took a different approach, however, instead going to great lengths to symbolically demonstrate his loyalty to the Spanish. During his visit to Granada, Briton released numerous captives, publicly accepted baptism, and entered into Christian marriage with a Spanish-speaking captive.[36] Admiral Dilson II, for his part, was less visible in Spanish towns, though he worked vigorously to secure new trade agreements, as well as to recruit defecting captains from the ranks of both Governor Briton and King George II. The growing size of Dilson's faction even warranted comment from Spanish inspectors, who noted that Dilson seemed to be drawing support away from Colville Briton.[37]

Ultimately, it was the governor who would cause these tensions to erupt into civil war. In May 1789, roughly a year after his highly publicized marriage, Briton met with the governor of Nicaragua to officially stake his claim as the preeminent ruler of the entire Mosquito Kingdom. Then, in a highly unprecedented bid for power, Briton asked his Spanish hosts for four hundred troops to assist him in forcing the other Mosquito leaders to recognize his authority.[38] Briton's explicit claim to rule the entire confederation, as well as his brazen invitation of foreign soldiers to occupy Mosquito sovereign territory, was apparently too much for the other Mosquito leaders to bear. Dilson and George allied against Briton, and early in 1791, launched a surprise attack on the governor's home village. Briton was killed and his following fragmented.[39]

With Colville Briton out of the way, Dilson II and George II now began to compete against each other to dominate the ailing confederation. In the summer of 1791, both Dilson and George met separately with Spanish agents in order to stake their own claims to preeminence. The Spanish were not sure of which leader to back, but ultimately, the competing factions settled the matter on their own. Both leaders tried to amass as many loyal soldiers as possible, but in the end, Dilson II's faction came up lacking. King George II was simply too strong, and by the end of the year, the king had killed Dilson II as well.[40] George II was left to consolidate his place as the dominant leader of the Mosquito, but the price of this victory was enormous. With the confederation fragmented and weakened, it would never recover its former imperial influence.

Spanish Reactions and Appeals for Mosquito Loyalty, 1775–1791

From the Spanish perspective, relations with the Mosquito were already showing marked improvement in the years leading up to the new outbreak of hostilities with Great Britain. Following the successful Costa Rican negotiations with the Mosquito in the 1760s, diplomatic efforts proliferated in the 1770s as other provinces followed Costa Rica's precedent. An interesting example occurred in 1775 when the Mosquito leaders King George and Governor Briton used an English agent to negotiate a treaty with the viceroy of Santa Fe. The terms were similar to the treaties previously negotiated in Costa Rica, offering trade licenses in exchange for guarantees of protection. Nonetheless, this was the first time that the Mosquito had negotiated directly with Spanish officials so far down the coast. Building on the new legal precedents that allowed these types of negotiations, the viceroy commissioned a follow-up expedition to visit the Mosquito Coast and finalize the terms with George and Briton directly.[41] The expedition arrived safely at the Mosquito governor's home in Tebuppy in March 1777, but by this time both King George and Governor Briton had already died.[42] Still, the new Mosquito governor treated the guests well, and representatives of the new mosquito king also arrived to participate in the negotiations.[43]

Furthermore, less than a year later in February 1778, the son of the previous admiral—also named Dilson—visited Cartago in person to update the ongoing peace agreements. Before this visit, Costa Rica had not hosted any formal diplomatic encounters with the Mosquito since the elder Admiral Dilson had sent representatives to Cartago in 1769. Still, Costa Rica remained on peaceful terms with the Mosquito, who had not raided the Matina Valley since 1766. The Costa Rican governor was glad to accept reassurances that peace would continue, though not surprised, having already sent orders to welcome Mosquito diplomats if any arrived.[44] The governor of Costa Rica gave the young admiral a warm welcome, greeting him with numerous gifts to demonstrate Costa Rica's continued goodwill.[45] Once the negotiations started, the new admiral asked for a series of trade agreements in exchange for keeping Matina safe, paralleling the treaty of the previous admiral in 1769.[46]

It was against this background of proliferating negotiations that the American merchant Jeremiah Terry arrived in Central America on a Crown-approved mission to negotiate a treaty with the Mosquito. Terry had lived on the Mosquito Shore earlier in the 1770s, and after being passed over by the English government for an official post in the region, Terry decided to offer his services to the Spanish Crown. After spending several months organizing the venture with Crown officials, Terry set out in a ship called the *Atlantico* and arrived at the mouth of the San Juan River in September of 1778 where he and the crew set to work constructing houses and a trading post.[47] Terry then sent word to the most powerful Mosquito leaders including Admiral Dilson, Governor Briton, and King George, who arrived for a general meeting in September where they signed a treaty allowing Terry to stay and facilitate trade between Spanish provinces and the Mosquito. Terry's previous rapport with Mosquito leaders certainly helped him to set up the meeting, though significantly, the terms largely represented a continuation of earlier negotiations that had taken place throughout the 1770s. In fact, the Mosquito signers specifically requested that the governors of Costa Rica and Nicaragua, as well as the viceroy of Santa Fe, be the first ones informed about the updated treaty.[48]

The news of Terry's success in negotiating the treaty was not surprising in Cartago given its own recent negotiations with the confederation, though it was still a welcome confirmation that the Mosquito were committed to maintaining the peace.[49] However, when the Mosquito later arrested Terry and turned him over to English authorities in Jamaica to face treason charges, the Costa Rican officials suddenly had cause for alarm: if the Mosquito had decided to invalidate Terry's treaty, then what about the previous peace negotiations? Desperate for more information on the state of the negotiations, authorities in Cartago interviewed members of Terry's crew in

December 1778 who had managed to make their way back to Costa Rica after the failed mission.[50] These interviews yielded little information as to why the Mosquito had suddenly broken the new treaty, though luckily, the Mosquito king George II took the initiative to send an envoy to Matina a few months later in June 1779. Helping to diffuse the tension, this delegation reassured local officials that the Terry incident did not indicate any malicious intentions toward Costa Rica.[51] Admiral Dilson also took initiative to reassure the Costa Ricans of his good intentions, sending another delegation led by his brother to visit Cartago in November 1779.[52] Ultimately, despite creating a brief controversy, the Terry expedition had little impact on the Spanish-Mosquito relations in practice, with local actors continuing to work with the Mosquito as before.

The ongoing Spanish conquest of Central America entered a new phase, however, when war broke out once again between the Spanish and English Crowns in 1779. Guatemala received word about the official declaration of war in August, and the president began making immediate preparations. On the one hand, Central America had long been a vulnerability of the Spanish Americas, and local officials knew that defensive preparations were necessary given the new likelihood of invasion. On the other hand, the war presented an opportunity to settle territorial disputes over the Mosquito Coast once and for all, and officials began planning offensive campaigns as well. Despite these efforts, the English took an early advantage, seizing two strategic fortifications within the first year: Fort San Fernando de Omoa on the northern coast of Honduras and Fort Inmaculada Concepción on the San Juan River.[53] Mosquito forces played important roles in both campaigns. The Zambo-Mosquito faction led by General Tempest—the same leader who had reportedly threatened to kill Luis Diez Navarro during the diplomatic visit in 1764—provided support for the Omoa attack.[54] The invasion up the San Juan River then utilized an even broader coalition of Mosquito leaders, including King George and Governor Colville Briton.[55]

Significantly, neither of these attacks violated the ongoing Mosquito peace with Costa Rica, though officials in Cartago began to fear that a joint English-Mosquito invasion of Matina was imminent. Accordingly, the Costa Rican governor took steps to fortify the Matina Valley, sending additional troops to reinforce a defensive trench in the region.[56] The Costa Ricans also began planning an offensive assault to try and secure the coast from Matina to the San Juan River. Reports indicated that the English position at Fort Inmaculada Concepción was highly vulnerable, with the garrison debilitated by disease and the fort open to a surprise attack if the invaders followed an alternate route along the Colorado River.[57] These reports turned out to be true, and when Costa Rica finally launched an expedition in August 1780, it encountered little resistance, routing a few small camps of English and Mosquito interlopers scattered along the coast.[58] Spanish offensives saw success on other fronts as well. Guatemala organized a much larger joint expedition of militias and regular troops in order to retake the Fort of San Fernando de Omoa, which capitulated to the Spanish in October 1780. Following this expedition, an invasion of Nicaraguan militia forces retook the debilitated Fort Inmaculada Concepción in December.[59]

It was against this background of scattered hostilities and increased Costa Rican aggression that the Mosquito Kingdom finally broke the longstanding truce with Costa Rica, invading Matina in October 1781. According to reports, no English soldiers participated in the raid. In fact, witnesses specified that the invasion was composed only of Mosquito soldiers of Amerindians descent, who numbered about two hundred.[60] The invasion had limited casualties, with only five deaths reported by Spanish officials. Still, the Mosquito devastated the valley, burning numerous properties, including the house of the Matina lieutenant, and then sailing off with twenty-five prisoners and a large cargo of cacao.[61] Around the same time, Mosquito forces also launched offensives in the provinces of Honduras and Nicaragua, attacking San Pedro de Sula in June 1781, as well as Juigalpa in early 1782.[62]

These localized operations ultimately had little bearing on the overall war effort, and when the conflict officially ended in 1783, the treaty recognized Spanish sovereignty over the disputed territories of Central America.[63] As in previous wars, however, the Mosquito Shore continued to be a source of controversy even after the treaty was signed. The agreement's wording implied that the Mosquito Shore should be included in the territories surrendered to the Spanish, yet English officials asserted that this was an accident and expected to keep the Mosquito Shore when the terms were clarified in future discussions.[64] Nonetheless, Spanish officials remained stubborn, arguing that the Mosquito Shore had always rightfully belonged to Spain and that the English Crown had finally recognized this fact in the new treaty.[65] Accordingly, Spanish officials in Central America took their own initiative to press these claims. For example, the president of Guatemala sent the commanding officer of Trujillo to visit Black River in December 1784, reminding the English of the treaty, as well as giving an even earlier deadline of February 1785 for evacuation.

Central American leaders understood, however, that even if the English did evacuate, the Mosquito still had effective control over the region. Indeed, the Trujillo commander was not allowed to approach the shore in Black River until General Tempest gave him permission.[66] Officials also understood that extensive precedents already existed for negotiating with the Mosquito. This was especially evident in Costa Rica, where King George had already taken the initiative to reopen formal diplomatic relations earlier in October 1784 by sending his uncle, Duke Isaac, to Matina to release Costa Rican prisoners taken during the 1781 attack. That King George would prioritize relations with Costa Rica is not surprising given the long-standing relationship between Costa Rica and the Mosquito. Duke Isaac had also been the one to visit Matina in 1779 to reassure the Costa Ricans after the Terry incident, and when he arrived again in 1784, Matina officials were already expecting him, having received word from a previous emissary about King George's peaceful intentions.

Despite following these previously established precedents, however, Isaac's 1784 visit was unique in one very important way: rather than negotiating on behalf of all Mosquito factions as he had done previously, Isaac's delegation harshly criticized the other Mosquito leaders. For example, Duke Isaac's translator, a Cuban-born captive of thirty years named Joseph Antonio Esguerra, testified that the Zambo-Mosquito under King George had declined to participate in the hostilities of the previous war. In contrast, the translator explained, the Mosquito Amerindians under Admiral Dilson and Governor Colville Briton alone had participated actively. Among other things, the Amerindian factions had been solely responsible for the invasion of Matina 1781, as well as the 1782 invasion of Juigalpa.[67] As proof of these claims, Duke Isaac released several captives from the Matina invasion who all corroborated that Dilson was in fact responsible. These witnesses further explained that the Zambo-Mosquito had opposed the invasion and that Duke Isaac had paid to free the Matina captives as soon as he found out that the treacherous Dilson was keeping them as slaves.[68]

At the time that Duke Isaac visited Costa Rica to reestablish the previous treaty on behalf of the king while simultaneously subverting Admiral Dilson, it remained unclear whether the English would renounce their claims to the Mosquito Shore and give in to Spanish pressure to evacuate. Indeed, English agents on the Mosquito Shore had held out hope throughout the entire year of 1785 that the treaty could be renegotiated to prevent the evacuation. Nevertheless, in July 1786, the English Crown officially clarified that the Mosquito Shore did indeed belong to the Spanish.[69] Word reached the Mosquito Shore in October 1786, and the English superintendent informed the settlers that the decision was final.[70] The process took several months, but in April 1787, a Spanish colonel arrived in Black River to oversee the official transfer of power to the Spanish.

This changeover, of course, was only in theory: many English settlers stayed on and the Mosquito were still the effective rulers of the territory. Significantly, the Spanish colonel tacitly recognized Mosquito authority, using this initial encounter to offer gifts and tributes to King George and General Tempest. Another Spanish captain then left to visit Governor Colville Briton in the settlement of Tebuppy, likewise offering gifts in hopes of winning over Mosquito trust.[71] Following these visits, Spanish authorities did try to make their seizure of the Mosquito Coast more tangible by populating the territory with Spanish settlers. As early as July 1787, settlers began arriving at the port of Trujillo, waiting to be spread out among settlements previously inhabited by the English. Over the next few months, as many as thirteen hundred settlers arrived.[72]

However, these efforts did little to shift the balance of power away from the Mosquito: the number of Spanish arrivals still paled in comparison to the Mosquito population, and the majority congregated at Black River, leaving the rest of the coast uncolonized.[73] Consequently, Spanish officials remained woefully dependent on the goodwill of Mosquito leaders to enact their new "colonization" project. Luckily, Mosquito leaders already had years of experience working with provincial governments, and they built on these previous relationships as the Spanish showed more willingness than ever to openly negotiate. As early as November 1787, for example, Governor Briton sent a delegation to meet with the Viceroy of Santa Fe at the port of Cartagena, and Admiral Dilson sent his own delegation the following year. These negotiations followed earlier patterns, stressing issues such as official titles and trade licenses.[74]

Nonetheless, Mosquito leaders continued Duke Isaac's newer precedent of negotiating separately, and in May 1789, Colville Briton wrote to the governor of Nicaragua requesting the support of Spanish troops in opposing his rivals. As Briton had proven the most cooperative Mosquito leader over the last few years, Spanish officials liked the idea of supporting Briton's bid to become the ruler of all Mosquito factions. Nonetheless, the Spanish still lacked the resources to implement such a change, leaving the governor to fend for himself. By 1791, hostilities finally broke out among Mosquito leaders, leaving both Governor Briton and Admiral Dilson dead. The Spanish played almost no direct role in these events, however, finding out about each leader's death long after it had occurred.[75]

Ultimately, as the century ended, the ongoing conquest of Central America remained incomplete, with the Mosquito Coast still representing a salient example of Spain's limited power. Even after the Mosquito civil war, Spanish officials lacked the resources to launch additional colonization efforts, and the project slowly withered. By 1800 the Spanish colonists were almost entirely reduced to Black River, and on September 4 of that year, the Mosquito king George attacked the struggling settlement, decisively negating Spain's tenuous claims to the region following the English evacuation.[76] Consequently, the Mosquito remained free as Spain's American colonial project began to give way to independence movements, leaving the Mosquito Coast as an object of conquest for later generations of consolidating nation states.

English Reactions and War with Spain, 1777–1786

From the perspective of the English settlements of the Mosquito Shore, the events leading up to the war with Spain and eventual evacuation only further highlighted the extent to which the English colonial project in the region depended on Mosquito support. In this context, the charge to maintain close ties to Mosquito leaders, as well as to react speedily to address any possible complication in this relationship, remained the job of the Mosquito Shore superintendent. When English officials finally made the decision to recall Robert Hodgson in 1776, longtime Black River resident James Lawrie became the new superintendent of the Mosquito Shore. Lawrie seemed to have a stronger rapport with Mosquito leaders than had Hodgson, in theory making the Mosquito more reliable allies. Moreover, with recent measures passed to regulate private slave-raiding ventures, English officials hoped to court additional indigenous allies as well. Together, these initiatives held the promise of solidifying England's mainland colonies, which since the official recognition of the Mosquito Shore Intendency in 1749 had struggled with the unpredictability caused by competing Spanish legal claims, as well as with the lingering possibility of Spanish attacks or Mosquito leaders pulling support. Nonetheless, the situation in practice remained largely unchanged during Lawrie's tenure: Mosquito leaders continued to make decisions independently, Spanish officials continued to press their claims in the region, and fear continued to mount that Mosquito authorities might abandon the alliance and leave the English colonists helpless.

As discussed above, these problems were already on display in March 1777—just one year after Hodgson's removal—when a group of Mosquito leaders hosted a Spanish delegation at the governor's residence in Tebuppy.[77] Then, to make matters worse, a Spanish coast guard vessel attacked an English ship near Bluefields soon after, and rumors spread that the Mosquito Confederation was secretly in league with the Spanish to wipe the English from the shore.[78] As late as December 1777, Mosquito leaders still faced scrutiny over the attack, obliging Colville Briton to write to Jamaica addressing the scandal yet again.[79] To the annoyance of the English, however, even in asserting their innocence of any conspiracy, Mosquito leaders did not cut off diplomatic relations with the Spanish. In fact, Admiral Dilson II visited the Costa Rican capital of Cartago only a few months later in February 1778 to continue the ongoing tribute negotiations. Word of the visit soon reached English settlers in Bluefields, and by May, rumors that Dilson was helping to plan a Spanish attack had reached Jamaica.[80]

It was against this background of renewed fear and distrust that Jeremiah Terry returned to the Mosquito Shore in the summer of 1778. However, unlike his previous stay when he had represented the English, this time Terry arrived representing the Spanish. After visiting London in 1775 with the Mosquito delegation that had presented complaints against Robert Hodgson, Terry had hoped to acquire the post of superintendent of the Mosquito Shore for himself. Passed over for the position, Terry then sought patronage from the Spanish instead, successfully acquiring a commission in 1777 to facilitate trade between the Spanish and the Mosquito.[81] As late as June 1778, Terry was still in Portobelo gathering supplies for the venture, but after outfitting a vessel, Terry made the short trip to the mouth of the San Juan River just to the south of Mosquito territory where he and his crew constructed houses and a trading post.[82] He then sent word requesting an audience with the principal Mosquito leaders, who indeed visited Terry's trading post in early September to sign a treaty giving Terry permission to facilitate trade between the Mosquito and the Spanish.[83]

By October, news of Terry's venture had reached English settlers at both Bluefields and Black River, and a familiar pattern of alarm set in. Some reports claimed that Terry himself had admitted that his goal was to turn the Mosquito against the English in order to forcefully remove the English settlers.[84] This interpretation was seemingly corroborated by other reports claiming that Terry had arrived with a large store of arms to distribute among the Mosquito.[85] Consequently, Superintendent Lawrie took the rumors seriously, and by November, he was convinced that the potential threat caused by Terry's presence required immediate action. Lawrie recognized, however, that the politics of the situation were far more complicated and that he could not simply make the decision to act against Terry on his own. Indeed, what made Terry so threatening in the first place was his potential to turn the Mosquito against the English. Diffusing the situation, therefore, required a course of action amenable to Mosquito leaders. And since nearly the entire confederation council had already approved of Terry's plan, arresting Terry risked provoking retaliation from Mosquito leaders—ironically, the exact situation that the English were trying to avoid.

Accordingly, Lawrie took his complaints directly to the Mosquito council in hopes of settling the dispute by working within the structures of Mosquito governance. This approach had mixed results. Having worked closely with Terry in the past and even traveled to England together in 1775, King George II apparently took no action. Fortunately for Lawrie, however, Colville Briton recanted his apparent support for Terry's treaty, taking the opportunity to perform superior loyalty to the English alliance in comparison to the other Mosquito leaders. The governor then accompanied Lawrie in confronting Terry, bringing an escort of Mosquito soldiers to arrest Terry in early November 1778.[86] The Mosquito governor then transported Terry to Jamaica to be interrogated by higher authorities.

During the interrogations, Terry generally downplayed the role of the Spanish, presenting himself more as a private merchant with nominal Spanish support rather than an agent of Spanish expansionism.[87] The governor of Jamaica found Terry's defense reasonable, concluding in his final report in April 1779 that "Mr. Lawrie's apprehensions of Mr. Terry's return to the Shore seem to be very ill-founded."[88] On the one hand, the Jamaican governor's assessment was reasonable. There is no evidence that Mosquito leaders ever agreed to turn on the English settlers, and they certainly never took any steps to put any such policy into practice. In fact, the treaty itself was not even novel since the Mosquito had negotiated various peace accords and commercial agreements with Spanish representatives since the Costa Rican reconciliation in 1763. On the other hand, given how poorly defended English settlements on the Mosquito Shore were, and how dependent they were on Mosquito support, it was not unreasonable that Lawrie and other English settlers would fear the worst at any hint of Mosquito disloyalty.

These long-standing fears were partially vindicated, moreover, since around the same time that the Jamaican governor was concluding that Terry posed no major threat, the Spanish and English Crowns on the other side of the ocean were declaring war on each other. What is more, officials on both sides began planning Central American operations that involved the Mosquito Coast. For their part, Spanish officials hoped that the English would be weakened by having diverted so many resources to putting down the revolt of the North American colonists, and in the summer of 1779, authorities in Guatemala began outfitting the fort at Omoa on the Honduran coast to serve as a base for offensive operations against the English settlers.[89] Moreover, English authorities were already envisioning their own offensive campaigns, and as early as June 1779, officials in London sent orders to Jamaica encouraging early strikes against key points such as the San Juan River, which connected the Caribbean to Lake Nicaragua and the Spanish interior. These plans, of course, depended on Mosquito support.[90]

Despite the revolution in North America, the English managed to strike first in the Central American theater, taking the Spanish fort of Omoa in October 1779. The established settlement at Black River, as well as the military alliance with the Mosquito themselves, proved vital to this operation. Before laying siege to the fort, British naval vessels stopped in Black River not only to stock up on supplies but also to secure a company of Mosquito soldiers led by the Mosquito General Tempest. Reports indicated that these troops were crucial to the success of the campaign, were aware of their worth, and negotiated accordingly. In fact, the English officers had to pay Tempest 100 pounds directly to guarantee his support, as well as covering transportation costs.[91]

The outbreak of war, therefore, placed in stark relief the extent to which the English strategy of relying on the Mosquito had become a double-edged sword. On the one hand, the support of the powerful confederation gave the English important advantages in manpower, logistics, and intelligence. On the other hand, losing these advantages could have dire consequences, leaving the English exposed to Spanish retaliation. Given these stakes, Tempest's material support for the English in the opening hostilities of the newly declared war did not fully assuage the lingering fears of Mosquito defection that had plagued the English colonists over the past two decades. Hoping to further solidify the alliance, Superintendent Lawrie met with King George

II to secure a written treaty declaring support for the English Crown against the Spanish.[92]

As the war progressed, English officers continued to place the Mosquito at the center of their plans. The English not only counted on the extra manpower and fighting prowess of Mosquito soldiers but also openly relied on Mosquito for specialized knowledge and technical support. When the English Captain John Polson set out from Jamaica in February 1780 with orders to take the Spanish fort on the San Juan River, he first went to the Mosquito Shore to outfit the expedition. In addition to needing soldiers, Polson lacked the specialized shallow water vessels needed to travel upriver, and he counted on the Mosquito for this fundamental aspect of the plan. The English also relied on the Mosquito for geographic knowledge, such as how to navigate upriver to Lake Nicaragua once past the fort guarding the river.[93] Polson hoped that this assistance would be forthcoming, but he also traveled ready to secure Mosquito support through compensation and gifts.[94]

Polson's initial campaign was successful, and the joint English—Mosquito forces took control of the Spanish fort on April 29, 1780. Polson complained bitterly about his Mosquito allies, however, who provided fewer vessels and soldiers than he had hoped and abandoned the arduous expedition rather than settling in for a long campaign, especially once the fort had already fallen. For his part, Polson suspected that Spanish agents were sowing distrust among Mosquito leaders and making them wary of English intentions.[95] In this way, Polson echoed the fears of many English colonists, which frequently erupted into accusations of defection when Mosquito leaders were reported to have had diplomatic meetings with the Spanish.

These supposed conspiracies had never manifested into any concrete event, though a related set of English fears did turn out to be warranted: that Black River was vulnerable to Spanish reprisals. Indeed, one of the reasons that securing Mosquito support had been so important in the first place was to provide military protection against a possible Spanish attack. Unfortunately for the English, this attack finally came in April 1780 when most English and Mosquito fighters were on the Polson expedition. After retaking the Fort at Omoa, Spanish forces launched a naval-based counterattack on the poorly defended Black River colony. Rather than trying to occupy and hold the colony, the invaders burned the settlement, and the colonists were forced to evacuate, either to the Island of Roatan or to the Mosquito interior.[96]

After the Spanish attack on Black River, English colonists became painfully aware of yet another dimension of their dependence: not only had English settlers long depended on the Mosquito goodwill for material and political support but they also depended on the labor of Amerindian and African slaves. Indeed, when Spanish delegate Luis Diez Navarro had visited Black River in 1764, he created various maps documenting the demographic diversity of the colony, where most of the colony residents were not White but rather Afro-descended, Amerindian-descended, or mixed race. Moreover, many of the Black and Indigenous residents were slaves, and it is possible that Black River was a majority slave colony despite lacking a developed plantation economy.[97] In the aftermath of the 1780 invasion, however, while the White colonists evacuated, a group of escaped slaves reestablished themselves in Black River and fortified the colony. Documents consulted for the present study leave it ambiguous whether the slaves took advantage of the chaos of the invasion to escape, or if their masters had forced the slaves to stay behind and fight as they themselves fled. Regardless, soon after the Spanish attack, reports began to circulate that the displaced settlers of Black River could not return because it was now controlled by a group of armed "negros."[98]

For the White slavers now living in exile in Roatan, this was a terrifying development. The Black River colony had long lived under the specter of a possible Spanish invasion or Mosquito betrayal and now faced a possible slave revolt. Accordingly, the White Black River colonists, along with settlers from Roatan and a group of "loyal slaves," organized an expedition in late June 1780 to retake the colony and reestablish the previous slave system. The English officer leading the expedition, a lieutenant named Richard Hoare, even sent a message to the principal leaders of the Mosquito asking for assistance.[99] The expedition set out from the island on June 20, and after making landfall and a brief march, Hoare sent a messenger to Black River, arranging to meet with the captains of the uprising on June 26. According to Hoare, these negotiations resulted in an amnesty agreement in which English authorities would give the slaves the benefit of the doubt and assume that they had taken up arms to defend the colony against the Spanish rather than to oppose their masters. However, Hoare refused to negotiate any possible freedom for the slaves, insisting under threat of force that the slaves be returned to their former masters.[100] In this way, Black River not only survived the Spanish assault but remained a slave-based colony.

After retaking Black River, the English worked to refortify their position on the mainland as the declared war with the Spanish remained ongoing.

This, of course, meant working to maintain the alliance with the Mosquito Kingdom, which had long been vital to English defense and more recently had provided support for English offensives in Honduras and Nicaragua. The harsh realities of war, however, had led to new tensions. And whereas the English had never been able to take Mosquito support for granted, they had to be even more attentive to the possibility of losing it as the war progressed. Not only did the Mosquito Kingdom approach the war with different strategic interests but they approached warfare with a different set of ideas and practices that sometimes clashed with English priorities. This was especially evident in Polson's expedition to the San Juan River, which resulted in heavy losses for the Mosquito—both in human lives and economic expenditures—for no apparent gains other than placating their English allies.

Signs of this brewing Mosquito dissatisfaction appeared as early as June 1780 when General Tempest demanded that the English recognize his contributions to the war effort by officially granting him a higher rank, as well as increased tribute payments.[101] Given that the English had long considered the general to be the strongest pro-English voice on the Mosquito Confederation council, these demands illustrated the growing discontent and sense of being underappreciated among Mosquito leaders.[102] This discontent then became even more overt in October when the principal leaders of the Mosquito Kingdom gathered for a general congress to air grievances against their English allies. Using longtime Mosquito Shore resident Colville Cairns as a mediator, the Mosquito leaders complained that after Polson's expedition, they had not received fair compensation either for the families of fallen Mosquito soldiers or for the use of Mosquito watercraft. They went on to declare that they would remain allied with the English, but that they would no longer participate in joint expeditions with English troops.[103] This declaration dictated the role of the Mosquito for the remainder of the war. The Mosquito leaders did not defect to the Spanish, and in fact Admiral Dilson invaded Costa Rica with a contingent of Mosquito troops in October 1781 in order to help the English war effort.[104] Nonetheless, Mosquito soldiers ceased to play a major role in English-planned operations.

Ultimately, despite offensive campaigns on both sides, neither the English nor the Spanish had made any decisive territorial gains in the Central American borderlands by the conclusion of the war. Whereas the English had seen early successes such as the capture of Fort Omoa in Honduras or the siege of Fort Inmaculada in Nicaragua, their forces were unable to hold either fort, and Spanish counteroffensives successfully drove English garrisons out. Likewise, even though Spanish forces overwhelmed Black River in a surprise assault, the English settlers soon returned, reestablishing slavery in the process. From the local perspective, therefore, the war at first seemed to have left the status quo intact, with each side settling back into its previous territorial positions. Nonetheless, as officials in Europe began debating how to interpret the terms of the treaty, the status of the Mosquito Shore Intendency was suddenly thrown into doubt. For their part, Spanish officials continued to press the same claims that Diez Navarro had made back in 1764 demanding that the English evacuate mainland settlements such as Black River. And whereas English settlers remained recalcitrant, authorities in England showed signs of relenting in the new postwar context.

As early as 1783, the governor in Jamaica understood that the Mosquito Shore Intendency losing its recognition from authorities in England was a real possibility. In July, for example, the governor received a request from loyalists in the North American plantation colony of South Carolina who hoped to bring their slaves to the Mosquito Shore in the wake of the American Revolution. The governor balked at the idea, however, admitting that the future of the colony was in flux and fearing that these relocated colonists might wind up stranded once again.[105] The governor's fears were further validated with the arrival of an October 1783 letter from officials in England confessing that negotiators had failed to clarify the status of the Mosquito Shore in the new treaty, instead wording the treaty in such a way as to place the future of the colony in jeopardy. The letter went on to say that the king's private opinion was that the English should keep the territory and that for the time being the colonists should stay. Nonetheless, the governor was under advisement that this status could change.[106]

The colony lasted one more year, but as previously discussed, in July 1786, Crown officials made their final decision: the British Crown renounced its recognition of the Mosquito Shore Intendency, Black River was ceded to the Spanish, and the English settlers were ordered to evacuate.[107] These orders arrived at Black River three months later in October 1786, and James Lawrie, the final Mosquito Shore superintendent, agreed to carry them out. Nonetheless, he first wrote to the governor of Jamaica expressing his frustration with the result. According to Lawrie, the decision was going to have disastrous consequences, and significantly, his elaboration of these dire predictions expressed a familiar set of fears. For example, Lawrie predicted that

Mosquito leaders would interpret the decision as a betrayal, likely inspiring them to kill the White settlers in revenge. Lawrie went on to explain that even if the Mosquito did not kill the English themselves, simply losing Mosquito protection was likely to lead to a slave revolt if Black River's slaves ever became aware of how weakened the English were.[108] Neither of these predictions ever came to pass, but they are fitting in that they offer a final reminder of how English efforts to colonize the Mosquito Shore had played out over the past several decades: the settlers had depended heavily on Mosquito support, they had been aware of this dependence, and fear had been a driving force in colonial decision-making.

Conclusion

Perhaps the most important contribution of this chapter has been to provide new insights into the events leading up the confederation's descent into civil war in 1791. Whereas previous research has long presumed that the English evacuation in 1786 was the driving force of the confederation's unraveling, the events described here cast doubt on several key aspects of this explanation. For example, previous studies have generally interpreted Mosquito negotiations with the Spanish after 1786 as a sign of Mosquito desperation caused by the new geopolitical context: an interpretation premised on the idea that the Mosquito had never seriously negotiated with the Spanish before.[109] However, the events described in the chapter—and indeed, throughout the entire book—show that these negotiations were not novel at all but rather drew from extensive precedents throughout the century. Moreover, the assumption that Mosquito negotiations with the Spanish signaled desperation has led some researchers to interpret this as evidence that the Mosquito had become economically and culturally dependent on the English, and that the supposed implosion of this dependency cycle afterward contributed to the civil war as Mosquito leaders competed for scarce resources.[110] Yet, this chapter has demonstrated that not only were Mosquito negotiations with the Spanish not unique to this period but the confederation negotiated from a position of strength with no evidence of resource shortages affecting daily life on the Mosquito Shore. Finally, this chapter has also provided evidence against the ethnic rivalry interpretation, which suggested that these resource shortages pitted Tawira and Zambo Mosquito factions against each other.[111] While tensions had long brewed among Mosquito leaders in the years leading up to the war, they had never taken place along ethnic lines, and the events of the civil war proved no exception.

Ultimately, even while recognizing the numerous ways that the Mosquito imperial project had become intertwined with the competing Spanish and English conquests, this chapter has helped to highlight the extent to which the Mosquito Confederation always followed a logic of its own. While Mosquito leaders maintained a keen awareness of Spanish and English activities, the Mosquito world never revolved around Europeans. True, without more access to sources showing the thoughts and feelings of the Mosquito themselves, questions remain regarding why personal grievances among council members became so acute as to explode into war. But a careful recounting of observable events and practices in Mosquito history reveals that the confederation was the arbiter of its own fate, and that Mosquito leaders brought this imperial project to an end on their own terms.

CONCLUSION AND HISTORIOGRAPHICAL CONSIDERATIONS

In 1899, just over one hundred years after the civil war that drastically reduced the power of the Mosquito Confederation, a former British resident of the Mosquito Shore named Charles Napier Bell published *Tangweera*: a semi-anthropological personal account of his life growing up in the region in the mid-nineteenth century. Even at the time of publication, some anthropologists questioned the reliability of the work's description of the Mosquito people given that the work relied on distant childhood memories. Nonetheless, anthropologists still welcomed the work as a start. As one reviewer put it while writing for the *Journal of the Anthropological Institute of Great Britain and Ireland*, "With these reservations, it is certainly a most interesting account of a people of whom we have little trustworthy information."[1] Given this early scrutiny, it is interesting that one of the most enduring claims of the book was not even a childhood recollection but rather an assumption about the central role of European technology in the origins of the Mosquito Kingdom over two centuries earlier. Without citing any evidence beyond common sense, Bell wrote, "I have no doubt that the course of affairs was similar to what happened in New Zealand; that is, that the Mosquito Indians living on the coast were the first to get hold of European weapons and with them they at once overpowered the interior tribes."[2]

Whereas the primary purpose of this book has been to detail the eighteenth-century rise and fall of the Mosquito Confederation, a secondary purpose has been to explain the implications of new archival evidence for previous understandings of the Mosquito. By way of conclusion, therefore, this final chapter provides an overview of the key findings of the book in comparison to the predominant ideas in previous research. Overall, whereas more recent studies have given Mosquito history a relatively robust theoretical treatment, the core premises of previous works have often relied on dubious assumptions from early studies for the basic facts of the narrative. A major contribution of this book, therefore, has been to incorporate just such new archival information, and indeed, these documents reveal that many of the previous assumptions about Mosquito history do not match the details of what was happening on the ground. Accordingly, this chapter examines four key sites of misunderstanding: the origins of Mosquito power, the presumed dependency on raiding, the presumed lack of negotiation with the Spanish, and the causes of the civil war.

Firearms and the Origins of Mosquito Power

Whereas most research has presumed that the decisive factor underpinning the power of the Mosquito was early access to European technology—especially firearms—the new archival evidence incorporated into the present study has demonstrated that Mosquito power over their neighbors derived far more from Indigenous knowledge and manpower. Indeed, eyewitness accounts and descriptions of specific events show that these factors were far more decisive than firearms in any specific military or diplomatic encounter, and a major contribution of this book has been to document chronologically how Mosquito leaders strategically assembled these advantages through the unified factions of the confederation, its allies, and its slaves. The assumption that Mosquito power simply derived from firearms, however, has largely obscured these core features of the confederation.

Whereas Bell's 1899 semi-anthropological memoir was perhaps the first work to posit that early access to firearms was a defining feature of Mosquito history, early twentieth-century historians Jose Dolores Gámez and Sofanías Salvatierra expanded the claim, at the same time characterizing the Mosquito as drunks and savages who jumped at the chance to get revenge on the Spanish when the English provided them with weapons.[3] In contrast to Bell's work, which mostly relied on anthropological fieldwork, these early histories did incorporate archival documents from the eighteenth century and accordingly made important contributions in writing other aspects of Central American history. However, regarding this specific claim about the

Mosquito, they followed Bell in relying on assumptions or stereotypes rather than historical examples or documentary evidence.

Echoing these early ideas, Troy Floyd's 1967 *The Anglo-Spanish Struggle for Mosquitia* gave a similar assessment, albeit placing less emphasis on firearms specifically while still claiming that Mosquito expansion depended primarily on European knowledge. In Floyd's interpretation, the buccaneers of the late seventeenth century "taught the Sambo-Miskitos an almost unforgettable lesson in pillaging," which became part of "the Indians' deeply rooted habits."[4] As a whole, Floyd's work gave nuanced analysis of English and Spanish activities. Nonetheless, the assessment of Mosquito raiding followed previous works in relying more on stock characterizations than rigorous evidence.

A shift in this discussion occurred in the late 1960s, however, when renowned anthropologist Mary Helms attempted to add more theoretical rigor to explanations of Mosquito raiding. Her body of work succeeded in removing many of the racially derogatory characterizations that had previously explained Mosquito behavior by instead treating Mosquito raiding as a rational ecological adaptation. Nonetheless, it is significant that Helm's work did not attempt to find new primary source evidence, taking for granted the factual accuracy of previous studies, including Bell's commonsense assumption that the key to Mosquito power was access to firearms.[5] Accordingly, Helms's update followed previous studies in completely overlooking the importance of the strategic knowledge-gathering and coordinated manpower of the confederation. In fact, Helms alleged the opposite: that the Mosquito were so disorganized that even having vastly superior weapons was barely enough to give them an advantage over their neighbors.[6]

The firearm thesis continued to appear as a premise in future studies, which tended to mention the Mosquito dependence on firearms as a passing fact in historical background sections. Claudia García's 2007 article, for example, focused primarily on the very late eighteenth century, though as a premise the article stated that firearms had long before become a "cultural necessity."[7] Wolfgang Gabbert's 2016 analysis of the authority of Mosquito leadership structures similarly took for granted that firearms were the "primary means of production" for the Mosquito.[8] In fact, the only work that has ever tried to attach archival research to Bell's classic claim about firearms was Ibarra's 2011 book *Del arco y la flecha a las armas de fuego*, though even these efforts were extremely limited, depending on a single letter from 1786 in which Mosquito leaders begged their English allies for powder and ammunition on the grounds that they were no longer accustomed to bows and arrows.[9] Ibarra's analysis never considers the possibility that this persuasive letter may have been exaggerating, but even if taken at face value, the letter was describing a specific situation in 1786. Nonetheless, following the established logic of the historiography, the book extrapolated this claim back to the previous 150 years, concluding that firearms had been the most important cause of social change since 1633.[10] It is also interesting to read this letter in the context of Bell's nineteenth-century recollections, which specifically mention the notable skill of the Mosquito with bows and arrows.[11]

This is not to say that all studies have passively accepted firearms as deterministic causal forces. Notably, Karl Offen's 2015 study on Mosquito raiding downplayed the role of firearms, alluding to evidence that the Mosquito often chose not to even use them on raids because they were noisy and prone to misfiring. In a major missed opportunity, however, Offen's article left intact the overarching narrative that the Mosquito rise to power depended on foreign knowledge, and that this shift in the Mosquito way of life left them dependent on European trade: "It was not so much the introduction of firearms to the Mosquito that changed the direction and volume of Amerindian captivity in their favor . . . but rather Mosquito experiences accompanying pirates and privateers on their raids against Spanish settlements. . . . The Mosquito became economically-dependent on this arrangement and I would argue that the capture and sale of human beings became constitutive of a broader Mosquito political ecology and way of life."[12] Nonetheless, Offen's work stands out for adding much needed nuance to previous assumptions regarding the role of firearms in Mosquito history.

Political, Economic, and Cultural Dependency

In addition to refuting previous interpretations of the origins of Mosquito power, this book has challenged the grand narrative that the eighteenth-century Mosquito lived in a constant state of dependence on foreign imports. Indeed, as García's, Gabbert's, and Ibarra's works indicate, a logical extension of the firearm hypothesis was that the Mosquito way of life from the seventeenth century was characterized by existential dependence on foreign imports. The most extreme version of this dependency narrative appeared in the early historical surveys that claimed that the Mosquito were politically dependent on the English, who allegedly appointed their leaders. Regarding political dependency, early historians such as Ayón and Dolores Gámez drew largely from racial stereotypes in claiming that the Mosquito had virtually no agency in creating their own political institutions. Ayón's 1882 history, for example, called the Mosquito kingship a "savage and farcical" monarchy deriving from a "ridiculous act" of the English.[13] Gaméz Dolores's 1915 history of the Mosquito Coast echoed this claim, calling the kingship a "grotesque farce" imposed by the "authority of Jamaica."[14] Floyd's 1967 monograph *The Anglo-Spanish Struggle for Mosquitia* moved away from the harsh rhetoric of earlier studies, though significantly, the book repeated the premise regarding Mosquito political dependence, stating in passing that "from this time [1687] onward, the Miskitos relied on the governor of Jamaica to choose their king, theoretically at least, from a list of several candidates."[15] References to the political dependence of the Mosquito continued to appear sporadically in subsequent studies. Naylor's 1989 monograph, for example, likewise treated the Mosquito kingship as an English invention, claiming that the first known Mosquito king, Jeremy, owed his position entirely to the English.[16]

More recent works have questioned the political dependence of the Mosquito, however, arguing instead that they were indeed an autonomous political unit despite their close ties to the English. This alternate line of thinking to some extent might be traced to Mary Helms's early research on the Mosquito kingship. Helms did not fully reject the political dependency premise, but she did take a middle ground approach, arguing that whereas the Mosquito king himself was dependent on the English for his title, the wider Mosquito people remained largely independent. Accordingly, Helms's analysis concluded that the king was more of a go-between than a monarch, and while the king might have been beholden to the English as previous studies had suggested, he and his English benefactors held little power over the Mosquito.[17] Helms's interpretation sparked a nuanced scholarly debate over the Mosquito kingship, with Olien arguing even more strongly against the political dependence interpretation. Olien agreed with Helms that the Mosquito were politically autonomous, though he disagreed with her approach to the kingship, arguing that the king was also autonomous and that he did indeed have command power within Mosquito politics.[18] This way of thinking remained influential, and in the 2000s, the notion that the Mosquito were politically autonomous became more widely accepted. One particularly innovative version of this argument appeared in Offen's 2007 article "Creating Mosquitia," which used colonial maps to argue persuasively that Europeans in the eighteenth century indeed recognized Mosquito autonomy given how they imagined and represented Central American spaces.[19]

At the same time, the assumption that the Mosquito were economically and culturally dependent has remained the predominant analytical framework for recounting Mosquito history. To a great extent, these trends can also be traced back to Helms's work, which hypothesized that the Mosquito entered into a cycle of raiding and trading in order to acquire foreign imports and that as they abandoned other activities in order to specialize in raiding, foreign imports became economic and cultural necessities. In a 1969 essay titled "The Purchase Society," Helms outlined a theoretical framework for this dependency model. In her words, "The channel that directs and influences all other activities, is the need ... for items of foreign manufacture. These goods quickly become cultural necessities, either because traditional crafts are forgotten, or because they become necessary for the psychological wellbeing of the group."[20]

This hypothesis was from its inception highly theoretical, depending less on specific historical examples and more on hypotheticals of what might occur if a society was indeed dependent on a cycle of raiding and trading due to a dependence on outside materials, and to be fair, the logic that this could happen in colonial encounters was not unreasonable. The problem, however, lay in the assertion that the colonial-era Mosquito indeed represented an example of this hypothetical model—a leap that the article made relying more on common assumptions about the Mosquito rather than historical evidence. The emerging framework, then, came to depend on circular logic: that the Mosquito must have been economically and culturally dependent on European materials because they were constantly raiding for trade goods. And they must have been constantly raiding for trade goods because they were economically and culturally dependent. Neither the constant raiding nor the dependency was rigorously documented in historical examples, yet each assumption functioned as a theoretical premise that seemed to prove the other.

To be fair, archival sources do indicate that the Mosquito liked foreign goods such as clothes and firearms enough to trade for them. Still, the assumption that these tastes were *needs* rather than wants requires a leap in logic that has yet to be filled with sound evidence. Likewise, there are examples of Mosquito raids in the historical record, but the assumption that these raids were part of a vicious cycle of raiding and trading necessary for economic and cultural subsistence would require far more evidence to confirm Helms's hypothetical model. Nonetheless, Helms's purchase society framework has remained an influential narrative for interpreting Mosquito history.

Raiding and Constant Warfare with the Spanish

Against this historiographical background, a major contribution of this book has been to test the purchase society hypothesis, not only by questioning assumptions about Mosquito dependency but also by reexamining the even more deeply rooted assumptions regarding Mosquito raiding—the alleged symptom of the Mosquito Kingdom's supposed economic and cultural dependency on foreign goods. Indeed, while the purchase society narrative depends on a very specific interpretation of Mosquito raiding as urgent, constant, and primarily extractive, new archival evidence demonstrates that these characterizations do not hold up well when considering a fuller inventory of specific events: not only was raiding far less constant or all-encompassing than previous studies have presumed, but the practice itself was part of a more complex set of geopolitical practices, including alliance-building, gunboat diplomacy, information gathering, and manpower accumulation.

Nonetheless, the above-mentioned firearms thesis and purchase society model have obscured these nuances, as has another long-standing premise that the present study challenges: the myth of constant warfare between the Mosquito and the Spanish. Indeed, the raiding and trading cycle seemed so self-evident in part due to the assumption that the Mosquito constantly raided Spanish settlements for slaves and trade goods. Leaving this premise unquestioned, the historiography has given relatively little attention to the question of *what* the Mosquito were doing, instead focusing more on theorizing *why*, and taking for granted that constant raiding to acquire trade goods—especially targeting the Spanish in Costa Rica—was a historical fact.

This myth of constant warfare between the Spanish and the Mosquito took shape in the early surveys of Central America, including Ayón's 1882 history of Nicaragua, Dolores Gámez's 1915 history of the Mosquito Coast, and Salvatierra's 1939 history of Central America. Ayón, for example, called the Mosquito a "savage race" that launched near constant incursions of "bloody revenge" against the Spanish from 1704 onward.[21] Dolores Gámez wrote that the Mosquito "never rested in their work of constant hostilities" against their "bitter enemies" the Spanish.[22] These works also emphasized Costa Rica as one of the main recipients of this violence, with Salvatierra claiming without any systematic attempt to compile examples that the Matina Valley was the "constant object of depredations."[23] These flat assumptions then continued in later studies, even as works used new archival sources to add nuanced interpretations of Spanish and English activities. Floyd's 1967 monograph on the Mosquito Coast, for example, echoed previous interpretations by claiming broadly without compiling a detailed list of specific events that "the Sambo-Miskitos took poorly to peaceful ways and welcomed the wars of the eighteenth century, in which they invariably took an active part [against the Spanish]."[24] Sorsby's 1968 study similarly treated Mosquito attacks as a generalizable norm, stating as a premise at the outset of the work that Mosquito "incursions, robberies, burnings and kidnappings had continued unabated since at least as early as 1699."[25]

The myth of constant warfare between Spanish and Mosquito also found its way into more nuanced analyses of Mosquito ecology. For example, Olien's 1983 article on Mosquito politics, while using a small body of published primary sources to offer nuanced analyses on power structures within Mosquito government, claimed without evidence that the Mosquito attacked Costa Rica "on an annual basis" as part of their seasonal subsistence practices.[26] Potthast's 1998 article escalated this claim, stating that the Mosquito attacked Costa Rica twice per year for nearly the entire eighteenth century.[27] To their credit, these studies eschewed the racial stereotypes that had been used to explain Mosquito raiding in earlier works, instead approaching raiding as a rational ecological adaptation. But it is still significant that neither Olien nor Potthast presented any systematic evidence cataloging specific events in support of their sweeping claims.

Here it is worth noting that Karl Offen's work, while not directly taking on this myth of constant warfare, did add nuance by explaining that Mosquito raids usually targeted other Indigenous groups rather than Spanish settlements.[28] I would argue that Offen's assessment of the scale of Mosquito raiding—which, as explained in chapter 1, relied on another scholar who extrapolated a dubious estimation from a single source in the 1720s to generalize raiding for the entire eighteenth century—likely still overstated how many raids actually occurred. Moreover, Offen's analysis, while giving excellent attention to the demographics of raiding, still presumed that raiding was almost exclusively for extracting slaves to be sold, whereas this book has presented extensive evidence that the Mosquito used raiding for gunboat diplomacy, as well as to keep the strategic knowledge and labor of slaves for themselves. Nonetheless, by clarifying the true targets of Mosquito raiding, as well as refusing to repeat the myth that the Mosquito attacked the Spanish annually in Costa Rica, Offen's research offered a valuable corrective in comparison to earlier works.

CONCLUSION 179

Another iteration of the myth of constant warfare worth mentioning here is the idea that Spanish and Mosquito territories formed a militarized frontier. This interpretation largely accepts the premise from the early historiography that the Spanish and the Mosquito were constantly fighting, but it adds in a defense component, assuming that the Mosquito had to constantly defend themselves against the advance of the Spanish conquest. Naylor's 1989 book made this claim in passing, stating that the Spanish had never been able to conquer the Mosquito, thus suggesting that they had indeed tried.[29] Ibarra's 2011 book used a similar approach, claiming that the Mosquito "fought tenaciously to defend themselves against the Spanish and maintain their power."[30] In place of presenting historical examples of Spanish incursions, however, both works operated on assumptions. In fact, there is no evidence that the Mosquito had any significant contact with the Spanish until the late seventeenth century. And when sustained contact did occur, it took place exclusively along waterways, primarily the Caribbean Coast, as the Mosquito expanded their territories rather than the Spanish expanding theirs. Consequently, the image of any interior overland frontier is highly misleading, distorting how these spaces operated in practice, as well as obscuring the important role that ongoing peace negotiations played in Spanish and Mosquito relations.

Moreover, the myth of constant warfare with the Spanish has not only contributed to broader misunderstandings regarding the extent and nature of Mosquito raiding but also inhibited understandings of the extent and nature of Mosquito diplomacy. Indeed, the events detailed in this book run counter to the bulk of the historiography, which has typically assumed that Mosquito negotiations with Spanish provinces were either sporadic, isolated, or nonexistent. This tendency to downplay Mosquito diplomacy with the Spanish emerged in the early historiography in studies which, somewhat ironically, demonstrated awareness of the negotiation efforts with Costa Rica that began back in 1711 yet chose to write off these negotiations as a ruse by perfidious savages. Dolores Gámez's widely cited 1915 study of the Mosquito Coast, for example, mentioned in passing the negotiations that began in 1711, yet the book concluded that this was simply a trap on the part of the Mosquito to lull their enemies into a false sense of security. This interpretation depended heavily on assuming that the Spanish had accepted the peace deal, and that the Mosquito had gone back on their word in attacking Matina in 1724.[31] As this book has shown, however, numerous archival documents reveal that it was actually the Costa Ricans who rejected the peace, and the Mosquito attack was a show of force intended to reinstate the peace agreement—not break it. Nonetheless, Dolores Gámez's interpretation continued to be the norm, with Salvatierra's 1939 book offering a similar interpretation and stressing the "perfidy" of the barbarous Mosquito. Salvatierra used this assumption as the basis to also write off future negotiations, dismissing a 1736 peace treaty from the Mosquito as "absurd."[32]

Later studies similarly downplayed Mosquito negotiations with the Spanish. Chacón de Umaña's biography of Costa Rican Governor Diego De la Haya Fernández, for example, while offering nuanced discussions of other aspects of Spanish policy using archival sources, made the same mistake of assuming that the Mosquito were the ones who broke off the negotiations in 1724. The book misinterpreted other events as well, labeling a Mosquito visit in 1720 as an invasion when it was actually a peaceful encounter.[33] Floyd's 1967 study echoed these interpretations, drawing from previous assumptions regarding Mosquito animosity, as well as a factual error in saying that the Guatemalan government had supported the Mosquito treaty, when in fact it had rejected the treaty—a move that provoked the 1724 Mosquito invasion.[34]

This tendency to downplay Mosquito diplomacy then continued as studies examined later periods as well. Sorsby's 1968 study, for example, echoed Salvatierra's interpretation of the 1736 peace offering, calling it "absurd" and "arrogant" given the supposed constant battery of Mosquito atrocities against the Spanish. Sorsby went on to characterize Terry's treaty negotiations as unprecedented, ignoring that the Mosquito had already been negotiating continuously with Costa Rica for over a decade and that they clearly saw Terry's treaty as a continuation of these discussions since the Mosquito asked that the treaty immediately to be sent to the Costa Rica governor.[35] In a similar vein, Potthast's 1998 article gave little credence to Mosquito negotiation by taking at face value the claims of English superintendents such as the Hodgsons that they had to constantly prevent the Mosquito from attacking the Spanish, even though in reality the English worked even harder to impede Mosquito negotiations with the Spanish.[36] Ibarra's 2011 study likewise offered sweeping generalizations about the supposed constant hostility between the Mosquito and the Spanish, dismissing any negotiations as "sporadic and fragile" without delving into a detailed list of examples.[37] And Williams's detailed article on the Mosquito civil war built its analysis on the flawed assumption that 1787 was the "initial period of sustained contact" between the Spanish and the Mosquito.[38]

The Mosquito Civil War

Finally, the new evidence presented in this book challenges the prevailing scholarly interpretations of the Mosquito Kingdom's civil war and subsequent decline in power, interpretations that have placed enormous causal emphasis on supposed external pressures that accompanied the British evacuation. In many ways, misunderstandings surrounding the civil war represent the culmination of several of the myths discussed above. Indeed, presuming that Mosquito power depended on access to foreign goods, and presuming that this dependence threw them into an unstable raiding and trading cycle, previous studies reasoned that the decline of Mosquito power was simply the inevitable result of this system finally crashing with the removal of English material support. Nonetheless, by showing that Mosquito dependence on foreign trade has been overstated, and by showing that Mosquito negotiations with the Spanish were robust long before the English evacuation, this book provides new evidence to question the core logic of these explanations.

For example, an early iteration of this logic appeared in the theoretical work of Mary Helms. Relying on secondary works and a small sample of published primary documents, Helms characterized the Mosquito in a 1983 article as holding "the most precarious position" in a system of raiding and trading.[39] Reasoning that this system was likely to be driven by the vicissitudes of boom and bust cycles, and taking for granted that the Mosquito had likely abandoned other economic practices to specialize in this system, the article went on to hypothesize that busts in the slave trade in the second half of the century precipitated the decline of Mosquito power.[40]

While establishing the logical basis for interpreting Mosquito decline as the result of a material crisis, Helms's work did not discuss the Mosquito civil war explicitly. The pioneering work of Karl Offen, however, did attempt to establish a direct connection between the civil war and the imploding raid-and-trade cycle described by Helms. Specifically, Offen's explanation of the civil war combined Helms's assumptions about resource pressure with another problematic theory mentioned in previous chapters, the ethnic rivalry thesis. Though Dennis and Olien's 1983 article on Mosquito kings mentioned in passing the likelihood of ethnic tensions, this theory truly gained force with Karl Offen's 2002 essay "The Sambo and Tawira Miskito."[41] While Offen's article focused primarily on the second half of the century, it suggested that ethnic tensions had limited unity throughout the entire century, becoming particularly acute with the ascension of the Zambo Peter to the kingship in 1729. Thornton's 2017 essay "The Zambos and the

Transformation of the Miskitu Kingdom" extended these claims, suggesting that there was actually a Mosquito civil war going on during the 1710s. Thornton's other contributions notwithstanding—such as being the only author I have seen to find archival sources to support the shipwreck hypothesis for the origins of the Zambo Mosquito—his more extreme version of the ethnic rivalry hypothesis never took a strong hold in the historiography. On the other hand, Offen's thesis did, with several studies repeating the claim as a premise.[42]

The ethnic rivalry thesis derived from several factual errors, such as the mistaken interpretation that Jeremy and Hannibal were negotiating separately during the 1720s, or the false assumption that Peter was the first Zambo king.[43] Still, Offen's explanation of the civil war incorporated assumptions about ethnic rivalry with additional assumptions about the crumbling raid and trade cycle. Presuming that the Tawira would have been suffering resource shortages for decades due to Zambo pressures limiting Tawira access to the slave trade, the logic then followed that after the British evacuation, the Tawira lost even the little access to outside trade that they did have, bringing the economic strain to a breaking point. The article also took for granted that the Mosquito did not have an ongoing relationship with the Spanish, and on these grounds interpreted Colville Briton's 1791 negotiations with the Spanish as an act of desperation. The article concludes, "I would suggest that the rapid transition of Spaniard as foe to Spaniard as friend intruded on an incipient Miskitu ethnic space."[44]

Later studies continued to interpret the decline of the Mosquito Confederation within the paradigm outlined by Helms and Offen, though without necessarily testing key premises against broader evidence, even while incorporating new archival sources to describe the events of the civil war itself. Caroline Williams's 2013 study of the Mosquito civil war is an illustrative example. Utilizing a large body of new archival sources discovered in the Spanish archives in Simancas, the article represents a major contribution in revealing the details of the civil war. In addition to compiling the sequence of events in the late 1780s and early 1790s, it provides insight into how Mosquito leaders manipulated the situation by playing the Spanish and English off each other to negotiate new tributes and privileges. The article's sources do not, however, provide any direct evidence that the Mosquito faced any material crisis, or that the Mosquito Kingdom had even depended on a raiding and trading cycle in the first place. Nonetheless, the article still concluded that this is what was happening, basing this part of the argument entirely on the secondary literature. Once again, the assumption that the Mosquito had not negotiated seriously with the Spanish before the 1786 English evacuation, and therefore that any Spanish negotiations after this should be interpreted as evidence of crisis, carried the weight of the argument. Citing the previous assumptions of authors such as Helms and Offen, Williams explained, "Miskitu promises of loyalty and allegiance [to the Spanish] after 1787 were of a different character, in the sense that they were driven by the pressing need, in the aftermath of the departure of all but a small number of their long-standing trading partners, to find new markets for local produce, as well as an alternative source of supply of European manufactured goods."[45]

Ibarra's 2011 book on the Mosquito used similar premises to characterize the decline of Mosquito power; indicating the continued influence of the European technology thesis, the work emphasized in particular the disruption in access to firearms. As stated above, the work does cite one Mosquito letter from the 1780s expressing in theory that losing access to English firearms would be detrimental, though the book does not cite any historical events either before or after the English evacuation to corroborate that firearms had been important to the rise of the Mosquito, or that their loss played any role in the Mosquito decline.[46] Gabbert's 2016 article further echoed these claims. In discussing Mosquito weakness at the end of the century, the article repeated the economic bust characterization with firearms at the center: "[The English evacuation] had a profound effect on the region's economy and balance of power and saw the temporary collapse of trade relations with the Indians and contraband activities with the Spanish.... For their part, the Miskitu were not prepared to risk major attacks on the Spanish without massive British support in the form of firearms, powder, and shot."[47]

Again, the present work does not assert that the English evacuation and broader geopolitical context played no role in how the Mosquito civil war played out. Nonetheless, the new evidence examined does call into question the extent to which these processes can be interpreted as the primary cause, especially since arguments treating these external forces as causes have depended on dubious assumptions regarding Mosquito economic dependency or ongoing ethnic rivalry. True, the geopolitical context affected the timing and nature of the Mosquito civil war, yet the new evidence presented here shows that the impact of this context was not to create pressures so much as to influence how Mosquito leaders perceived opportunities to strike against confederation rivals. Moreover, the British evacuation did not cause these rivalries, nor did it seem to place the Mosquito into a position of weakness. Indeed, the subsequent negotiations with the Spanish seemed to occur from a position of strength as the Spanish rushed to meet Mosquito demands rather than the other way around.

Ultimately, in addition to providing new evidence to question the premise that the Mosquito were caught in an unstable cycle of raiding and trading, this book has also shown that Mosquito negotiations after the British evacuation actually fit into a broader pattern of reconciliation that began in Costa Rica in 1763. This reconciliation included negotiations with the entire confederation—not just the Tawira or Zambo—and was not an isolated event but rather continuously informed Spanish and Mosquito relations in subsequent decades. Accordingly, this new evidence suggests that the fall of the Mosquito Confederation had little to do with external pressures, either economic or political, and more to do with internal rivalries that emerged in spite of the confederation's stable bases of power. Perhaps future research will uncover new evidence as to why Mosquito leaders began competing for power. But the detailed events described in this book demonstrate that the traditional explanations—ethnic rivalry, economic desperation, or political affinity for the English—do not align with what we now know was happening on the ground. Moving forward, the historiography will need to reevaluate long-standing premises such as the presumed dependence on raiding and trading in order to better contextualize these events, and indeed, the entire narrative arc of the Mosquito Confederation.

EPILOGUE

Central America and Legacies of Conquest

After the Mosquito civil war of 1791, the confederation's powerful fleet system never fully recovered. Along with it, the imperial orbit of the Mosquito Confederation shrank dramatically. Mosquito relations with Costa Rica provide a salient example. Whereas the Mosquito Confederation had exercised significant influence over Costa Rica's Matina Valley since King Jeremy II had first initiated diplomatic relations in 1711, contact between Costa Rica and Mosquito leaders dramatically declined in the 1790s. Moreover, the balance of power shifted in favor of the Costa Ricans. By the turn of the nineteenth century, officials in Matina had already suspended traditional gifts and tribute payments to the Mosquito, and while rumors circulated in 1819 that Mosquito leaders were planning to raid Matina in what would have been the first incursion since 1781, the attack never manifested.[1] Accordingly, the Mosquito ceased to represent a military threat to Costa Rica, and over the next few years, national officials became far less concerned with Mosquito aggression and more concerned with how Mosquito settlements might inconvenience colonization projects for agricultural expansion.[2]

This represented a stark contrast to the situation in the eighteenth century, when the Mosquito Confederation had been characterized by its overwhelming manpower, its nimble fleet system, and its geopolitical assertiveness. Indeed, throughout the eighteenth century, the frontier provinces of Spanish Central America had almost always negotiated with the Mosquito from positions of weakness, allowing the confederation to dictate the terms of war, peace, tribute, and trade. By the 1840s, however, the balance of power had shifted so much that Mosquito leaders even began petitioning Costa Rican authorities for support to maintain access to traditional fishing waters.[3]

In May 2018, two leaders of the Miskitu people—the present-day descendants of the Mosquito Confederation—visited Costa Rica, now in a very different context than the visits of the eighteenth century. Rather than arriving at the head of a fleet to demand trade privileges, they flew in to speak at the meeting of the Conference of Latin American Geographers. Donaldo Allen González, the president of Confederación de Pueblos Autóctonos de Honduras (CONPAH), discussed the current situation of the Miskitu in Honduras; and Brooklyn Rivera, a long-time Miskitu political organizer and representative of the National Congress of Nicaragua, discussed conditions for Miskitu in Nicaragua. Significantly, a common theme in both talks was the looming threat of displacement. Indeed, in both Honduras and Nicaragua, the Miskitu have long had to confront government officials and private industries working together to erode protected lands and impose more centralized state control.[4] Moreover, a report by the International Center for Justice and Rights (CEJIL) released the following year further corroborated these concerns, documenting in particular a disturbing pattern of Daniel Ortega's regime in Nicaragua allowing paramilitary violence and illegal settlements to steal rightful Miskitu lands.[5]

The primary focus of this book has been to tell the story of the eighteenth-century Mosquito conquest, reflecting on its implications for the competing Spanish and English conquests in the same region. Nonetheless, even though the central narrative arc concludes at the close of the eighteenth century when the Mosquito conquest came to an end, this is certainly not to suggest that Central America's Caribbean borderlands ceased to be a site of conquest. Quite the opposite, in fact: by emphasizing how many peoples and territories remained beyond the control of European colonizers at the close of the colonial period, this book contributes to a broader theme of borderlands research to reflect on how nation-states participated in the conquest just as vigorously as empires did. Perhaps even more vigorously, in fact, as nation-states applied new weapons and "distance-demolishing technologies" in a widespread assault on Indigenous peoples and nonstate spaces that empires may have claimed but never actually conquered.[6]

At stake in revealing the limitations of European conquests, therefore, is also highlighting the true legacy of conquest that empires and nation-states share. Of course, I am not the first historian to suggest that empires and nation-states may not actually be that different in practice.[7] But I would add to this discussion by suggesting that conquest in particular is an important framework for exploring the continuities that spanned the colonial and national eras.

This framework certainly applies to Central America's Caribbean borderlands. Mounting evidence shows that the Honduran government, for example, continues efforts to dispossess the Afro-Indigenous Garifunas of their lands in service of private tourism and agro-industrial interests.[8] And the conquest of the Mosquito Coast continues as well. Even though the region had remained semiautonomous since the colonial period, efforts to incorporate this territory into the Nicaraguan nation-state accelerated under the modernizing visions of the Sandinista government in the 1980s.[9] This led to numerous violent confrontations, and while the Miskitu in theory still maintain some degrees of legal autonomy, the situation has become precarious under Daniel Ortega's regime, which has systematically ignored property rights of Miskitu communities.

Ultimately, whereas this book has described European and Indigenous conquests of the eighteenth century, the current situation on the Mosquito Coast indicates the disturbing extent to which conquest continues to shape how people experience Central America's Caribbean borderlands today. For many Central Americans, conquest is not a distant memory of a colonial past but a lived reality that continues in the present.

ACKNOWLEDGMENTS

Numerous institutions deserve recognition for supporting the years of research behind this book. To begin, I am grateful for the financial support offered by the History Department of the University of Houston, which provided generous scholarships throughout my graduate studies, as well as travel funding for dissertation research in Central America and Europe. I am further indebted to the archives that welcomed my research and allowed me access to their collections: the National Archive of Costa Rica, the General Archive of Central America in Guatemala, and The National Archives in the U.K., and the General Archive of the Indies in Spain. Among these, the National Archives of Costa Rica merits special thanks for sponsoring my application for a Fulbright grant, working with me for ten months, and going above and beyond to make sure that I was able to access the most critical documents for this research. I am also grateful to the NYU Center for Latin American and Caribbean Studies for supporting my work with a postdoctoral fellowship, during which time I developed the earliest versions of this book manuscript. Moreover, special thanks are also due to my current institution, Vassar College, for providing generous financial support to bring this book all the way to publication.

So many of my colleagues also deserve praise for their contributions to this project. First, I would like to thank Susan Kellogg for her intellectual and professional guidance throughout my graduate studies and early career as a professor. I am also grateful for my professors at the University of Houston who first encouraged me to explore new ways of thinking about borderlands, imperialism, and Latin American history in general. In particular, I would like to thank Raúl Ramos, Mark Goldberg, Thomas O'Brien, Xiaoping Cong, José Angel Hernández, John Hart, Philip Howard, and Natalia Milanesio. I would also like to thank my colleague, Rikki Bettinger, whose constant willingness to collaborate and share ideas during the dissertation phase greatly enriched this project. In Costa Rica, I owe a debt of gratitude to Aaron Arguedas, whose willingness to share his expertise in Central American archives shaped this project from its inception. Moreover, at the University of Georgia Press, Nate Holly deserves special thanks for giving such insightful feedback on so many manuscript drafts. Finally, I am grateful to John Thornton for showing interest in my work, for encouraging me to continue it, and even generously sharing his own collection of documents from the AGI for use in this book.

So many of my friends and family have also supported this book in indirect yet vital ways. To my parents, David and Betty Mendiola, thank you for teaching me to love learning and to see education, not simply as a path to a career, but as a way of enriching my life. To my best friend, Franco Matinez, thank you for always being there for me since we first started college in Houston, and for putting me on the path to becoming the Latin American historian that I am today. And to my wife, Silvia Solis Pesantez, thank you for bringing so much joy to my life as I completed this book, for contributing so much to my work at Vassar, for helping us to build such a wonderful community in Poughkeepsie, and for inspiring me with so many ideas for the future.

NOTES

Preface

1. See for example: Ayón, *Historia de Nicaragua*, 194; Gámez, *Historia de la costa de Mosquitos*, 82; Salvatierra, *Contribución a la historia de Centroamérica*, 422; Olien, "Miskito Kings and the Line of Succession," 205; Potthast-Jutkeit, "Centroamérica y el contrabando," 508; Ibarra, *Del arco y la flecha*, xxxii; Williams, "Living between Empires," 255.
2. Hämäläinen, *Comanche Empire*.
3. For more on the importance of ANCR documents in debunking the myth of constant warfare, see Mendiola, "El Reino Mosquito"; Segovia Rivera, "Los Mosquitos y La Provincia de Costa Rica."
4. Helms, "Cultural Ecology," 81–82; Williams, "Living between Empires," 225; Ibarra, *Del arco y la flecha*, 230; García, "Ambivalencia de las representaciones coloniales," 674; Gabbert, "'God Save the King'," 75–77; Offen, "Mapping Amerindian Captivity," 45.

Introduction

1. "Declaración de Christobal de Guadalupe Cap. Del Guaymi," Cartago, May 9, 1719, ANCR, CO 223, fols. 9r–10v.
2. Mendiola, "Rise of the Mosquito Kingdom."
3. Warren, *Iranun and Balangingi*, 26; Scott, *Art of Not Being Governed*, 49.
4. Woodward, *Central America*; Pérez Brignoli, *Brief History of Central America*; Restall, *Maya Conquistador*; Matthew, *Memories of Conquest*.
5. Offen, "Sambo and Tawira Miskitu," 331.
6. Henry Darby, court proceedings at Brookshire House, Providence Island, June 21, 1637, TNA, CO 124/2, fol. 150r.
7. M. W., "Familiar Description," 288; Exquemelin, *Buccaneers of America*, 234, 250.
8. Exquemelin, *Buccaneers of America*, 250.
9. Peralta, *Costa Rica y costa de Mosquitos*, 57; Uring, *Voyages and Travels*, 154.
10. Offen, "Sambo and Tawira Miskitu," 336.
11. Helms, *Middle America*; Romero Vargas, *Historia de la Costa Atlántica*.
12. Solorzano and Romero Vargas, "Declaración de Carlos Casarola"; Olien, "General, Governor, and Admiral"; Offen, "Sambo and Tawira Miskitu."

13. "Gastos hechos en el hermano del Almoral," Santiago de Guatemala, April 23, 1778, AGCA, AI (6), Legajo 3, Expediente 28, fols. 1r–5v.

14. Peter the King, "King Peter to Governor Robert Hunter," Sandy Bay, October 3, 1729, TNA, CO 137/18, fol. 68r; "Declaration of Edward King of the Mosquito Indians," Dacora, March 16, 1740, TNA, CO 123/1, fol. 52r.

15. Offen, "Sambo and Tawira Miskitu," 337; Gabbert, "'God Save the King'," 71–72.

16. Burbank and Cooper, *Empires in World History*, 8.

17. Hämäläinen, "Shapes of Power," 44.

18. "An Account of the Road Cut from Black River on the Moskito Shore toward Opening a Commerce with Guatemala," Jamaica, December 19, 1743, TNA, CO 137/48, fol. 90r.

19. Lázaro de Castro to the president of Guatemala, Villa de San Cruz de Yoro, 1705, AGCA, AI (4), Legajo 50, Expediente 492, fol. 1r; "Autos hechos para averiguar si piraguas de la isla de mosquitos trajeron contrabando," Cartago, December 7, 1711, ANCR, CO 188, fol. 1r; Satisfacer de la Real Cédula, Guatemala, February 9, 1708, AGI, Guatemala 299, fol. 6r; President of Guatemala, "Autos," Guatemala, April 25, 1725, AGI, Guatemala 302, fol. 150r.

20. Mendiola, "Constructing Imperial Spaces," 205–15.

21. Hearn, *Theorizing Power*, 10.

22. Woodward, *Central America*, 36–38.

23. Lockhart, *Nahuas after the Conquest*; Quezada, *Maya Lords and Lordship*; Lovell, *Strange Lands and Different Peoples*.

24. Gibson, *Aztecs under Spanish Rule*; H. Scott, *Contested Territory*.

25. Woodward, *Central America*, 26–29; Clendinnen, *Ambivalent Conquests*, chap. 1.

26. Lovell, *Strange Lands and Different Peoples*; Hall and Pérez Brignoli, *Historical Atlas*.

27. Kupperman, "Errand to the Indies."

28. Offen, "Sambo and Tawira Miskitu," 340.

29. Kupperman, "Errand to the Indies," 86.

30. Pestana, "Early English Jamaica."

31. Offen, "Mapping Amerindian Captivity," 37.

32. Ayón, *Historia de Nicaragua*; Dolores Gámez, *Historia*; Salvatierra, *Contribución*.

33. Floyd, *Anglo-Spanish Struggle for Mosquitia*.

34. Sorsby, "British Superintendency."

35. Helms, "Cultural Ecology," 76–84; Helms, "Miskito Slaving and Culture Contact"; Helms, "Of Kings and Contexts"; Dennis and Olien, "Kingship among the Miskito"; Olien, "Miskito Kings and the Line of Succession"; Olien, "General, Governor, and Admiral."

36. Potthast's primary publishing language is German, though for a Spanish-language example of her contributions to the historiography, see Potthast-Jutkeit, "Centroamérica y el contrabando."

37. Offen, "Sambo and Tawira Miskitu."

38. Ibarra, *Del arco y la flecha*, 230.

39. See, for example, General Archive of the Indies (AGI), Guatemala 302.

40. See, for example, ANCR, CO 283, CO 286, CO 290, CO 295, CO 303.

41. Scott, *Art of Not Being Governed*, chap. 1.

42. Kellogg, *Weaving the Past*, 1.

43. Gabbert, "'God Save the King'," 75; Williams, "Living between Empires," 240–41; Ibarra, *Del arco y la flecha*, 230; Helms, "Miskito Slaving and Culture Contact," 179–97.

44. Ayón, *Historia*, 194; Dolores Gámez, *Historia de la costa de Mosquitos*, 82; Salvatierra, *Contribución*, 422; Floyd, *Anglo-Spanish Struggle for Mosquitia*, 22; Sorsby, "British Superintendency," 22; Olien, "Miskito Kings and the Line of Succession"; Potthast-Jutkeit, "Centroamérica y el contrabando," 508; Ibarra, *Del arco y la flecha*, xxxii; Offen, "Sambo and Tawira Miskitu," 352; Williams, "Living between Empires," 255; Gabbert, "'God Save the King'," 76–79.

45. Ayón, *Historia*, 191; Dolores Gámez, *Historia de la costa de Mosquitos*, 70; Floyd, *Anglo-Spanish Struggle for Mosquitia*, 62; Naylor, *Penny Ante Imperialism*, 31; Helms, "Cultural Ecology," 76–78; Ibarra, *Del arco y la flecha*; García, "Ambivalencia de las representaciones coloniales," 674; Gabbert, "'God Save the King'," 75–77; Offen, "Mapping Amerindian Captivity," 45.

46. Helms, "Miskito Slaving and Culture Contact," 191; Offen, "Sambo and Tawira Miskitu," 350; Williams, "Living between Empires," 255; Ibarra, *Del arco y la flecha*, 230.

Chapter 1. The Formation and Expansion of the Mosquito Confederation, 1687–1713

1. "Declaración de Joseph Jimenez," Cartago, June 26, 1711, ANCR, GA 144, fols. 9v–11r; Joseph Carrasola y Cordova (lieutenant of Matina) to Joseph Guthierrez (fiscal of Guatemala), Cartago, July 1, 1711, ANCR, GA 144, fols. 7r–8v; "Testimonio de Cap. Juan Francisco de Ybarra, vecino de este ciudad de 30 años," Cartago, May 25, 1713, ANCR, CO 188, fol. 11r–v; "Declaración del ayudante Joseph de Chevarria," July 6, 1713, ANCR, CO 192, fols. 4r–5v.

2. Gabbert, "'God Save the King'," 75; Williams, "Living between Empires," 240–41; Ibarra, *Del arco y la flecha*, 230; Helms, "Miskito Slaving," 179–97.

3. Duke of Albermarle to committee, Jamaica, February 11, 1688, TNA, CO138/6, fols. 42r–43r; Sloane, *Voyage to the Islands*, lxxvi.

4. Uring, *Voyages and Travels*, 160.

5. M. W., "Familiar Description," 288.

6. "Auto del Capitan Castellano del Castillo," Castillo de la Inmaculada (Rio San Juan), March 19, 1709, AGI, Guatemala 299, fols. 85v–88v; "Declaración de Joseph de Cordoba," Castillo de la Inmaculada (Rio San Juan), March 19, 1709, AGI, Guatemala 299, fols. 93r–96r; Peralta, *Costa Rica y Costa de Mosquitos*, 58.

7. "Junta de Guerra," Cartago, August 17, 1698, ANCR, CO 97, fols. 1r–2r; Antonio de Monforte to Juan Jeronimo Guardo, Comayagua, October 22, 1705, AGCA, A1, legajo 4061, expediente 31561, fols. 1r–3r; "Testimonio de los autos hechos sobre la entrada del Sambo en los pueblos del Peten," Guatemala, September 24, 1708, AGI, Guatemala 299, fols. 13r–14v.

8. "Declaración de Michaela Gomez mulata libre," Nueva Segovia, January 2, 1717, AGI, Guatemala 301, fols. 254r–55v.

9. "Testimonio de Los autos hechos por el gobernador y teniente de Capitán General de la provincia de Nicaragua," Granada, August 7, 1709, AGI, Guatemala 299, fol. 645r; "Declaración del Indio Don Juanillo," Granada, August 5, 1709, AGI, Guatemala 299, fols. 678v–82r.

10. M. W., "Familiar Description," 288.

NOTES TO CHAPTER ONE

11. Uring, *Voyages and Travels*, 156.
12. Romero Vargas, *Sociedades del Atlántico de Nicaragua*, 279; Offen, "Mapping Amerindian Captivity," 37–38.
13. "Declaración de Joseph Jimenez," Cartago, June 26, 1711, ANCR, GA 144, fols. 9v–10r.
14. "Declaración de Miguel del Camino, negro esclavo," Esparza, May 7, 1720, ANCR, CO 272, fols. 11r–12r.
15. Helms, "Miskito Slaving," 185; Offen, "Mapping Amerindian Captivity," 38; Gabbert, "'God Save the King'," 75.
16. Diego de la Haya Fernández, "Orden," Cartago, March 8, 1722, ANCR, CO 290, fols. 4v–5r.
17. Thomas Handyside (governor of Jamaica) to the Board of Trade, Jamaica, August 29, 1707, TNA, CO 137/7, fol. 227r.
18. "Declaración de Joseph Jiménez," Cartago, June 26, 1711, ANCR, GA 144, fol. 10r.
19. "Declaración de Andres," Catacamas, January 21, 1712, ANCR, GN 144, fol. 29r.
20. M. W., "Familiar Description," 287–88.
21. Offen, "Sambo and Tawira Miskitu"; Thornton, "Zambos and the Transformation" "Declaración de Joseph Jimenez," Cartago, June 26, 1711, ANCR, GA 144, fols. 10v-r.
22. "Declaración de Andres," Catacamas, January 21, 1712, ANCR, GN 144, fols. 28v–29v.
23. Uring, *Voyages and Travels*, 154.
24. "Declaración de Francisco Corella prisionero," July 3, 1713, ANCR, CO 192, fol. 2v; "Declaración del ayudante Joseph de Chevarria," July 6, 1713, ANCR, CO-192, fols. 4v–5v.
25. Woodward, *Central America*, 47–49.
26. Peralta, *Costa Rica y Costa de Mosquitos*, 85.
27. Fonseca, Alvarenga Venutolo, and Solórzano, *Costa Rica en el siglo XVIII*, 365.
28. Woodward, *Central America*, 52.
29. Author unknown, October 29, 1698, Santiago de Guatemala, AGCA, A1 (4), legajo 161, expediente 1688, fol. 1r.
30. Fray Reyundo Barrientos, Orica, March 30, 1701, AGCA, A1 (4), legajo 1, expediente 3, fol. 1r; author unknown, Olancho, March 22, 1700, AGCA, A1 (4), legajo 161, expediente 1689, fol. 1r.
31. "Título," Santiago de Guatemala, July 22, 1700, AGCA, A1, legajo 1571, expediente 10,215, fol. 211r; León, *Colección de documentos*, 7–10; Fonseca, Alvarenga Venutolo, and Solórzano, *Costa Rica en el siglo XVIII*, 351–65.
32. Lázaro de Castro to the president of Guatemala, Villa de San Cruz de Yoro, 1705, AGCA, A1 (4), legajo 50, expediente 492, fol. 1r.
33. Alcalde y Regidor del Pueblo de Letegua, 1709, AGCA, A1 (4), legajo 50, expediente 493, fol. 2r.
34. Ysidrio Espinoza to the president of Guatemala, February 4, 1710, AGCA, A1, legajo 4061, expediente 31,564, fol. 1r.
35. "Testimonio de los autos hechos sobre la entrada del Sambo en los pueblos del Peten," Guatemala, September 24, 1708, AGI, Guatemala 299, fols. 13r–14v; Joseph de Aguilar Galeano, "Carta," Nuestra Señora de los Dolores, August 24, 1708, AGI, Guatemala 299, fols. 26r–27r.
36. Peralta, *Costa Rica y Costa de Mosquitos*, 351.
37. "Declaración del Yndio Mosquito," May 2, 1710, AGCA, A1, legajo 77, expediente 632, fols. 9v–11r.

38. Fernández, *Colección de documentos*, 72–119.
39. "Auto para tomar sus declaraciones a los cinco indios llegados que son de esta ciudad," Granada, October 15, 1707, AGI, Guatemala 299, fol. 146r.
40. "Declaraciones de los indios," Granada, October 18, 1707, AGI, Guatemala 299, fols. 147r–48v.
41. Junta de guerra, Guatemala, October 10, 1708, AGI, Guatemala 299, fol. 40r.
42. "Carta del Capitán Frances, Santa Maria Magdalena," October 2, 1708, AGI, Guatemala 299, fols. 42v–43r; "Respuesta del Fiscal," Guatemala, October 15, 1708, AGI, Guatemala 299, fol. 44r.
43. "Carta de Francisco Thomas del Castillo," Guatemala, October 20, 1708, AGI, Guatemala 299, fols. 55v–57v.
44. "Carta," Castillo de la Inmaculada (Rio San Juan), March 4, 1709, AGI, Guatemala 299, fol. 77r–v.
45. "Declaración de Joseph de Córdoba, Castillo de la Inmaculada" (Rio San Juan), March 19, 1709, AGI, Guatemala 299, fols. 93r–96r.
46. "Auto del Capitan Castellano del Castillo," Castillo de la Inmaculada (Rio San Juan), March 19, 1709, AGI, Guatemala 299, fols. 85v–88v.
47. "Testimonio de Los autos hechos por el gobernador y teniente de Capitán General de la provincia de Nicaragua," Granada, August 7, 1709, AGI, Guatemala 299, fol. 645r; "Declaración del Indio Don Juanillo," Granada, August 5, 1709, AGI, Guatemala 299, fols. 678v–82r.
48. Don Thorivio Cosio (president of Guatemala) to king, Guatemala, December 12, 1710, AGI, Guatemala 299, fol. 8r.
49. Pestana, "Early English Jamaica without Pirates," 336.
50. Hanna, *Pirate Nests*.
51. Pestana, "Early English Jamaica without Pirates."
52. Thomas Handyside (governor of Jamaica) to the Commission of Trade and Plantations, Jamaica, July 20, 1704, TNA, CO 137/6, fol. 306v.
53. Thomas Handyside (governor of Jamaica) to the Board of Trade, Jamaica, August 29, 1707, TNA, CO 137/7, fol. 227r.
54. Henry Darby, court proceedings at Brookshire House, Providence Island, June 21, 1637, TNA, CO 124/2, fol. 150r.
55. M. W., "Familiar Description," 288.
56. Duke of Albermarle to the committee, Jamaica, February 11, 1688, TNA, CO138/6, fols. 42r–43r.
57. Uring, *Voyages and Travels*, 160.
58. Uring, *Voyages and Travels*, 157–58; Peralta, *Costa Rica y Costa de Mosquitos*, 59.
59. Felipe de Mesa to Diego de la Haya Fernández (governor of Costa Rica), Matina, April 11, 1719, ANCR, CO 223, fol. 2r.
60. "Declaración de Miguel del Camino, negro esclavo," Esparza, May 7, 1720, ANCR, CO 272, fols. 11r–12r.
61. M. W., "Familiar Description," 286–88.
62. Joseph Carrasola y Cordova (lieutenant of Matina) and Antonio Granda de Balbín (governor of Costa Rica), Cartago, July 4, 1711, ANCR, GA 144, fols. 3r–5r.
63. Joseph Carrasola y Cordova (lieutenant of Matina) to Joseph Guthierrez (fiscal of Guatemala), Cartago, July 1, 1711, ANCR, GA 144, fols. 7r–8v.
64. "Declaración de Joseph Jimenez," Cartago, June 26, 1711, ANCR, GA 144, fols. 9v–11v.

65. "Testimonio de Cap. Juan Francisco de Ybarra, vecino de esta ciudad de 30 años," Cartago, May 25, 1713, ANCR, CO 188, fol. 11r–v; "Testimonio del Cap. Don Joseph de Bonilla vecino de esta ciudad de edad de 36 años," Cartago, June 20, 1712, ANCR, CO 188, fol. 12r–v; "Testimonio de Marcos Daniel vecino de esta ciudad de edad de 35 años," Cartago, June 21, 1712, ANCR, CO 188, fol. 13r–v.

66. Letter from José Antonio Lacayo de Briones y Palacios (governor of Costa Rica), Cartago, July 4, 1713, ANCR, CO 192, fol. 1r.

67. "Declaración de Francisco Corella prisionero," Cartago, July 3, 1713, ANCR, CO 192, fols. 1v–3v.

68. Juan Francisco de Ibarra to Antonio Lacayo de Briones y Palacios (governor of Costa Rica), Matina, July 31, 1713, ANCR, ANCR 144, fols. 46r–47r.

69. Juan Francisco de Ibarra to Antonio Lacayo de Briones y Palacios (governor of Costa Rica), Matina, August 1, 1713, ANCR, CO 192, fol. 17r–v.

70. "Declaración del ayudante Joseph de Chevarria," July 6, 1713, ANCR, CO 192, fols. 4r–5v; Joseph Carrasola y Cordova (lieutenant of Matina) to Joseph Guthierrez (fiscal of Guatemala), Cartago, July 1, 1711, ANCR, ANCR 144, fols. 7r–8v.

71. Joseph Carrasola y Cordova (lieutenant of Matina) and Antonio Granda de Balbín (governor of Costa Rica), Cartago, July 4, 1711, ANCR, GA 144, fols. 3r–5r.

72. Fiscal Joseph Guthierrez (fiscal of Guatemala) to Antonio Granda de Balbín (governor of Costa Rica), Santiago de Guatemala, August 20, 1711, ANCR, GA-144, fols. 16r–18v.

73. Woodward, *Central America*, 48; Chacón de Umaña, *Don Diego de la Haya Fernández*, 70–78; Murga, "Between Fidelity and Pragmatism," 103–5.

74. Joseph Guthierrez (fiscal of Guatemala), "Junta de guerra," Santiago de Guatemala, October 5, 1711, ANCR, GA-144, fols. 20r–21v.

75. Junta de Real Hacienda, Santiago de Guatemala, November 9, 1708, AGI, Guatemala 299, fol. 70r.

76. "Carta del Obispo Fray Benito Garret y Arlovi," Granada, November 30, 1711, AGI, Guatemala 300, fols. 8v–34v.

77. Francisco Serrano de Reina to Matina, Cartago, December 7, 1711, ANCR, CO 188, fol. 1r–v.

78. Antonio Lacayo de Briones y Palacios (governor of Costa Rica), "Autos para examinar a Francisco Corella," Cartago, July 4, 1713, ANCR, CO 192, fol. 1r; Juan Francisco de Ibarra to Antonio Lacayo de Briones y Palacios, July 31, 1713, ANCR, CO 192, fol. 16r–v.

79. "Declaración de Francisco Corella prisionero," Cartago, July 3, 1713, ANCR, CO 192, fols. 1v–3v; "Declaración del ayudante Joseph de Chevarria," July 6, 1713, ANCR, CO 192, fols. 4r–5v.

80. Joseph Guthierrez (fiscal of Guatemala) to Antonio Lacayo de Briones y Palacios (governor of Costa Rica), Santiago de Guatemala, October 16, 1713, ANCR, CO 192, fols. 20r–24v.

Chapter 2. Consolidating the Mosquito Imperial System, 1713–1729

1. "Junta de Guerra," Matina, March 30, 1722, ANCR, CO 290, fol. 8r–v; Francisco Ibarra (sergeant major of Matina) to Diego de la Haya Fernández (governor of Costa Rica), Matina, April 9, 1722, ANCR, CO 290, fols. 7r–8v.

NOTES TO CHAPTER TWO

2. Letter from José Antonio Lacayo de Briones y Palacios (governor of Costa Rica), Cartago, July 4, 1713, ANCR, CO 192, fol. 1r.

3. "Declaración de Christobal de Guadalupe Cap. Del Guaymi," Cartago, May 9, 1719, ANCR, CO 223, fols. 9r–10v.

4. "Declaración de Miguel del Camino, negro esclavo," Esparza, May 7, 1720, ANCR, CO 272, fols. 11r–12r.

5. "Declaración de Christobal de Guadalupe Cap. Del Guaymi," Cartago, May 9, 1719, ANCR, CO 223, fols. 9r–10v.

6. Felipe de Mesa to Diego de la Haya Fernández (governor of Costa Rica), Matina, April 11, 1719, ANCR, CO 223, fol. 2r–v; "Declaración del alférez Miguel del Castillo de edad de 24 años," Cartago, April 24, 1719, ANCR, CO 223, fols. 4v–5r.

7. Francisco Espinoza to Diego de la Haya Fernández (governor of Costa Rica), Matina, January 3, 1719, ANCR, CO 219, fol. 1r–v.

8. "Declaración de Miguel del Camino, negro esclavo," Esparza, May 7, 1720, ANCR, CO 272, fols. 11r–12r; "Declaración de Francisco Corella mulato español e ynterprete de la lengua Mosquito," Esparza, May 7, 1720, ANCR, CO 272, fols. 12v–13v.

9. Antonio de Arlegui to Diego de la Haya Fernández (governor of Costa Rica), Matina, May 6, 1720, ANCR, CO 272, fol. 18r–v.

10. Joseph Carrasola y Cordova (lieutenant of Matina) and Antonio Granda de Balbín (governor of Costa Rica), Cartago, July 4, 1711, ANCR, GA 144, fol. 4r–v.

11. "Extracto," Guatemala, December 9, 1720, AGI, Guatemala 301, fol. 648r–49v.

12. "Agreement of Governor Nicholas Lawes and Jeremy King of the Mosquito," Jamaica, June 25, 1720, TNA, CO 137/13, fols. 277r–78r.

13. Nicholas Lawes (governor of Jamaica) to the Lords Commissioners of Trade, Jamaica, November 13, 1720, TNA, CO 137/13, fol. 289r.

14. Peralta, *Costa Rica y costa de Mosquitos*, 63–74.

15. "Dictamen Fiscal y resolución del Rey sobre el exterminio de los Zambos Mosquitos la consequencia de representaciones del Presidente de Guatemala y del Obispo de Nicaragua," Madrid, February 25, 1714, AGI, Guatemala 300, fols. 2r–7v.

16. Jose de Almezaga to Fray Benito Garret y Arlovi, Panama, July 8, 1715, AGCA, A1, legajo 4061, expediente 31,566, fol. 1r–v.

17. "Consulta sobre donativo para exterminio de indios en la isla Mosquitos," Manila, December 12, 1719, AGI, Filipinas, 94, N. 100, fols. 1r–2v, http://pares.mcu.es/ParesBusquedas20/catalogo/show/3073004.

18. "Autos sobre la pérdida de otras Piraguas," Honduras, June 1717, AGI, Guatemala 301, fol. 634r; "Declaración de Antonio Rodríguez," San Pedro de Sula, July 17, 1717, AGI, Guatemala 301, fol. 635r.

19. Francisco Rodriguez de Rivas (president of Guatemala) "Petecíon y presentación," Guatemala, September 15, 1717, AGI, Guatemala 301, fol. 1r; "Testimonio de las listas de las compañias del Capitan de Mar y Guerra Don Joseph Christobal de Otrera y del Capitan de Mar y Guerra Enrique Andres Juan Sol Osseli que se levantaron en el pueblo de Sacapa y su jurisdiccion para el armamento de las piraguas que se fabricaron," Guatemala, January 26, 1718, fol. 163r; "Testimonio de los autos hechos sobre la exploración y desalojo de los enemigos Zambos de la Isla de Mosquitos, y providencias dadas por su señoria el señor Don Francisco Rodriguez de Rivas," Guatemala, January 26, 1718, AGI, Guatemala 301, fol. 198r.

20. "Consejo en 3 de Diciembre de 1718, como lo dice el señor Fiscal," Madrid, December 3, 1718, AGI, Guatemala 301, 613r.

21. "Declaración de Michaela Gomez, Mulata Libre," Nueva Segovia, January 2, 1717, AGI, Guatemala 301, fol. 245r.

22. Francisco Espinoza to Diego de la Haya Fernández (governor of Costa Rica), Matina, January 3, 1719, ANCR, CO 219, fols. 1r–2r.

23. Felipe de Mesa to Diego de la Haya Fernández (governor of Costa Rica), Matina, April 11, 1719, ANCR, CO 223, fol. 2r–v.

24. "Declaración del alférez Miguel del Castillo de edad de 24 años," Cartago, April 24, 1719, ANCR, CO 223, fols. 4v–5r.

25. "Declaración del Cap. Gregorio de Mesa de edad de 19 años," Cartago, April 24, 1719, ANCR, CO 223, fols. 5v–6v.

26. "Parecer de los Sar. Mayores Don Joseph Morales y Don Pedro de Alvarado y de los capitanes Fran. Mariano Phelipe de Mesa, Don Antonio y Don Dionisio Pacheco," Cartago, October 17, 1721, ANCR, CO 286, fol. 27r–v.

27. Antonio de Arlegui to Diego de la Haya Fernández (governor of Costa Rica), Matina, May 6, 1720, ANCR, CO 272, fol. 18r–v.

28. Joseph Bonilla Phelipe de Mesa to Diego de la Haya Fernández (governor of Costa Rica), Matina, April 3, 1721, ANCR, CO 283, fols. 1r–2v; Junta de guerra, Cartago, April 18, 1721, ANCR, CO 282, fols. 77r–79v.

29. Diego de la Haya Fernández, "Relación hecha al rey, relativa a los zambos Mosquitos," Cartago, 1721, ANCR, CC 4963, fol. 7r.

30. "Razon, dada por el Cap. Varona de ser 26 piraguas con 507 hombres Mosquitos," Cartago, October 27, 1721, ANCR, CO 286, fols. 43v–44r.

31. Pedro Ximenez, Pedro Joseph de los Rios, and Bernardo Pacheco to Diego de la Haya Fernández (governor of Costa Rica), Matina, October 10, 1721, ANCR, CO 286, fol. 3r–v; "Declaración de don Manuel de Rojas," Matina, October 10, 1721, ANCR, CO 286, fol. 4r–v.

32. Diego de la Haya Fernández, "Relación hecha al rey, relativa a los zambos Mosquitos," Cartago, 1721, ANCR, CC 4963, fol. 17v.

33. Bernardo Pacheco, Pedro Ximenez, and Joseph de los Rios to Diego de la Haya Fernández (governor of Costa Rica), Matina, October 10, 1721, ANCR, CO 286, fol. 3r–v; "Declaración de Don Manuel de Rojas," Matina, October 10, 1721, ANCR, CO 286, fol. 4r–v.

34. Bernardo Pacheco to Diego de la Haya Fernández (governor of Costa Rica), Matina, November 18, 1721, ANCR, CO 286, fols. 63r–65r; Diego de la Haya Fernández, "Testimonio de la Patente para Gov. Anibel," Cartago, November 1, 1721, ANCR, CO 286, fols. 57r–59v.

35. "Declaración, el negro congo Antonio de edad al parecer 32," Cartago, March 8, 1722, ANCR, CO 290, fols. 3r–4v; Joseph de los Ríos and Francisco Corella to Francisco Ybarra, Mosquitia, April 25, 1722, ANCR CO 290, fols. 32r–33r; "Declaración de Francisco Corella pardo libre," Cartago, June 8, 1722, ANCR, CO 290, fol. 41r–v.

36. Jeremy, Hannibal, and Peter to Diego de la Haya Fernández (governor of Costa Rica), Dacora, May 11, 1722, ANCR, CO 290, fol. 34r.

37. Joseph de los Ríos and Francisco Corella to Francisco Ybarra, Mosquitia, April 25, 1722, ANCR CO 290, fols. 32r–33r.

38. "Declaración de Francisco Corella pardo libre," Cartago, June 8, 1722, ANCR, CO 290, fols. 41r–42v.
39. Jeremy, Hannibal, and Peter to Diego de la Haya Fernández (governor of Costa Rica), Dacora, May 11, 1722, ANCR, CO 290, fol. 34r.
40. Bernardo Pacheco to Diego de la Haya Fernández (governor of Costa Rica), Matina, May 29, 1722, ANCR, CO 290, fol. 31r–v; Bernardo Pacheco to Diego de la Haya Fernández, Matina, June 7, 1722, ANCR, CO 290, fols. 35r–39v.
41. "Declaración de Christobal de Guadalupe Cap. Del Guaymi," Cartago, May 9, 1719, ANCR, CO 223, fol. 9r–v.
42. Domingo de Quesada to Diego de la Haya Fernández (governor of Costa Rica), Matina, January 12, 1723, ANCR, CO 295, fols. 92r–93v; Domingo de Quesada to Diego de la Haya Fernández, Matina, January 16, 1723, ANCR, CO 295, fols. 94r–95r.
43. Francisco de Ybarra to Diego de la Haya Fernández (governor of Costa Rica), Matina, April 23, 1723, ANCR, CO 295, fol. 98r–v; Joseph de Bonilla to Diego de la Haya Fernández, Matina, undated, ANCR, CO 295, fol. 100r–v; "Declaración de Martin Tenorio," Cartago, May 28, 1723, ANCR, CO 295, fols. 103r–4r.
44. "Declaración de Christobal de Guadalupe Cap. Del Guaymi," Cartago, May 9, 1719, ANCR, CO 223, fol. 9r–v.
45. "Declaración de Miguel del Camino, negro esclavo," Esparza, May 7, 1720, ANCR, CO 272, fols. 11r–12r; "Declaración de Francisco Corella mulato español e ynterprete de la lengua Mosquito," Esparza, May 7, 1720, ANCR, CO 272, fols. 12v–13v.
46. Diego de la Haya Fernández (governor of Costa Rica), "Orden," Esparza, April 28, 1720, ANCR, CO 272, fol. 9r–10r.
47. Sebastián de Arancibia y Sasi (governor of Nicaragua) to Diego de la Haya Fernández (governor of Costa Rica), Granada, December 28, 1720, ANCR, CO 282, fol. 1r; Diego de la Haya Fernández, "Auto," Cartago, January 20, 1721, ANCR, CO 282, fol. 3r.
48. "Extracto," Guatemala, December 9, 1720, AGI, Guatemala 301, fols. 648r–49v.
49. Diego de la Haya Fernández (governor of Costa Rica), "Auto para que se forme junta de guerra," Cartago, January 21, 1721, ANCR, CO 282, fols. 10v–11r.
50. Alvaro de Quevara and Joseph de Bonilla to Diego de la Haya Fernández (governor of Costa Rica), Matina, April 3, 1721, ANCR, CO 282, fol. 76r–v.
51. Diego de la Haya Fernández (governor of Costa Rica), "Junta de guerra," Cartago, April 18, 1721, ANCR CO-282, fols. 77v–79r.
52. Bernardo Pacheco, Pedro Ximenez, and Joseph de los Ríos to Diego de la Haya Fernández (governor of Costa Rica), Matina, October 10, 1721, ANCR, CO 286, fols. 1r–3v; "Declaración de Don Manuel de Rojas," Matina, October 10, 1721, ANCR, CO 286, fols. 4r–5v.
53. "Parecer de los Sar. Mayores Don Joseph Morales y Don Pedro de Alvarado y de los capitanes Fran. Mariano Phelipe de Mesa, Don Antonio y Don Dionisio Pacheco," Cartago, October 17, 1721, ANCR, CO 286, fol. 27r–v; "Declaración del Sarg. Manuel Arlegui," Cartago, October 18, 1721, ANCR, CO 286, fols. 37v–38v.
54. Bernardo Pacheco to Diego de la Haya Fernández (governor of Costa Rica), Matina, November 18, 1721, ANCR, CO 286, fols. 63r–65v; Diego de la Haya Fernández, "Testimonio de la Patente para Gov. Anibel," Cartago, November 1, 1721, ANCR, CO 286, fols. 57v–59v; Diego de la Haya Fernández, "Relación hecha al rey, relativa a los zambos Mosquitos," Cartago, 1721, ANCR, CC 4963, fol. 17v.

55. Diego de la Haya Fernández, "Orden," Cartago, October 19, 1721, ANCR, CO 286, fols. 41v–43v.
56. "Carta, escrita por el gobernador y Capitan General de Comayagua al señor presidente," Comayagua, February 8, 1722, AGI, Guatemala 302, fols. 66r–68r.
57. "Declaración, el negro congo Antonio de edad al parecer 32," March 8, 1722, ANCR, CO 290, fols. 3r–4v.
58. Diego de la Haya Fernández (governor of Costa Rica), "Orden," Cartago, March 2, 1722, ANCR, CO 295, fol. 8r–v.
59. Francisco Ibarra (sergeant major of Matina) to Diego de la Haya Fernández (governor of Costa Rica), Matina, April 9, 1722, ANCR, CO 290, fol. 7r–v; Joseph de los Rios and Francisco Corella to Francisco Ibarra, Mosquitia, April 25, 1722, ANCR, CO 290, fols. 32r–33v.
60. "Declaración de Francisco Corella pardo libre," Cartago, June 8, 1722, ANCR, CO 290, fols. 40v–42v.
61. Jeremy, Hannibal, and Peter to Diego de la Haya Fernández (governor of Costa Rica), Dacora, May 11, 1722, ANCR, CO 290, fol. 34r.
62. Bernardo Pacheco to Diego de la Haya Fernández (governor of Costa Rica), Matina, May 29, 1722, ANCR, CO 290, fol. 30r–v.
63. Bernardo Pacheco to Diego de la Haya Fernández (governor of Costa Rica), Matina, June 7, 1722, ANCR, CO 290, fols. 35r–39v.
64. "Junta de guerra," Matina, June 11, 1722, ANCR, CO 290, fols. 60r–61v.
65. Bartolomé Trujillo and Ximenez Mondragon, "Obedicimiento," Matina, June 21, 1722, ANCR, CO 295, fols. 4r–5r.
66. Diego de la Haya Fernández (governor of Costa Rica), "Junta de guerra," Cartago, June 9, 1722, ANCR, CO 290, fols. 52r–53v.
67. Diego de la Haya Fernández (governor of Costa Rica), "Orden," Cartago, June 10, 1722, ANCR, CO 290, fol. 56r; Gerónimo Manuel Ramos to Diego de la Haya Fernández, Matina, June 25, 1722, ANCR, CO 290, fol. 76r.
68. Peralta, *Costa Rica y Costa de Mosquitos*, 95.
69. "Real Cédula," November 13, 1722, AGCA, A1, legajo 4063, fol. 32r.
70. "Real Cédula," October 15, 1723, AGCA, A1, legajo 4063, fol. 56r.
71. "Declaración de Gregorio Lopez de edad de 22, indio y desertor de los mosquitos," Cartago, April 24, 1724, ANCR, CO 303, fols. 30v–31v.
72. Domingo de Quesada (captain of Matina) to Diego de la Haya Fernández (governor of Costa Rica), Matina, April 17, 1724, ANCR, CO 303, fol. 1r; Domingo de Quesada to Diego de la Haya Fernández, Matina, April 20, 1724, ANCR, CO 303, fol. 17r.
73. Pedro de Molina to Domingo de Quesada (captain of Matina), Matina, April 19, 1724, ANCR, CO 303, fol. 19r–v; Hannibal (governor of the Mosquito) to Domingo de Quesada, Matina, April 19, 1724, ANCR, CO 303, fol. 21r.
74. "Declaración de Joseph Antonio," Cartago, January 17, 1725, ANCR, CO 310, fols. 1v–2r.
75. "Declaración de Faustino," Olancho, April 16, 1725, AGCA, A1 (4), legajo 50, expediente 496, fols. 4r–5v.
76. "Declaración de Joseph Antonio," Cartago, January 17, 1725, ANCR, CO 310, fols. 1r–3v.
77. "Declaración de Julian Solano, de edad de 30 años," Cartago, January 17, 1725, ANCR, CO 310, fol. 4r–v; "Declaración de Domingo de Quesada de edad 35," Cart-

ago, January 18, 1725, ANCR, CO-310, fol. 5r; "Declaración de Pedro de Acuña de edad 30 años," Cartago, January 18, 1725, ANCR, CO 310, fols. 5v–6r.

78. Diego de la Haya Fernández (governor of Costa Rica) to Phelipe de Mesa, Cartago, March 5, 1725, ANCR, CO 313, fol. 41r–v.

79. Phelipe de Mesa to Diego de la Haya Fernández (governor of Costa Rica), Matina, March 16, 1725, ANCR, CO 313, fol. 2r–v; "Declaración del sargento Joseph de Córdoba de 30 años," Cartago, March 20, 1725, ANCR, CO 313, fols. 3r–4v.

80. Diego de la Haya Fernández (governor of Costa Rica) to the fiscal of Guatemala, Cartago, March 10, 1726, ANCR, GA212, fols. 1r–2r; "Declaración de prisionero de los dos últimos," Cartago, March 12, 1728, ANCR, CO 325, fol. 27r–v.

81. "Declaración, de Joseph Alexos Fernandez de 22 años, prisionero que vino de los mosquitos," Cartago, July 19, 1727, ANCR, CO 325, fols. 13r–14v.

82. Phelipe de Mesa (captain of Matina) to Balthasar Francisco de Valderrama (governor of Costa Rica), Matina, June 7, 1727, ANCR, CO 325, fol. 1r.

83. Phelipe de Mesa (captain of Matina) to Balthasar Francisco de Valderrama (governor of Costa Rica), Matina, June 16, 1727, ANCR, CO 325, fol. 7r.

84. Phelipe de Mesa (captain of Matina) to Balthasar Francisco de Valderrama (governor of Costa Rica), Matina, August 1727, ANCR, CO 325, fols. 16r–17v; Antonio de Soto y Baraona to Balthasar Francisco de Valderrama, Matina, January 30, 1728, ANCR, 325 CO, fols. 22r–23v.

85. "Declaración de Gregorio Lopez de edad de 22, indio y desertor de los mosquitos," Cartago, April 25, 1724, ANCR, CO 303, fols. 30v–31v.

86. Domingo de Quesada to Diego de la Haya Fernández (governor of Costa Rica), Matina, January 12, 1723, ANCR, CO 295, fols. 92r–93v.

87. Domingo de Quesada to Diego de la Haya Fernández, Matina, January 16, 1723, ANCR, CO 295, fols. 94r–95r.

88. Diego de La Haya Fernández (governor of Costa Rica), "Orden," Cartago, January 21, 1723, ANCR, CO 295, fol. 95r.

89. Joseph de Bonilla to Diego de la Haya Fernández (governor of Costa Rica), Matina, April 23, 1723, ANCR, CO 295, fol. 96r; Francisco Ibarra to Diego de la Haya Fernández, Matina, April 23, 1723, ANCR, CO 295, fol. 98r.

90. Francisco Ibarra to Diego de la Haya Fernández (governor of Costa Rica), Matina, April 23, 1723, ANCR, CO 295, fol. 98r; Joseph de Bonilla to Diego de la Haya Fernández, Matina, [undated], ANCR, CO 295, fol. 100r.

91. "Declaración de Martin Tenorio," Cartago, May 28, 1723, ANCR, CO 295, fols. 103r–4r.

92. Domingo de Quesada (captain of Matina) to Diego de la Haya Fernández (governor of Costa Rica), Matina, April 17, 1724, ANCR, CO 303, fol. 1r.

93. "Autos, del recibo de la carta y providencia mandados," Cartago, April 20, 1724, ANCR, CO 303, fol. 3r–v; Diego de la Haya Fernández (governor of Costa Rica), "Orden," Cartago, April 21, 1724, ANCR, CO 303, fol. 5r.

94. Diego de la Haya Fernández (governor of Costa Rica), "Orden," Cartago, April 22, 1724, ANCR, CO 303, fol. 8r–10v; Diego de la Haya Fernández, "Llegada en el sitio de Santiago," Cartago, April 23, 1724, ANCR, CO 303, fol. 11v.

95. Diego de la Haya Fernández (governor of Costa Rica), Santiago, April 23, 1724, ANCR, CO 303, fol. 14r.

96. Domingo de Quesada to Diego de la Haya Fernández (governor of Costa Rica),

Matina, April 20, 1724, CO 303, fol. 17v; Pedro de Molina to Don de Quesada, Matina, April 19, 1724, ANCR, CO 303, fol. 19r.

97. Hannibal (governor of the Mosquito) to Domingo de Quesada, Matina, April 19, 1724, ANCR, CO 303, fol. 21r.

98. Fernández, *Colección de documentos*, 163.

99. "Declaración de Joseph Antonio," Cartago, January 17, 1725, ANCR, CO 310, fol. 1r; "Declaración de Julián Solano de edad de 30 años," January 17, 1725, CO 310, fol. 4r.

100. "Declaración del Capitán Domingo de Quesada," January 18, 1725, ANCR, CO 310, fol. 5r; "Declaración de Pedro de Acuña de edad de 30 años cavo," Cartago, January 18, 1725, ANCR, CO 310, fols. 5v–6v; "Declaración de Juan Calvo de 45 años," Cartago, January 18, 1725, ANCR, CO 310, fol. 7r.

101. Diego de la Haya Fernández (governor of Costa Rica), "Orden," Cartago, March 5, 1725, ANCR, CO 313, fol. 41r.

102. Garido to Diego de la Haya Fernández (governor of Costa Rica), Matina, March 30, 1725, ANCR, CO 313, fols. 43v–45r; Alvarado de Jirales to Diego de la Haya Fernández, Matina, March 30, 1725, ANCR, CO 313, fol. 47r.

103. Diego de la Haya Fernández (governor of Costa Rica) to the fiscal of Guatemala, Cartago, March 10, 1726, ANCR, GA 212, fol. 1r; "Declaración de prisionero de los dos últimos," Cartago, March 12, 1728, ANCR, CO 325, fol. 27r–v.

104. "Declaración, de Joseph Alexos Fernández de 22 años, prisionero que vino de los mosquitos," Cartago, July 19, 1727, ANCR, CO 325, fols. 13r–14v.

105. Balthasar Francisco de Valderrama (governor of Costa Rica), "Testimonio de la orden que han de observar el cabo principal del Valle de Matina," Cartago, June 18, 1727, ANCR, CO 325, fols. 4r–5r.

106. Phelipe de Mesa to Balthasar Francisco Valderrama (governor of Costa Rica), Matina, June 16, 1727, ANCR, CO 325, fol. 7r; Phelipe de Mesa to Balthasar Francisco Valderrama, Matina, August 1727, ANCR CO 325, fols. 16r–17r.

107. De Soto y Baraona and Luis Gutierrez to Balthasar Francisco Valderrama (governor of Costa Rica), Matina, January 30, 1728, ANCR, CO 325, fols. 22r–23v.

108. Antonio de Soto y Baraona to Balthasar Francisco de Valderrama (governor of Costa Rica), Matina, March 1, 1728, ANCR, CO 325, fols. 25r–26v; Antonio de soto y Baraona to Balthasar Francisco de Valderrama, Matina, April 16, 1728, ANCR, CO 325, fols. 40r–41r; Antonio de Soto y Baraona to Balthasar Francisco de Valderrama, Matina, May 4, 1728, ANCR, CO 325, fols. 43r–44v; Antonio de Soto y Baraona to Balthasar Francisco de Valderrama, Matina, June 15, 1728, ANCR, CO 325, fols. 70v–71r; Phelipe Bermudez to Balthasar Francisco de Valderrama, Matina, December 26, 1728, ANCR CO-325, fols. 87r–88v.

109. Balthasar Francisco de Valderrama (governor of Costa Rica), "Ordenes," Cartago, August 4, 1728, ANCR, CO 325, fols. 78v–79r.

110. Offen, "Sambo and Tawira Miskitu," 324, 342; Thornton, "Zambos and the Transformation," 14–20.

111. Sorsby, "British Superintendency of the Mosquito Shore," 13, 183, 244; Potthast-Jutkeit, "Centroamérica y el contrabando," 503; Ibarra, *Del arco y la flecha*, xxxii; Offen, "Sambo and Tawira Miskitu," 352; Williams, "Living between Empires," 255; Gabbert, "'God Save the King'," 76–79; Dziennik, "Miskitu, Military Labour, and the San Juan Expedition," 167.

112. Dolores Gámez, *Historia de la costa de Mosquitos*, 86; Salvatierra, *Contribución*, 422.

Chapter 3. New Challenges and the Recovery of the
Confederation, 1728–1749

1. Carta to Balthasar Francisco de Valderrama (governor of Costa Rica), Matina, March 19, 1736, ANCR, CO 325, fol. 265r–v; "Declaración de Joseph Nicolas Roman Zambo de edad de 23 años poco más o menos," Cartago, April 16, 1736, ANCR, CO 325, fol. 271r–v.

2. Juan Días de Herrera to Francisco Antonio de Carrandi y Menán (governor of Costa Rica), Matina, January 16, 1737, ANCR, CO 325, fol. 286r; Antonio de Carrandi y Menan, "Auto," Cartago, January 20, 1737, ANCR, CO 325, fol. 285 r–v.

3. "Declaración de prisionero de los dos últimos," Cartago, March 12, 1728, ANCR, CO 325, fols. 27r–28v.

4. Phelipe Bermudez (captain of Matina) to Balthasar Francisco de Valderrama (governor of Costa Rica), Matina, December 26, 1728, ANCR, CO 325, fols. 87r–88r.

5. "Declaración del Negro Manuel García de edad de 55 años poco más o menos," Cartago, December 20, 1733, ANCR, CO 325, fols. 240r–41v.

6. De Soto y Baraona to Balthasar Francisco de Valderrama (governor of Costa Rica), Matina, April 16, 1728, ANCR, CO 325, fols. 40r–41r.

7. "Declaración de los indios el uno de 24 a 26 años y el otro de 18 a 20 años," Cartago, February 12, 1730, ANCR, CO 325, fols. 131r–32v.

8. Peter (king of the Mosquito) to Robert Hunter (governor of Jamaica), Sandy Bay, October 3, 1729, TNA, CO 137/18, fol. 68r.

9. Offen, "Sambo and Tawira Miskitu," 324–28, 342; Thornton, "Zambos and the Transformation," 16–18, 24.

10. "Declaración de los indios el uno de 24 a 26 años y el otro de 18 a 20 años," Cartago, February 12, 1730, ANCR, CO 325, fol. 132r.

11. "Declaración de Francisco Corella prisionero," Cartago, July 3, 1713, ANCR, CO 192, fol. 2r–v; Jeremy, Hannibal, and Peter to Diego de la Haya Fernández (governor of Costa Rica), Dacora, May 11, 1722, ANCR, CO 290, fol. 34r.

12. Uring, *Voyages and Travels*, 155.

13. Diego de la Haya Fernández, "Relación hecha al rey, relativa a los zambos Mosquitos," 1721, ANCR, CC 4963, fol. 19r; Francisco Corella to Francisco de Ybarra, April 25, 1722, ANCR, CO 290, fol. 32v; Garido to Diego de la Haya Fernández (governor of Costa Rica), Matina, March 30, 1725, ANCR, CO 313, fol. 43v.

14. Diego de Barros y Carbajal to Balthasar Francisco de Valderrama (governor of Costa Rica), Matina, February 16, 1733, ANCR, CO 325, fol. 219r.

15. "Declaración de Lazaro de Guido indio de edad 48 años," Matagalpa, March 8, 1730, AGCA, A1, legajo 77, expediente 634, fol. 1r; "An Account of the Road Cut from Black River on the Moskito Shore toward Opening a Commerce with Guatemala," Jamaica, December 19, 1743, TNA, CO 137/48, fol. 90r.

16. Captain Charles Hobby to the governor of Jamaica, July 17, 1731, TNA, CO 137/19, fol. 115r.

17. Offen, "Mapping Amerindian Captivity," 140.

18. "Declaración del negro Manuel García de edad de 55 años poco más o menos," Cartago, December 20, 1733, ANCR, CO 325, fol. 240r.

19. Balthasar Francisco de Valderrama (governor of Costa Rica), "Auto para que se forme junta de guerra," Cartago, April 24, 1734, ANCR, CO 325, fols. 242r–243v.

20. "Traducción de la Carta del Rey Mosquito, Guatemala, 17 Oct. 1736," Guatemala, October 17, 1736, AGI, Guatemala, fol. 954r–v; Peralta, *Costa Rica y Costa de Mosquitos*, 103.

21. Juan Días de Herrera to Francisco Antonio de Carrandi y Menán (governor of Costa Rica), Matina, January 16, 1737, ANCR, CO 325, fol. 286r.

22. "Declaración de Joseph Nicolas Roman Zambo de edad de 23 años poco más o menos," Cartago, April 16, 1736, ANCR, CO 325, fol. 271r–v.

23. "Declaración del Negro Manuel García de edad de 55 años poco más o menos," Cartago, December 20, 1733, ANCR, CO 325, fol. 240r.

24. "Declaration of Edward King of the Mosquito Indians," Dacora, March 16, 1740, TNA, CO 123/1, fol. 52r.

25. Robert Hodgson (elder) to Edward Trelawny (governor of Jamaica), Santiago de la Vega, November 28, 1740, TNA, CO 137/57, fols. 35r–39v.

26. "Declaración de Francisco Javier de Vera, pardo libre y vecino del Pueblo de Penonome," Cartago, August 1, 1740, ANCR, CO 432, fol. 18r–v; "Declaración de Juan Lorenzo Gonzales de 30 años y Pedro Pascual de 24 años ambos naturales y tributarios del pueblo de Penonome," Cartago, August 1, 1740, ANCR, CO 432, fol. 19r; "Declaración de Juan Inocente Pascual Zambo libre y vecino del Pueblo de Penonome de 25 años," August 1, 1740, ANCR, CO 432, fol. 20r.

27. Robert Hodgson (elder) to Edward Trelawny (governor of Jamaica), Santiago de la Vega, November 28, 1740, TNA, CO 137/57, fols. 35r–39v.

28. "Auto y declaración de Antonio Cespedes," Cartago, July 18, 1740, ANCR, CO 432, fol. 1r–v; "Declaración de Juan Matias de Baraono, mulato libre," Cartago, July 19, 1740, ANCR, CO 432, fol. 6r–v; "Declaración de Ayudante Miguel Castillo," Cartago, July 21, 1740, ANCR, CO432, fol. 8r–v; "Carta del teniente General del Valle de Matina," Matina, July 17, 1740, ANCR, CO 432, fol. 9r–v.

29. Manuel Francisco Cubera to Juan Gemmir y Lleonart (governor of Costa Rica), July 16, 1740, ANCR, CO 432, fols. 4r–5v; "Declaración de Ayudante Miguel Castillo," Cartago, July 21, 1740, ANCR, CO 432, fol. 8r–v.

30. Dionisio Pacheco (lieutenant of Matina) to Juan Gemmir y Lleonart (governor of Costa Rica), Matina, July 17, 1740, ANCR, CO 432, fols. 9r–10r.

31. Colville Briton, "Advertisement That Is to Give Notice to All the British Subjects Settled on the Southern Part of the Mosquito Shore," November 29, 1776, TNA, CO 123/31, fols. 17r–18v.

32. Manuel Francisco Cubera to Juan Gemmir y Lleonart (governor of Costa Rica), July 16, 1740, ANCR, CO 432, fols. 4r–5v; "Declaración de Ayudante Miguel Castillo," Cartago, July 21, 1740, ANCR, CO 432, fol. 8r–v.

33. "Declaración del Capitán y general del fuerte de San Fernando del Valle de Matina," Matina, April 26, 1745, ANCR, CO 468, fol. 1r; "Autos," Cartago, May 11, 1745, ANCR, CO 468, fol. 23r.

34. Esteban Ruiz Mendoza to Juan Gemmir y Lleonhart (governor of Costa Rica), Matina, April 23, 1747, ANCR, CC 3588, fol. 2r–v; Francisco Rodríguez to Juan Gemmir y Lleonhart, Fuerte San Fernando, April 24, 1747, ANCR, CC 3588, fols. 3v–4r; "Declaración de Francisco Ramos de edad de 22 años," Cartago, May 22, 1747, ANCR CO-3588, fols. 22r–24r.

35. "Declaración de Nicolas Román," Cartago, August 17, 1747, ANCR, CO 482, fols. 5r–8r; "Declaración del cabo de escuadra Manuel de Campo," Cartago, August 31, 1747, ANCR, CO 483, fols. 1r–4v; "Declaración de Antonio de Alva," Cartago, September 18,

1747, ANCR, CO 483, fols. 9r–16v; "Declaración de Joseph Nicolas Camayo," Cartago, August 23, 1747, ANCR, CO 482, fols. 38r–40v.

36. Manuel Guzman to Luis Diez Navarro (governor of Costa Rica), Matina, June 8, 1749, ANCR CO-493, fol. 16r–v; "Declaración de Nicolas Román, prisionero del Moscos," Cartago, June 16, 1749, ANCR, CO 493, fol. 19r–v.

37. "Declaración de Lázaro de guido indio de edad de 48 años," Matagalpa, March 8, 1730, AGCA, A1, legajo 77, expediente 634.

38. The Hispanicized name "Bretan" refers to the same governor who is called "John Briton" in English sources. "Declaración de los indios el uno de 24 a 26 años y el otro de 18 a 20 años," Cartago, February 12, 1730, ANCR, CO 325, fol. 131r–v.

39. "Declaración del negro Manuel García de edad de 55 años poco mas o menos," Cartago, December 20, 1733, ANCR, CO 325, fol. 240r–v.

40. "Traducción de la Carta del Rey Mosquito, Guatemala, 17 Oct. 1736," Guatemala, October 17, 1736, AGI, Guatemala fol. 954r–v.

41. Pedro de Rivera (president of Guatemala) to king, Guatemala, May 10, 1737, AGI, Guatemala 302, fols. 943r–49r.

42. Peralta, *Costa Rica y Costa de Mosquitos*, 98–112.

43. "Carta to Balthasar Francisco de Valderrama" (governor of Costa Rica), Matina, March 19, 1736, ANCR, CO 325, fol. 265r–v; "Declaración de Joseph Nicolas Roman Zambo de edad de 23 años poco mas o menos," Cartago, April 16, 1736, ANCR, CO 325, fol. 271r–v.

44. Juan Días de Herrera to Francisco Antonio de Carrandi y Menán (governor of Costa Rica), Matina, January 16, 1737, ANCR, CO 325, fol. 286r.

45. Antonio de Carrandi y Menan, "Auto," Cartago, January 20, 1737, ANCR, CO 325, fol. 285 r–v.

46. Francisco Antonio Carrandi y Menan, "Avaluo y calculo de materiales para la construcción de un fuerte que defienda aquel valle," Cartago, August 23, 1736, fol. 1039r.

47. Sorsby, "British Superintendency," 11–14.

48. "Declaración de Juan Matias de Baraona, mulato libre," Cartago, July 17, 1740, ANCR, CO 432, fols. 6r–7v; "Auto y declaración, Antonio Cespedes de 30 años," Cartago, July 18, 1740, ANCR, CO 432, fol. 1r–v.

49. Manuel Francisco Cubera to Juan Gemmir y Lleonart (governor of Costa Rica), July 16, 1740, ANCR, CO 432, fols. 4r–5v; "Declaración de Ayudante Miguel Castillo," Cartago, July 21, 1740, ANCR, CO 432, fols. 8r–10v.

50. Balthasar Francisco de Valderrama (governor of Costa Rica), "Orden," Cartago, 1729, ANCR, CC 5958, fol. 1r.

51. Francisco Antonio de Carrandi y Menán (governor of Costa Rica), "Auto," Matina, January 20, 1737, ANCR, CO 325, fol. 285r.

52. Fernández, *Colección de documentos*, 276–81.

53. "Declaración de Lanani, Negro de edad de 24 años," Cartago, December 2, 1744, ANCR, CO 455, fol. 21r–22v; "Declaración de Maria Francisca Negra Ladina al parecer de edad de 30 a 35 años," Cartago, December 2, 1744, ANCR, CO 455, fols. 35r–36v.

54. "Carta escrita por el Cap. del fuerte de San Fernando del Valle de Matina," Matina, April 26, 1745, ANCR, CO 468 fol. 1r–v; "Copia de la carta respuesta al Capitán y Alcalde de Fuerte de San Fernando," Matina, May 1, 1745, ANCR, CO 468, fol. 9r.

55. Juan Gemmir y Lleonhart (governor of Costa Rica), "Auto," Cartago, November 20, 1745, ANCR, CO 470, fol. 14r; "Declaración del artillero del fuerte," Cartago, November 22, 1745, ANCR, CO 470, fols. 15v–17r.

56. Esteban Ruiz Mendoza to Juan Gemmir y Lleonhart (governor of Costa Rica), Matina, April 23, 1747, ANCR, CC 3588, fol. 2r; Francisco Rodríguez to Juan Gemmir y Lleonhart, Fuerte San Fernando, April 24, 1747, ANCR, CC 3588, fol. 3r.

57. Esteban Ruiz Mendoza to Juan Gemmir y Lleonhart (governor of Costa Rica), Matina, April 26, 1747, ANCR, CC 3588, fols. 4v–5r.

58. "Declaración de Francisco Ramos de edad de 22 años," Cartago, May 22, 1747, ANCR, CO 3588, fols. 22r–24v.

59. Juan Gemmir y Lleonhart (governor of Costa Rica), "Orden," Cartago, May 1, 1747, ANCR, CO 3588, fols. 12v–13v.

60. "Declaración del soldado Nicolás Román," Cartago, August 17, 1747, ANCR, CO 482, fols. 5r–9v; "Declaración del cabo de escuadra Manuel de Campo," Cartago, August 31, 1747, ANCR, CO 483, fols. 1r–4v; "Declaración de Antonio de Alva," Cartago, September 18, 1747, ANCR, CO 483, fols. 9v–12v.

61. "Declaración del segundo correo," Cartago, August 20, 1747, ANCR, CO 482, fols. 24v–26r; Joseph de Flores to Juan Gemmir y Lleonhart (governor of Costa Rica), Matina, August 22, 1741, ANCR, CO 482, fol. 52r.

62. "Declaración de Joseph Nicolas Camayo," Cartago, August 23, 1747, ANCR, CO 482, fol. 39r–v.

63. Uring, *Voyages and Travels*, 160.

64. "Agreement of Governor Nicholas Lawes and Jeremy King of the Mosquito," Jamaica, June 25, 1720, TNA, CO 137/13, fols. 277r–78r.

65. Nicholas Lawes (governor of Jamaica) to the Lords Commissioners of Trade, Jamaica, November 13, 1720, TNA, CO 137/13, fol. 291r.

66. "Declaración de Francisco Corella mulato español e ynterprete de la lengua Mosquito," Esparza, May 7, 1720, ANCR, CO 272, fol. 13r.

67. "Declaración de Francisco Corella pardo libre," Cartago, June 8, 1722, ANCR, CO 290, fols. 41v–42r.

68. Anibel to Captain del Valle Domingo de Quezada, Matina, April 19, 1724, CO 303, fol. 21r.

69. Dawson, "William Pitt's Settlement."

70. Offen, "British Logwood Extraction from the Mosquitia," 127–28.

71. Captain Charles Hobby to the Governor of Jamaica, July 17, 1731, TNA, CO 137/19, fol. 115r.

72. Hanna, *Pirate Nests*.

73. Edward Trelawny (governor of Jamaica) to duke of Newcastle, Jamaica, November 25, 1738, TNA, CO 137/56, fol. 156r–v.

74. "Declaration of Edward King of the Mosquito Indians," Dacora, March 16, 1740, TNA, CO 123/1, fol. 52r.

75. Edward Trelawny (governor of Jamaica) to the Board of Trade, Jamaica, March 16, 1741, TNA, CO 137/57, 33r.

76. Sorsby, "British Superintendency," 26–30.

77. Robert Hodgson (elder) to Edward Trelawny (governor of Jamaica), Santiago de la Vega, November 28, 1740, TNA, CO 137/57, fols. 35r–39v.

78. Edward Trelawny (governor of Jamaica) to Robert Hodgson, Jamaica, December 11, 1741, TNA, CO 323/11, fol. 70r.

79. Edward Trelawny (governor of Jamaica) to Andrew Sloane, Jamaica, July 20, 1743, TNA, CO 137/57, fol. 349r–v.

80. Edward Trelawny (governor of Jamaica) to the duke of Newcastle, Jamaica, July 20, 1743, TNA, CO 137/57, fols. 351r–52r.
81. Edward Trelawny (governor of Jamaica) to duke of Newcastle, Jamaica, December 10, 1743, TNA, CO 137/57, fols. 361r–63r.
82. Edward Trelawny (governor of Jamaica) to the Board of Trade, Jamaica, December 19, 1743, TNA, CO 137/48, fol. 87r–v.
83. "Letter from Lieutenant Hodgson to the Board, containing a distinct account of the Mosquito Shore," Bay of Honduras, April 3, 1744, TNA, CO 323/11, fols. 67v–68v.
84. "Declaración de Francisco Ramos de edad de 22 años," Cartago, May 22, 1747, ANCR, CC 3588, fols. 23r–24r.
85. "Declaración de Joseph Nicolas Camayo," Cartago, August 23, 1747, ANCR, CO 482, fols. 39r–40r.
86. Duke of Bedford to Edward Trelawny (governor of Jamaica), Whitehall, October 5, 1749, TNA, CO 137/48, fol. 186r.
87. Robert Hodgson (elder, superintendent of the Mosquito Shore) to Adworth, Jamaica, February 3, 1750, TNA, CO 137/59, fol. 10r–v.
88. For discussions of the 1736 treaty in particular, see for example Salvatierra, *Contribución*, 426; Sorsby, "British Superintendency," 13.
89. Helms, "Cultural Ecology," 81–82; Ibarra, *Del arco y la flecha*, 230; Gabbert, "'God Save the King'," 75–77.
90. García, "Ambivalencia de las representaciones coloniales," 674; Williams, "Living between Empires, 241; Offen, "Mapping Amerindian Captivity," 45.
91. "Declaración de Gregorio Lopez de edad de 22, indio y desertor de los mosquitos," Cartago, April 25, 1724, ANCR, CO 303, fol. 32v; "Declaración de Joseph Antonio," Cartago, January 17, 1725, ANCR, CO 310, fol. 2r.
92. Robert Hodgson, "The First Account of the State of That Part of America Called the Mosquito Shore in the Year 1757," London, August 30, 1759, TNA, CO 123/1, fols. 64, 68, 78.

Chapter 4. Mosquito Aggression and Reconciliation with Costa Rica, 1747–1763

1. Joseph Hilario Polo to Joseph Antonio de Oriamuno (governor of Costa Rica), Barvilla, June 9, 1763, ANCR, CO 562, fol. 1r–v; "Carta del Señor Rei y Governador de los Moscos," June 8, 1763, ANCR, CO 562, fol. 2r–v.
2. "Declaración de Antonio Morales," Cartago, September 18, 1752, ANCR, CO 501, fols. 1r–3r; "Declaración de Thomasa Gutierrez," Cartago, September 18, 1752, ANCR, CO 501, fols. 3v–4v; "Declaración de Agustina Morales," Cartago, September 18, 1752, ANCR, CO 501, fol. 5r.
3. Hurtado y Plaza, *Memorial de mi vida*, 69–70; Incer Barquero, *Nicaragua, viajes, rutas y encuentros*, 375–76.
4. "Declaración de Francisco Garcia Romero Español que salió por Matina de prisionero del Mosco," Cartago, July 22, 1749, ANCR, CO 493, fols. 22v–23r.
5. William Pitt to Edward Trelawny (governor of Jamaica), Mosquito Shore, April 8, 1751, TNA, CO 137/57, fols. 544r–45r.
6. Edward Trelawny (governor of Jamaica) to Lord Holderness, Jamaica, November 25, 1751, TNA, CO 137/57, fol. 565r–v.

7. Olien, "General, Governor, and Admiral," 288–89.
8. Sorsby, "British Superintendency," 89.
9. Joseph de los Ríos and Francisco Corella to Francisco Ybarra, Mosquitia, April 25, 1722, ANCR CO 290, fols. 32r–33r.
10. Luis de Mendoza to Cristóbal Ignacio de Soria (governor of Costa Rica), Matina, May 27, 1753, ANCR, CO 504, fol. 1r; "Declaración de Manuel edad de 30 años," Cartago, May 31, 1753, ANCR, CO 504, fols. 2v–3r.
11. Esteban Ruiz de Mendoza to Cristóbal Ignacio de Soria (governor of Costa Rica), Barbilla, June 7, 1753, ANCR, CO 505, fol. 1r; "Declaración de Mathias Bonilla, Theniente del Valle de Matina," Cartago, undated, ANCR CO-505, fols. 4v–5v.
12. Charles Knowles (governor of Jamaica) to the earl of Holdernesse, Jamaica, January 12, 1754, TNA, CO 137/60, fol. 66r–v; Joseph Hilario Polo (lieutenant of Matina) to Robert Hodgson (elder, superintendent of the Mosquito Shore), Matina, February 19, 1755, TNA, CO 137/60, fol. 190r.
13. Joseph Hilario Polo (lieutenant of Matina) to Joseph Antonio de Oriamuno, Barbilla, July 2, 1756, ANCR, CO 521, fols. 7v–8r; "Declaración de Antonio Bernardo guerrero de 17 años," Cartago, July 12, 1756, ANCR, CO 521, fols. 20r–21v.
14. Juan Lozano Cadenas to Joseph Antonio Oriamuno, Matina, September 26, 1756, ANCR, CO 521, fol. 40r–v; "Declaración de Juan Antonio de la Riva, negro criollo, natural de esta ciudad y esclavo," Cartago, October 8, 1756, ANCR, CO 521, fols. 42r–44r.
15. "Declaración de Bernardo Silva," Santiago de Guatemala, May 8, 1761, ANCR, CO 548, fols. 11r–15v; Manuel Lopez de Llano to Joseph Nicolas Bonilla, León, September 30, 1759, ANCR, CO 539, fols. 1r–4v.
16. An escaped captive who traveled with the expedition testified later that it was led by an "Indian Mosquito named Almar." Other clues from the testimony, such as the fact that the prisoners reached Matina in only four days after escaping, indicate that the captive was held in the admiral's territory, which was the farthest south. Accordingly, Almar must be a reference to either Admiral Dilson himself, or one of his captains. Either way, these actions can be safely attributed to Dilson's faction. See "Declaración de Pedro Marselo de la Concepción Gracia," Cartago, December 1, 1761, ANCR, CO 553, fols. 1r–3v; "Declaración de Luis Sanches," Cartago, December 1, 1761, ANCR, CO 553, fols. 4r–6v.
17. "Declaración de Fermín Quesada," Cartago, February 23, 1763, ANCR, CO 558, fols. 2v–3v.
18. "Declaración de Juan Joseph Rodríguez de edad de 30 años," Cartago, September 29, 1762, ANCR, CO 556, fols. 14v–17v.
19. Joseph Antonio de Oriamuno (governor of Costa Rica), "Auto," Cartago, September 16, 1762, ANCR, CO 556, fols. 4r–5r; "Declaración de Gregorio Solano," Cartago, September 20, 1762, ANCR, CO 556, fols. 11v–12v; "Declaración de Juan de Dios Iglesias," Cartago, November 15, 1762, ANCR, CO 557, fols. 2r–7v.
20. "Declaración de Ramon Corrales de edad de 28 años," Cartago, September 12, 1762, ANCR, CO 556, fols. 1v–3v.
21. "Declaración del then. de infantería Don Joseph Hilario Polo de edad de 40 años," Cartago, February 26, 1763, ANCR, CO 558, fols. 6r–7v.
22. Joseph Hilario Polo to Joseph Antonio de Oriamuno (governor of Costa Rica), Barvilla, June 9, 1763, ANCR, CO 562, fol. 1r–v.
23. "Carta del Señor Rei y Governador de los Moscos," June 8, 1763, ANCR, CO 562,

fol. 2r–v; the letter used the name "Almar," which was the Hispanicized name used for either Admiral Dilson or one of his captains. See note 16 above.

24. Sorsby, "British Superintendency," 51.

25. Edward Trelawny (governor of Jamaica) to Alonso Fernández y Heredia (governor of Nicaragua), Jamaica, October 16, 1750, TNA, CO 137/59, fols. 44r–45r.

26. Alonso Fernández de Heredia (governor of Nicaragua) to the marqués de Iscar (governor of Yúcatan), Granada, April 26, 1751, TNA, CO 137/59, fol. 119r.

27. Hurtado y Plaza, *Memorial de mi vida*, 69–70; Incer Barquero, *Nicaragua, viajes, rutas y encuentros*, 375–76.

28. Alonso Fernández y Heredia (governor of Nicaragua) to Robert Hodgson (superintendent of the Mosquito Shore), Granada, June 22, 1750, TNA, CO 137/57, fol. 90v.

29. Robert Hodgson (elder, superintendent of the Mosquito Shore) to Alonso Fernández y Heredia (governor of Nicaragua), Black River, December 3, 1750, TNA CO 137/57, fol. 548r.

30. Alonso Fernández y Heredia (governor of Nicaragua) to Edward Trelawny (governor of Jamaica), Granada, June 23, 1750, TNA CO 137/59, fol. 43r.

31. Edward Trelawny (governor of Jamaica) to duke of Newcastle, Jamaica, July 20, 1743, TNA, CO 137/57, fol. 352r.

32. Peralta, *Costa Rica y Costa de Mosquitos*, 145.

33. William Pitt to Edward Trelawny (governor of Jamaica), Mosquito Shore, April 8, 1751, TNA, CO 137/57 fols. 544r–45r.

34. Sorsby, "British Superintendency," 66.

35. Edward Trelawny (governor of Jamaica) to Lord Holderness, Jamaica, November 25, 1751, TNA, CO 137/57, fol. 565r–v.

36. Alonso Fernández de Heredia (governor of Nicaragua) to the viceroy of Mexico, Granada, April 30, 1751, TNA CO 137/57, fol. 572r–v.

37. "Declaración de Francisco Ocampo que salió de Matina de prisionero de los moscos," Cartago, May 8, 1749, ANCR, CO 493, fol. 10v; "Declaración de Francisco García Romero Español que salió por Matina de prisionero del Mosco," Cartago, July 22, 1749, ANCR, CO 493, fols. 22v–23r; "Declaración de Nicolás Granda que salió a Vigía de Matina," Cartago, July 29, 1749, ANCR, CO 493, fol. 24r.

38. "Declaración de Antonio Morales," Cartago, September 18, 1752, ANCR, CO 501, fols. 1r–3r; "Declaración de Tomasa Gutierrez," Cartago, September 18, 1752, ANCR, CO 501, fols. 3v–4v; "Declaración de Agustina Morales," Cartago, September 18, 1752, ANCR, CO 501, fol. 5r.

39. Luis de Mendoza to Cristóbal Ignacio de Soria (governor of Costa Rica), Matina, May 27, 1753, ANCR, CO 504, fol. 1r; "Declaración de Manuel edad de 30 años," Cartago, May 31, 1753, ANCR, CO 504, fols. 2v–3r; Esteban Ruiz de Mendoza to Cristóbal Ignacio de Soria (governor of Costa Rica), Barbilla, June 7, 1753, ANCR, CO 505, fol. 1r; "Declaración de Mathias Bonilla, Theniente del Valle de Matina," Cartago, undated, ANCR CO-505, fols. 4v–5v.

40. Charles Knowles (governor of Jamaica) to the earl of Holdernesse, Jamaica, January 12, 1754, TNA, CO 137/60, fol. 66r–v.

41. Joseph Icario Polo (lieutenant of Matina) to Robert Hodgson (elder, superintendent of the Mosquito Shore), Matina, February 19, 1755, TNA, CO 137/60, fol. 190r.

42. Peralta, *Costa Rica y Costa de Mosquitos*, 148.

43. Francisco Fernández de Pastora (governor of Costa Rica) to Joseph Antonio Oria-

muno, Matina, June 17, 1756, ANCR, CO 521, fol. 1r; Joseph Antonio de Oriamuno, "Auto," Cartago, June 20, 1756, ANCR, CO 521, fol. 2r–v.

44. Francisco Fernández de Pastora (governor of Costa Rica) to Joseph Antonio Oriamuno, Matina, June 27, 1756, ANCR, CO 521, fol. 5r; Joseph Antonio de Oriamuno, "Notificación," Cartago, July 4, 1756, ANCR, CO 521, fol. 6r.

45. Joseph Hilario Polo to Joseph Antonio de Oriamuno, Barbilla, July 2, 1756, ANCR, CO 521, fols. 7r–8r; "Declaración de Antonio Bernardo Guerrero de 17 años," Cartago, July 12, 1756, ANCR, CO 521, fols. 20r–21v.

46. Juan Lozano Cadenas to Joseph Antonio Oriamuno, Matina, September 26, 1756, ANCR, CO 521, fol. 41r; "Declaración de Juan Antonio de la Riva, negro criollo, natural de esta ciudad y esclavo," Cartago, October 8, 1756, ANCR, CO 521, fols. 42r–44v.

47. "Declaración de Bernardo Silva," Santiago de Guatemala, May 8, 1761, ANCR, CO 548, fols. 11r–15v.

48. Peralta, *Costa Rica y Costa de Mosquitos*, 164–70.

49. León, November 28, 1760, AGCA, A1, legajo 3, expediente 36, fol. 1r; Francisco Xavier de Oriamuno to president of Guatemala, Cartago, July 14, 1761, ANCR, CO 550, fol. 2r; "Declaración de Luis Sanches," Cartago, December 1, 1761, ANCR, CO 553, fols. 5v–6r.

50. The name "Almar" appears in Spanish documents on several occasions in reference to Admiral Dilson. The escaped slave who referenced Almar also reported arriving in Matina only four days after escaping, indicating that he had been in the closest Mosquito settlement in the Pearl Key Lagoon, which was the home of Dilson. The variant "Almoral" also appears. See for example "Gastos hechos en el hermano del Almoral," Santiago de Guatemala, April 23, 1778, AGCA, A1 (6), legajo 3, expediente 28, fol. 1r.

51. "Declaración de Pedro Marselo de la Concepción Gracia," Cartago, December 1, 1761, ANCR, CO 553, fols. 1v–4v.

52. "Declaración de Fermín Quesada," Cartago, February 23, 1763, ANCR, CO 558, fols. 2v–3r; "Declaración de Juan Joseph Rodríguez de edad de 30 años," Cartago, September 29, 1762, ANCR, CO 556, fol. 15r.

53. Joseph Antonio de Oriamuno (governor of Costa Rica), Joseph Antonio de Bonilla, and Luis Arnesto de Troya, "Autos," Cartago, September 16, 1762, ANCR, CO 556, fol. 4r; Joseph Antonio de Oriamuno, "Auto," Cartago, September 18, 1762, ANCR, CO 556, fol. 6r; "Declaración de Juan de Dios de la Trinidad Ubiedo de edad de 27 años," Cartago, September 18, 1762, ANCR, CO 556, fols. 9r–10v.

54. "Declaración de Gregorio Solano," Cartago, September 20, 1762, ANCR, CO 556, fol. 12r.

55. "Declaración de Juan de Dios Iglesias," Cartago, November 15, 1762, ANCR, CO 557, fols. 2v–4r.

56. "Declaración del then. de infantería Don Joseph Ylario Polo de edad de 40 años," Cartago, February 26, 1763, ANCR, CO 558, fols. 6r–7v.

57. Joseph Joaquín de Nava (governor of Costa Rica) to Admiral Dilson, Cartago, May 23, 1769, TNA, CO 137/65, fols. 10r–11v.

58. Joseph Hilario Polo to Joseph Antonio de Oriamuno (governor of Costa Rica), Barvilla, June 9, 1763, ANCR, CO 562, fol. 1r–v; "Carta del Señor Rei y Governador de los Moscos," June 8, 1763, ANCR, CO 562, fol. 2r–v.

59. "Junta de vecinos," Cartago, June 13, 1763, ANCR, CC 330, fol. 2r–v; Joseph Antonio de Oriamuno, "Auto," Cartago, June 16, 1763, ANCR, CC 330, fol. 4r.

60. William Pitt to Edward Trelawny (governor of Jamaica), Mosquito Shore, July 17, 1749, TNA, CO 137/57, fols. 530r–31r.
61. "An Extract of Gov. Trelawny's Instructions to Capt. Hodgson, Superintendent of the Mosquito Shore," Jamaica, April 14, 1750, TNA, CO 137/57, fol. 536r.
62. Hurtado y Plaza, *Memorial de mi vida*, 69–70; Incer Barquero, *Nicaragua, viajes, rutas y encuentros*, 375–76.
63. Alonso Fernández y Heredia (governor of Nicaragua) to Robert Hodgson (superintendent of the Mosquito Shore), Granada, June 22, 1750, TNA, CO 137/57, fol. 90v.
64. Edward Trelawny (governor of Jamaica) to duke of Bedford, Jamaica, April 14, 1750, TNA, CO 137/57, fol. 533v.
65. William Pitt to Edward Trelawny (governor of Jamaica), Mosquito Shore, April 8, 1751, TNA, CO 137/57 fols. 544r–45r.
66. Robert Hodgson (elder, superintendent of the Mosquito Shore) to Alonso Fernández y Heredia (governor of Nicaragua), Black River, December 3, 1750, TNA, CO 137/57, fol. 548r.
67. Alonso Fernández y Heredia (governor of Nicaragua) to the marqués de Iscar (governor of Yúcatan), Granada, January 12, 1750, TNA, CO 137/59, fol. 137r.
68. Alonso Fernández y Heredia (governor of Nicaragua) to Edward Trelawny (governor of Jamaica), Granada, June 23, 1750, TNA, CO 137/59, fol. 43r–v.
69. Alonso Fernández y Heredia (governor of Nicaragua) to Robert Hodgson (elder, superintendent of the Mosquito Shore), Granada, September 17, 1750, TNA, CO 137/59, fol. 94r.
70. Edward Trelawny (governor of Jamaica) to Alonso Fernández y Heredia (governor of Nicaragua), Jamaica, October 16, 1750, TNA, CO 137/59, fols. 44r–45r.
71. Robert Hodgson (elder, superintendent of the Mosquito Shore) to Alonso Fernández y Heredia (governor of Nicaragua), Black River, December 3, 1750, TNA, CO 137/57, fol. 548r.
72. Alonso Fernández de Heredia (governor of Nicaragua) to the marqués de Iscar (governor of Yúcatan), Granada, April 26, 1751, TNA, CO 137/59, fol. 119r.
73. Pablo Ruiz to Alonso Fernández de Heredia (governor of Nicaragua), Cartago, March 7, 1751, TNA, CO 137/59, fols. 127r–28v.
74. William Pitt to Edward Trelawny (governor of Jamaica), Mosquito Shore, April 8, 1751, TNA, CO 137/57, fols. 544r–45r.
75. James Lawrie and Richard Jones to Edward Trelawny (governor of Jamaica), Black River, April 9, 1751, TNA, CO 137/57, fols. 546r–47r.
76. Robert Hodgson (elder, superintendent of the Mosquito Shore) to the secretary of state, Jamaica, April 21, 1751, TNA, CO 137/57, fols. 550r–51v.
77. Alonso Fernandez de Heredia (governor of Nicaragua) to the viceroy of Mexico, Granada, April 30, 1751, TNA, CO 137/57, fol. 572r–v; Alonso Fernandez de Heredia (governor of Nicaragua) to marqués de Iscar (governor of Yúcatan), April 26, 1751, TNA, CO 137/57, fols. 572v–73r.
78. Edward Trelawny (governor of Jamaica) to the duke of Bedford, Jamaica, July 17, 1751, TNA, CO 137/57, fols. 552r–54v.
79. Edward Trelawny (governor of Jamaica) to Lord Holdernesse, Jamaica, November 25, 1751, TNA, CO 137/57, fol. 565r–v.
80. Joseph Vasquez Prego (president of Guatemala) to Edward Trelawny (governor of Jamaica), November 25, 1752, TNA, CO 137/60, fols. 33r–38r.

81. Robert Hodgson (elder, superintendent of the Mosquito Shore) to Charles Knowles (governor of Jamaica), Mosquito Shore, January 19, 1753, TNA, CO 137/60, fol. 25r–v.
82. Charles Knowles (governor of Jamaica) to the earl of Holdernesse, Jamaica, January 10, 1753, TNA, CO 137/60, fol. 1r–v.
83. Charles Knowles (governor of Jamaica) to Robert Hodgson (elder, superintendent of the Mosquito Shore), Jamaica, January 24, 1753, TNA, CO 137/60, fol. 23r.
84. Charles Knowles (governor of Jamaica) to the earl of Holdernesse, Jamaica, March 26, 1753, TNA, CO 137/60, fols. 17r–18r.
85. "Copy of a Letter from Captain Hodgson Commanding the Detachment of Col. Trelawny's Regiment on the Mosquito Shore to Governor Knowles," Mosquito Shore, December 19, 1752, TNA, CO 137/60, fols. 20v–21v.
86. Charles Knowles (governor of Jamaica) to the earl of Holdernesse, Jamaica, October 13, 1753, TNA, CO 137/60, fol. 53r.
87. Charles Knowles (governor of Jamaica) to Robert Hodgson (elder, superintendent of the Mosquito Shore), Jamaica, October 8, 1753, TNA, CO 137/60, fol. 55r–v.
88. Joseph Icario Polo (lieutenant of Matina) to Robert Hodgson (elder, superintendent of the Mosquito Shore), Matina, February 19, 1755, TNA, CO 137/60, fol. 190r.
89. Charles Knowles (governor of Jamaica) to the earl of Holdernesse, Jamaica, January 12, 1754, TNA, CO 137/60, fol. 66r–v.
90. Robert Hodgson (elder, superintendent of the Mosquito Shore) to Charles Knowles (governor of Jamaica), Black River, March 16, 1755, TNA, CO 137/60, fol. 162r–v.
91. Joseph Hilario Polo to Joseph Antonio de Oriamuno, Barbilla, July 2, 1756, ANCR, CO 521, fols. 7v–8r; "Declaración de Antonio Bernardo guerrero de 17 años," Cartago, July 12, 1756, ANCR CO 521, fols. 20r–21v.
92. Juan Lozano Cadenas to Joseph Antonio Oriamuno, Matina, September 26, 1756, ANCR, CO 521, fol. 40r; "Declaración de Juan Antonio de la Riva, negro criollo, natural de esta ciudad y esclavo," Cartago, October 8, 1756, ANCR CO 521, fols. 42r–44v.
93. "Extract of a Letter from George Haldane to the Board of Trade," Santiago de la Vega, July 20, 1759, TNA, CO 137/48, fol. 289r–v.
94. Dirk Halifax and James Oswald (Lords of Trade) to William Pitt, Whitehall, November 16, 1759, TNA, CO 137/48, fol. 286r.
95. Deposition of Peter Steward, Kingston, November 8, 1759, TNA, CO 137/48, fols. 296r–97v.

Chapter 5. The Mosquito Confederation and New Internal Tensions, 1763–1775

1. Joseph Otway (superintendent of the Mosquito Shore) to the earl of Halifax, Black River, April 25, 1764, TNA, CO 137/61, fols. 275r–76v.
2. Antonio de la Fuente to Joseph Joachin de Nava (governor of Costa Rica), Matina, June 16, 1765, ANCR, CO 566, fols. 2v–4v; "Declaración de Don Bentura Barraganes de edad de 25 años," Barbilla, July 6, 1765, ANCR, CO 566, fols. 6v–7v; "Declaración de Don Francisco Javier de la Riva de edad de 25 años," Barbilla, July 6, 1765, ANCR, CO 566, fols. 9v–10v.
3. "Declaración de Bartolome Garcia y Casas," Cartago, February 6, 1767, ANCR, CO 572, fols. 14v–16v.

4. Robert Hodgson, "Diary of Captain Hodgson's Tour Along the Mosquito Shore, Commencing Dec. 17, 1769 and ending March 2, 1770," Punta Gorda, March 2, 1770, TNA, CO 137/65, fols. 240r–41v.

5. "Declaración de Felix Joachin de Alvarado Girón," Cartago, January 27, 1767, ANCR, CO 572, fols. 11v–13v.

6. Colville Briton, "Advertisement That Is to Give Notice to All the British Subjects Settled on the Southern Part of the Mosquito Shore," November 29, 1776, TNA, CO 123/31, fols. 17r–18v.

7. Olien, "General, Governor, and Admiral," 289, 298, 305.

8. "Deposition of Henry Corrin," Jamaica, May 28, 1768, TNA, CO 137/63, fol. 56r.

9. Richard Jones, "An Account of the Late Expected Insurrection of the Indians on the Mosquito Shore," Jamaica, July 25, 1768, TNA, CO 137/64, fols. 3r–7v.

10. Joseph Joaquín de Nava (governor of Costa Rica) to Admiral Dilson, Cartago, May 23, 1769, TNA, CO 137/65, fols. 10r–11v.

11. Joseph Joaquín de Nava to president of Guatemala, Cartago, July 11, 1769, AGCA A1, legajo 117, expediente 2475, fols. 3r–5v.

12. Joseph Joaquín de Nava (governor of Costa Rica) to Admiral Dilson, Cartago, May 23, 1769, TNA, CO 137/65, fols. 10r–11v; "Declaración de Felix Joachin de Alvarado Girón," Cartago, January 27, 1767, ANCR, CO 572, fols. 11v–13v.

13. Luis Diez Navarro to the president of Guatemala, Guatemala, November 9, 1769, AGCA, A1, legajo 117, expediente 2475, fols. 15r–16v.

14. "Petition to the King from His Majesty's Principal Subjects inhabiting the British Settlement on the Mosquito Shore," Black River, October 17, 1769, TNA CO 137/65, fols. 75r–76r.

15. Admiral Dilson to Roberto Hodgson (superintendent of the Mosquito Shore), September 16, 1769, TNA, CO 137/65, fol. 261r.

16. George (king of the Mosquito) to Robert Hodgson (superintendent of the Mosquito Shore), October 30, 1769, TNA, CO 137/65, fol. 263r–v; George (king of the Mosquito) to William Trelawny (governor of Jamaica), Cape Gracias a Dios, February 28, 1770, TNA, CO 137/65, fol. 204r–v; Richard Jones, "A Report of the Proceedings of Mr. Jones to the Governor of Jamaica, during the Time He Was on the Mosquito Shore," April 4, 1770, TNA CO 137/65, fols. 183r–84r; Robert Hodgson, "Diary of Captain Hodgson's Tour along the Mosquito Shore, Commencing Dec. 17, 1769 and ending March 2, 1770," Punta Gorda, March 2, 1770, TNA, CO 137/65, fols. 240r–41v.

17. Robert Hodgson, "Diary of Capt. Hodgson's Tour along the Mosquito Shore on to Jamaica, Commencing April 16 1774 and Ending June 12 Following," TNA, CO 137/69, fols. 213r–14v.

18. Sorsby, "British Superintendency," 219.

19. Richard Jones, "A Report of the Proceedings of Mr. Jones to the Governor of Jamaica, during the Time He was on the Mosquito Shore," April 4, 1770, TNA, CO 137/65, fols. 183r–85v.

20. Briton (governor of the Mosquito) to Basil Keith (governor of Jamaica), Tebuppy, November 10, 1773, TNA, CO 137/69, fol. 187r.

21. "Interrogations to put to Mr. Jeremiah Terry," Jamaica, March 15, 1779, TNA, CO 137/74, fol. 229v.

22. Robert Hodgson (younger, superintendent of the Mosquito Shore) to earl of Dartmouth, Portobelo, July 24, 1775, TNA, CO 137/70, fols. 161r–62r.

23. Briton (governor of the Mosquito) to Basil Keith (governor of Jamaica), Tebuppy, November 10, 1773, TNA, CO 137/69, fol. 187r.

24. "Declaración de Gregorio Lopez de edad de 22, indio y desertor de los mosquitos," Cartago, April 25, 1724, ANCR, CO 303, fol. 32r–v.

25. Robert Hodgson, "The First Account of the State of That Part of America Called the Mosquito Shore in the Year 1757," London, August 30, 1759, TNA, CO 123/1, fols. 64, 68, 78.

26. John Dalling (governor of Jamaica), "Invoice of Presents for the Mosquitto Indians," Kingston, October 8, 1778, TNA, CO 137/73, fol. 231r.

27. Colville Briton (governor of the Mosquito) to John Dalling (governor of Jamaica), Tebuppy, December 8, 1777, TNA, CO 137/73, fol. 203r–v.

28. Olien, "Miskito Kings," 211–13.

29. Joseph Otway (superintendent of the Mosquito Shore) to the earl of Halifax, Black River, April 25, 1764, TNA CO 137/61, fols. 275r–76v; Sorsby, "British Superintendency," 135–36.

30. Antonio de la Fuente to Joseph Joachin de Nava (governor of Costa Rica), Matina, June 16, 1765, ANCR, CO 566, fols. 2v–4v; "Declaración de Don Bentura Barraganes de edad de 25 años," Barbilla, July 6, 1765, ANCR, CO 566, fols. 6v–7r; "Declaración de Don Juan de Sierra de edad de 25 años," Barbilla, July 6, 1765, ANCR, CO 566, fols. 8r–9r; "Declaración de Bartolomé García y Casasola de edad de 22 años," Barbilla, July 6, 1765, ANCR, CO 566, fols. 12v–13r.

31. Joseph Joachin de Nava (governor of Costa Rica), "Auto," Cartago, September 1766, ANCR, CO 572, fols. 1r–2v; "Declaración de Felix Joachin de Alvarado Giron," Cartago, January 27, 1767, ANCR, CO 572, fols. 11v–13r; "Declaración de Bartolomé García y Casas," Cartago, February 6, 1767, ANCR, CO 572, fols. 14v–16r.

32. Joseph Joaquín de Nava (governor of Costa Rica) to Admiral Dilson, Cartago, May 23, 1769, TNA, CO 137/65, fols. 10r–11v.

33. Joseph Joachin de Nava (governor of Costa Rica) to the president of Guatemala, Cartago, July 11, 1769, AGCA, A1, legajo 117, expediente 2475, fols. 3r–5v.

34. "Junta de vecinos," Cartago, June 13, 1763, ANCR, CC 330, fol. 2r–v.

35. Luis Diez Navarro to the president of Guatemala, Guatemala, November 9, 1769, AGCA, A1 legajo 117, expediente 2475, fols. 15r–16v.

36. "Patente de Gobernador de los indios Mosquitos, de la provincia de Cartago, a favor de Almiral Dilson," Ciudad de Guatemala, December 29, 1769, AGCA, A1 legajo 4043, expediente 31,216, fol. 9r.

37. "Real Orden," San Ildefonso, September 17, 1770, AGCA, A1, legajo 117, expediente 2473, fol. 59r.

38. "Decreto," Guatemala, February 19, 1771, AGCA, A1, legajo 117, expediente 2473, fol. 61r.

39. Robert Hodgson, "Diary of Captain Hodgson's Tour along the Mosquito Shore, Commencing Dec. 17, 1769 and ending March 2, 1770," Punta Gorda, March 2, 1770, TNA, CO 137/65, fols. 240r–42v.

40. Robert Hodgson (superintendent of the Mosquito Shore) to Joaquin de Nava (governor of Costa Rica), Grindstone Bay, January 23, 1770, TNA, CO 137/65, fols. 247r–49v.

41. Joseph Joachin de Nava (governor of Costa Rica), "Auto," Cartago, February 12, 1770, AGCA, A1, legajo 119, expediente 4831, fols. 5r–6v; Joseph Joachin de Nava, "Auto," Cartago, February 15, 1770, AGCA, A1, legajo 119, expediente 4831, fol. 8r.

NOTES TO CHAPTER FIVE

42. Joseph Joachin de Nava (governor of Costa Rica), Cartago, "Auto," September 15, 1771, AGCA, A1, legajo 119, expediente 4831, fols. 10r–11v.
43. "Ocurro de Don Miguel de Villanueva Martinez," Guatemala, February 28, 1769, AGCA, A1, legajo 117, expediente 2475, fols. 1r–5v.
44. "Real Orden," Madrid, January 16, 1774, AGCA, A1, legajo 4629, fol. 129r.
45. Sorsby, "British Superintendency," 123.
46. Joseph Otway (superintendent of the Mosquito Shore) to William Lyttelton (governor of Jamaica), Black River, November 11, 1763, TNA, CO 137/61, fol. 217r–v.
47. Joseph Otway (superintendent of the Mosquito Shore) to the earl of Halifax, Black River, April 25, 1764, TNA, CO 137/61, fol. 275r.
48. Joseph Otway (superintendent of the Mosquito Shore) to the Lords Commissioners of Trade and Plantations, Black River, July 12, 1765, TNA, CO 137/33, fol. 232v.
49. "Deposition of Henry Corrin," Jamaica, May 28, 1768, TNA, CO 137/63, fol. 56r.
50. Richard Jones, "An Account of the Late Expected Insurrection of the Indians on the Mosquito Shore," Jamaica, July 25, 1768, TNA, CO 137/64, fols. 3r–7v.
51. Joseph Joaquín de Nava (governor of Costa Rica) to Admiral Dilson, Cartago, May 23, 1769, TNA, CO 137/65, fols. 10r–11v.
52. Joseph Joaquín de Nava to president of Guatemala, Cartago, July 11, 1769, AGCA, A1, legajo 117, expediente 2475, fols. 3r–5v.
53. Admiral Dilson to Roberto Hodgson (younger, superintendent of the Mosquito Shore), September 16, 1769, TNA, CO 137/65, fol. 261r.
54. "Memorial of the Sundry Inhabitants Residing on the Windward Part of the Mosquito Shore," Pearl Bay Lagoon, October 7, 1769, TNA, CO 137/65, fol. 12r–v.
55. "Petition to the King from His Majesty's Principal Subjects Inhabiting the British Settlement on the Mosquito Shore," Black River, October 17, 1769, TNA, CO 137/65, fols. 75r–76r.
56. George (king of the Mosquito) to Robert Hodgson (younger, superintendent of the Mosquito Shore), October 30, 1769, TNA, CO 137/65, fol. 263r–v.
57. William Trelawny (governor of Jamaica), "The Governor of Jamaica's Orders to Richard Jones," St. Iago de la Vega, November 20, 1769, TNA, CO 137/65, fol. 14r–v.
58. Robert Hodgson, "Diary of Captain Hodgson's Tour along the Mosquito Shore, Commencing Dec. 17, 1769 and Ending March 2, 1770," Punta Gorda, March 2, 1770, TNA, CO 137/65, fols. 240r–42v.
59. Admiral Dilson to Roberto Hodgson (younger, superintendent of the Mosquito Shore), September 16, 1769, TNA, CO 137/65, fol. 261r.
60. Richard Jones, "A Report of the Proceedings of Mr. Jones to the Governor of Jamaica, during the Time He Was on the Mosquito Shore," April 4, 1770, TNA, CO 137/65, fols. 183r–85v.
61. Robert Hodgson, "Diary of Captain Hodgson's Tour along the Mosquito Shore, Commencing Dec. 17, 1769 and ending March 2, 1770," Punta Gorda, March 2, 1770, TNA, CO 137/65, fols. 241r–42v; Robert Hodgson (younger, superintendent of the Mosquito Shore) to Joaquin de Nava (governor of Costa Rica), Grindstone Bay, January 23, 1770, TNA CO 137/65, fols. 247r–49v.
62. Richard Jones, "A Report of the Proceedings of Mr. Jones to the Governor of Jamaica, during the Time He Was on the Mosquito Shore," April 4, 1770, TNA, CO 137/65, fol. 185r; John Dilson (admiral of the Mosquito) to Joaquin de Nava (governor of Costa Rica), Bluefields, February 4, 1770, TNA, CO 137/65, fols. 192r–93v.

63. Robert Hodgson (younger, superintendent of the Mosquito Shore) to Abraham Gill, Punta Gorda, February 20, 1770, TNA, CO 137/65, fols. 271r–72r.

64. Lord Hillsborough to Lord Weymouth, Whitehall, February 10, 1770, TNA, CO 137/65, fol. 45r.

65. Richard Jones, "A Report of the Proceedings of Mr. Jones to the Governor of Jamaica, during the Time he Was on the Mosquito Shore," April 4, 1770, TNA, CO 137/65, fols. 185v–86v.

66. Robert Hodgson (younger, superintendent of the Mosquito Shore) to Lord of Hillsborough, Punta Gorda, March 10, 1770, TNA, CO 137/65, fol. 272r; Abraham Tonoston to Robert Hodgson (younger, superintendent of the Mosquito Shore), Mosquito Shore, February 27, 1770, TNA, CO 137/65, fol. 277r.

67. Robert Hodgson (younger, superintendent of the Mosquito Shore) to William Trelawny (governor of Jamaica), October 7, 1770, TNA, CO 137/66, fols. 100r–101r; "The Diary of Captain Hodgson's Tour along the Mosquito Shore," Black River, October 7, 1770, TNA, CO 137/66, fols. 102r–11v.

68. Robert Hodgson (younger, superintendent of the Mosquito Shore) to Abraham Gill, Punta Gorda, February 20, 1770, TNA, CO 137/65, fol. 271v.

69. Jeremiah Terry to Robert Hodgson (younger, superintendent of the Mosquito Shore), Tebuppy, March 13, 1774, TNA, CO 137/69, fol. 209r–v.

70. Robert Hodgson (younger, superintendent of the Mosquito Shore), "Diary of Capt. Hodgson's Tour along the Mosquito Shore on to Jamaica, Commencing April 1, 1774 and ending June 12 Following," TNA, CO 137/69, fol. 209v.

71. Robert Hodgson (younger, superintendent of the Mosquito Shore), "Diary of Capt. Hodgson's tour along the Mosquito Shore on to Jamaica, Commencing April 1, 1774 and Ending June 12 Following," TNA, CO 137/69, fols. 212r–14v.

72. Richard Jones, "A Report of the Proceedings of Mr. Jones to the Governor of Jamaica, during the Time He Was on the Mosquito Shore," April 4, 1770, TNA, CO 137/65, fol. 184r.

73. Robert Hodgson (superintendent of the Mosquito Shore) to Juan Fernández de Bobadilla (governor of Costa Rica), Harbor of Nicaragua, April 20, 1774, TNA, CO 137/69, fol. 204r.

74. Robert Hodgson (superintendent of the Mosquito Shore) to the Lieutenant of the Matina Valley, Matina, May 5, 1774, TNA, CO 137/69, fol. 206r.

75. Robert Hodgson (superintendent of the Mosquito Shore), "Diary of Capt. Hodgson's tour along the Mosquito Shore on to Jamaica, commencing April 16 1774 and ending June 12 following," TNA, CO 137/69, fols. 220r–26v.

76. Briton (governor of the Mosquito) to Basil Keith (governor of Jamaica), Tebuppy, November 10, 1773, TNA, CO 137/69, fol. 187r.

77. Robert White to the earl of Dartmouth (principal secretary of state for America), London, June 24, 1774, TNA, CO 137/69, fol. 172r.

78. "Interrogations to Put to Mr. Jeremiah Terry," Jamaica, March 15, 1779, TNA, CO 137/74, fol. 229v.

79. "The Memorial of Jeremiah Terry on Behalf of the Indian Ambassadors and Himself," Whitehall, August 29, 1775, TNA, CO 137/70, fols. 148r–51v.

80. George (son and heir to the king of the Mosquito Shore) to earl of Dartmouth, Whitehall, November 10, 1775, TNA, CO 137/70, fol. 155r–v.

81. Sorsby, "British Superintendency," 201–3.

82. Edward Trelawny (governor of Jamaica) to duke of Bedford, Jamaica, April 14, 1750, TNA, CO 137/57, fols. 532r–34r.
83. Joseph Otway (superintendent of the Mosquito Shore) to the Lords Commissioners of Trade and Plantations, Black River, July 12, 1765, TNA, CO 137/33, fol. 233v.
84. Colville Briton, "Advertisement That Is to Give Notice to All the British Subjects Settled on the Southern Part of the Mosquito Shore," November 29, 1776, TNA, CO 123/31, fols. 17r–18v.
85. Sorsby, "British Superintendency," 198.
86. Offen, "Sambo and Tawira Miskitu," 352.
87. Helms, "Miskito Slaving," 191; Williams, "Living between Empires," 241.

Chapter 6. The Mosquito Confederation and Civil War, 1776–1791

1. "Declaración de Carlos Cubero," Cartago, October 15, 1784, ANCR, CO 793, fols. 3r–4v; "Otra de Joseph Menir," Cartago, October 15, 1784, ANCR, CO 793, fol. 4r–v; "Otra de Juan de Dios Roman," Cartago, October 15, 1784, ANCR, CO 793, fol. 5r.
2. Helms, "Miskito Slaving," 191; Offen, "Sambo and Tawira Miskitu," 350; Williams, "Living between Empires," 255; Ibarra, *Del arco y la flecha*, 230.
3. Edward Trelawny (governor of Jamaica) to duke of Bedford, Jamaica, April 14, 1750, TNA, CO 137/57, fols. 532r–34r.
4. George (son and heir to the king of the Mosquito Shore) to earl of Dartmouth, Whitehall, November 10, 1775, TNA, CO 137/70, fol. 155r–v.
5. Colville Briton, "Advertisement That Is to Give Notice to All the British Subjects Settled on the Southern Part of the Mosquito Shore," November 29, 1776, TNA, CO 123/31, fols. 17r–18v.
6. Colville Cairns to James Lawrie (superintendent of the Mosquito Shore), Tebuppy, May 10, 1777, TNA, CO 137/73, fols. 197r–202v.
7. Colville Briton (governor of the Mosquito) to John Dalling (governor of Jamaica), Tebuppy, December 8, 1777, TNA, CO 137/73, fol. 203r–v.
8. George II (king of the Mosquito) to Basil Keith (governor of Jamaica), Sandy Bay, April 12, 1777, TNA, CO 137/73, fols. 205r–6r.
9. Colville Cairns to James Lawrie (superintendent of the Mosquito Shore), Tebuppy, May 10, 1777, TNA, 137/73, fols. 197r–202v.
10. Juan Fernández de Bobadilla (governor of Costa Rica), Cartago, February 12, 1778, ANCR, MU146, fol. 1r; "Gastos hechos en el hermano del Almoral," Santiago de Guatemala, April 23, 1778, AGCA, A1 (6), legajo 3, expediente 31, fol. 1r.
11. Fernández, *Colección de documentos*, 56–62.
12. Deposition of John Hooker, Jamaica, May 14, 1778, TNA, CO 137/73, fol. 193r.
13. Jeremiah Terry, Memorial, August 29, 1775, TNA, CO 137/70, fol. 148r.
14. Sorsby, "British Superintendency of the Mosquito Shore," 232–38.
15. George II (king of the Mosquito), Duke Isaac, Colville Briton (governor of the Mosquito), Dilson (admiral of the Mosquito, General John Smee, and Admiral Frederick, Treaty Signed with Jeremiah Terry, St. Johns, September 5, 1778, TNA, CO 123/2, fol. 2r–v.
16. Deposition of Joseph Wood by Colville Cairns, Mosquito Shore, October 27, 1778, TNA, CO 137/74, fol. 296r; Deposition of Jonathan Worth by Colville Cairns, Mos-

quito Shore, October 26, 1778, TNA, CO 137/74, fol. 204r; Deposition of Abraham Gill by Colville Cairns, Mosquito Shore, October 23, 1778, TNA, CO 137/74, fol. 213r.

17. Colville Briton (governor of the Mosquito) to John Dalling (governor of Jamaica), St. John's, November 7, 1778, TNA, CO 137/74, fol. 221r–v.

18. James Lawrie (superintendent of the Mosquito Shore) to John Dalling (governor of Jamaica), St. Johns, November 8, 1778, TNA, CO 137/74, fols. 225r–26v; "The Examination of Robert Campbell," Kingston, March 20, 1779, TNA, CO 137/74, fol. 233r.

19. Colville Briton (governor of the Mosquito) to John Dalling (governor of Jamaica), St. John's, November 7, 1778, TNA, CO 137/74, fol. 221r.

20. Fernández, *Colección de documentos*, vol. 10, 84.

21. Fernández, *Colección de documentos*, vol. 10, 79–85.

22. "Gastos hechos en el hermano del Almoral y sus compañeros," Cartago, November 8, 1779, AGCA, AI (6), legajo 3, expediente 31, fols. 1r–3v.

23. Captain William Dalrymple to John Dalling (governor of Jamaica), Fort Fernando de Omoa, October 20, 1779, TNA CO 137/77, fol. 9r.

24. Chiefs of the Mosquito Nation to John Dalling (governor of Jamaica), Black River, November 10, 1779, TNA CO 137/77, fols. 26r–27r.

25. "The Journal of Captain John Polson," February 3 to April 29, 1780, TNA, CO 137/77, fols. 166r–70r.

26. Captain John Polson to John Dalling (governor of Jamaica), St. John's Fort, April 30, 1780, TNA, CO 137/77, fol. 158r.

27. Colville Cairns, "Proceedings at a General Congress," Tebuppy, October 1, 1780, TNA, CO 137/79, fols. 165r–67r.

28. Arguedas, "Kingdom of Guatemala," 147.

29. Juan Flores, Cartago, October 8, 1781, ANCR, CO 776, fol. 1r; "Declaración del Sarg. Antonio Rivas," Cartago, October 8, 1781, ANCR, CO-776, fol. 5r.

30. "Otra de Juan de Dios Román," Cartago, October 15, 1784, ANCR, CO 793, fol. 5r.

31. "Declaración de Carlos Cubero," Cartago, October 15, 1784, ANCR, CO 793, fols. 3r–4v.

32. "Declaración de Antonio Esguerra," Cartago, October 14, 1784, ANCR, CO 793, fols. 1r–2r.

33. Lord Sydney to Alfred Clarke (governor of Jamaica), Whitehall, July 31, 1786, TNA, CO 137/86, fol. 72r; James Lawrie (superintendent of the Mosquito Shore) to Alfred Clarke (governor of Jamaica), Black River, October 14, 1786, TNA, CO 137/86, fols. 156r 58v.

34. The Spanish never established a strong enough presence on the Mosquito Shore to inhibit British trade, and they allowed some British officials to stay, including former superintendent Robert Hodgson Jr. Accusations of contraband trade continued, including against Hodgson himself. See "Informe," 1790, AGCA, AI, legajo 6056, expediente 53, 642.

35. Williams, "Living between Empires," 245–55.

36. "Real Orden," Madrid, December 15, 1789, AGCA, AI legajo 1532, fol. 551–52.

37. Williams, "Living between Empires," 254.

38. Williams, "Living between Empires," 260–64.

39. Offen, "Sambo and Tawira Miskitu," 352.

40. Williams, "Living between Empires," 259, 265; Offen, "Creating Mosquitia," 353.

41. Sorsby, "British Superintendency," 219–21.

42. "Tuapi" is a Hispanicized version of the name of the Mosquito governor's home. In English sources, it is called "Tebuppy."

43. Colville Briton (governor of the Mosquito) to John Dalling (governor of Jamaica), Tebuppy, December 18, 1777, TNA, CO 137/73, fol. 203r–v; George II (king of the Mosquito) to Basil Keith (governor of Jamaica), Sandy Bay, April 12, 1777, TNA, CO 137/73, fols. 205r–6r.

44. Fernández, *Colección de documentos*, 56.

45. "Auto," Guatemala, April 24, 1778, AGCA, A1 (6), legajo 3, expediente 28, fol. 1r.

46. Fernández, *Colección de documentos*, 60–72.

47. "Declaración de Don Gabriel de Oñate," Cartago, December 27, 1778, ANCR, CO 713, fols. 1v–4r.

48. George II (king of the Mosquito), Duke Isaac, Colville Briton (governor of the Mosquito), Dilson (admiral of the Mosquito), General John Smee, and Admiral Frederick, Treaty Signed with Jeremiah Terry, St. Johns, September 5, 1778, TNA CO 123/2, fol. 2r–v.

49. Fernández, *Colección de documentos*, 78.

50. "Declaración de Juan de Cerda Gorda," Cartago, December 27, 1778, ANCR, CO 713, fols. 5r–7v; "Declaración de Matheo Larson," Cartago, September 25, 1779, ANCR, CO 738, fols. 1r–3v.

51. Fernández, *Colección de documentos*, 79–84.

52. "Gastos hechos en el hermano del Almoral," Santiago de Guatemala, April 23, 1778, AGCA, A1 (6), legajo 3, expediente 28, fols. 1r–5v.

53. Arguedas, "Kingdom of Guatemala," 122–37.

54. Captain William Dalyrymple to John Dalling (governor of Jamaica), Fort Fernando de Omoa, October 20, 1779, TNA, CO 137/77, fol. 9r.

55. Captain John Polson to John Dalling (governor of Jamaica), St. John's Fort, April 30, 1780, TNA CO 137/77, fol. 158r.

56. Juan Fernández de Bobadilla, "Auto," Cartago, January 1, 1780, ANCR, CO-743, fol. 1r; Arguedas, "Kingdom of Guatemala," 143–44.

57. "Declaración de Manuel Dionisio Vanegas," Cartago, August 12, 1780, ANCR, CO 754, fol. 2r–3v; "Declaración de Juan Pablo Gómez, natural de la ciudad de Havana," Cartago, August 13, 1780, ANCR, CO 754, fols. 3v–4v.

58. "Declaración de Joseph," Cartago, October 12, 1780, ANCR, CO 757, fols. 1v–3r.

59. Arguedas, "Kingdom of Guatemala," 129–48.

60. "Declaración de Cayetano Ramírez," October 8, 1781, ANCR, CO 776, fols. 1r–2v.

61. "Declaración del Sargento Nicolás Antonio Rivas," Cartago, October 8, 1781, ANCR, CO 776, fols. 5v–7r.

62. Arguedas, "Kingdom of Guatemala," 149; "Real Orden," Madrid, December 15, 1789, AGCA, A1, Legajo 1532, fol. 551r.

63. Sorsby, "British Superintendency," 291–95; Arguedas, "Kingdom of Guatemala," 165.

64. Lord North to Archibald Campbell (governor of Jamaica), Whitehall, October 3, 1783, TNA, CO 137/83, fols. 131r–32v.

65. "Translation," Madrid, January 5, 1785, TNA, FO 72/3, fols. 377r–78v.

66. James Lawrie (superintendent of the Mosquito Shore) to Alfred Clarke (governor of Jamaica), Black River, December 22, 1784, TNA, CO 137/85, fols. 102r–4v; Josef Estacherria (president of Guatemala) to the commander of Black River, Guatemala, April 30, 1784, TNA, CO 137/85, fol. 95r.

67. "Declaración de Antonio Esguerra," Cartago, October 14, 1784, ANCR, CO 793, fols. 1r–2r.

68. "Declaración de Carlos Cubero," Cartago, October 15, 1784, ANCR, CO 793, fols. 3r–4v; "Otra de Joseph Menir," Cartago, October 15, 1784, ANCR, CO 793, fol. 4r; Otra de Juan de Dios Román," Cartago, October 15, 1784, ANCR, CO 793, fol. 5r.

69. Lord Sydney to Alfred Clarke (governor of Jamaica), Whitehall, July 31, 1786, TNA, CO 137/86, fol. 72r.

70. James Lawrie (superintendent of the Mosquito Shore) to Alfred Clarke (governor of Jamaica), Black River, October 14, 1786, TNA, CO 137/86, fols. 156r–58v.

71. Williams, "Living between Empires," 244–46.

72. Sorsby, "Spanish Colonization of the Mosquito Coast," 146.

73. Arguedas, "Kingdom of Guatemala," 174–75.

74. Williams, "Living between Empires," 255.

75. Williams, "Living between Empires," 258–64.

76. Robert Sproat to Brigadier General Richard Bassett, Belize, September 27, 1800, TNA, CO 137/105, fols. 19r–21v.

77. George II (king of the Mosquito) to Basil Keith (governor of Jamaica), Sandy Bay, April 12, 1777, TNA, CO 137/73, fols. 205r–6r.

78. Colville Cairns to James Lawrie, Tebuppy, May 10, 1777, TNA, CO 137/73, fols. 197r–202v.

79. Colville Briton (governor of the Mosquito) to John Dalling (governor of Jamaica), Tebuppy, December 18, 1777, TNA, CO 137/73, fol. 203r–v.

80. Deposition of John Hooker, Jamaica, May 4, 1778, TNA, CO 137/73, fol. 193r.

81. Sorsby, "British Superintendency," 231–35.

82. Jeremiah Terry to Manuel Antonio de Flores (governor of New Granada), Portobelo, June 7, 1778, TNA, CO 137/74, fol. 219r.

83. George II (king of the Mosquito), Duke Isaac, Colville Briton (governor of the Mosquito), Dilson (admiral of the Mosquito), General John Smee, and Admiral Frederick, Treaty Signed with Jeremiah Terry, St. Johns, September 5, 1778, TNA CO 123/2, fol. 2r–v.

84. Deposition of Joseph Wood by Colville Cairns, Mosquito Shore, October 27, 1778, TNA, CO 137/74, fol. 296r; Deposition of Jonathan Worth by Colville Cairns, Mosquito Shore, October 26, 1778, TNA, CO 137/74, fol. 204r; Deposition of Abraham Gill by Colville Cairns, Mosquito Shore, October 23, 1778, TNA, CO 137/74, fol. 213r.

85. Deposition of John Young by James Lawrie (superintendent of the Mosquito Shore), Black River, October 10, 1778, TNA, CO 137/74, fol. 210r; Deposition of Samuel Butler by Colville Cairns, St. John's, November 2, 1778, TNA CO 137/74, fol. 209r.

86. Colville Briton (governor of the Mosquito) to John Dalling (governor of Jamaica), St. John's, November 7, 1778, TNA, CO 137/74, fol. 221r–v; James Lawrie (superintendent of the Mosquito Shore) to John Dalling (governor of Jamaica), St. Johns, November 8, 1778, TNA, CO 137/74, fols. 225r–26v.

87. "Interrogations Put to Mr. Jeremiah Terry," March 15, 1779, Jamaica, TNA, CO 137/74, fols. 227r–32r.

88. John Dalling (governor of Jamaica) to Lord George Germain, Jamaica, April 1, 1779, TNA, CO 137/74, 196v.

89. Arguedas, "Kingdom of Guatemala," 121–27.

90. Extract of the secretary of state's letters, Whitehall, June 17, 1779, TNA, CO 137/78, fol. 231r.

91. Captain William Dalyrymple to John Dalling (governor of Jamaica), Fort Fernando de Omoa, October 20, 1779, TNA CO 137/77, fol. 9r.
92. Chiefs of the Mosquito Nation to John Dalling (governor of Jamaica), Black River, November 10, 1779, TNA, CO 137/77, fols. 26r–27r.
93. "Heads of a Talk with Some Indian Chiefs by Sir Alexander Leith," Pearl Key Lagoon, August 18, 1780, TNA, CO 137/78, fols. 293r–96v.
94. "The Journal of Captain John Polson," February 3 to April 29, 1780, TNA, CO 137/77, fols. 166r–70r.
95. Captain John Polson to John Dalling (governor of Jamaica), St. John's Fort, April 30, 1780, TNA, CO 137/77, fol. 158r.
96. Robert White to George Germaine (secretary of state for America), London, September 13, 1780, TNA, CO 137/78, fol. 148r–v.
97. Offen, "Mapping Amerindian Captivity in Colonial Mosquitia," 37.
98. "By Order of Lieutenant Richard Hoare, Commanding at Rattan," Roatan, June 16, 1780, TNA, CO 137/78, fol. 301r–v; Richard Hoare, "To Jeffery and All the Head Men, Also to All the Negros, on Black River, Now in Arms," Roatan, undated, TNA, CO 137/78, fols. 302v–3r.
99. Richard Hoare to General Thomas Lee and all the Mosquito chiefs, Roatan, undated, TNA, CO 137/78, fol. 304r–v.
100. Richard Hoare to John Dalling (governor of Jamaica), Black River, July 5, 1780, TNA, CO 137/78, fols. 298r–300v.
101. Robert White to George Germaine (secretary of state for America), June 1, 1780, TNA, CO 137/77, fol. 120r.
102. Offen, "Sambo and Tawira Miskitu," 347.
103. Colville Cairns, "Proceedings at a General Congress," Tebuppy, October 1, 1780, TNA, CO 137/79, fols. 165r–67r.
104. Juan Flores, Cartago, October 8, 1781, ANCR, CO-776, fol. 1r; "Declaración del Sarg. Antonio Rivas," Cartago, October 8, 1781, ANCR, CO 776, fol. 5r; "Otra de Juan de Dios Roman," Cartago, October 15, 1784, ANCR, CO 793, fol. 5r.
105. Archibald Campbell (governor of Jamaica) to Lord North, Jamaica, July 14, 1783, TNA, CO 137/83, fols. 120r–21v.
106. Lord North to Archibald Campbell (governor of Jamaica), Whitehall, October 3, 1783, TNA, CO 137/83, fols. 131r–32v.
107. Lord Sydney to Alfred Clarke (governor of Jamaica), Whitehall, July 31, 1786, TNA, CO 137/86, fol. 72r.
108. James Lawrie (superintendent of the Mosquito Shore) to Alfred Clarke (governor of Jamaica), Black River, October 14, 1786, TNA CO 137/86, fols. 156r–58v.
109. Ibarra, *Del arco y la flecha*, xxxii; Williams, "Living between Empires," 255.
110. Helms, "Miskito Slaving and Culture Contact," 191; Williams, "Living between Empires," 241.
111. Offen, "Sambo and Tawira Miskitu," 350–52.

Conclusion and Historiographical Considerations

1. Crooke, "Review of Tangweera."
2. Bell, *Tangweera*, 18.
3. Dolores Gámez, *Historia de la costa de Mosquitos*, 79; Salvatierra, *Contribución*, 425.

4. Floyd, *Anglo-Spanish Struggle for Mosquitia*, 67.
5. Helms, "Purchase Society"; Helms, "Miskito Slaving and Culture Contact."
6. Helms, "Cultural Ecology of a Colonial Tribe," 81.
7. García, "Ambivalencia de las representaciones coloniales," 674.
8. Gabbert, "'God Save the King'," 75–77.
9. Ibarra, *Del arco y la flecha*, 230.
10. Ibarra, *Del arco y la flecha*, 215.
11. Bell, *Tangweera*, 39.
12. Offen, "Mapping Amerindian Captivity in Colonial Mosquitia," 45.
13. Ayón, *Historia de Nicaragua*, 191.
14. Dolores Gámez, *Historia de la costa de Mosquitos*, 70.
15. Floyd, *Anglo-Spanish Struggle for Mosquitia*, 62.
16. Naylor, *Penny Ante Imperialism*, 31.
17. Helms, "Cultural Ecology of a Colonial Tribe," 76–78.
18. Olien, "Miskito Kings and the Line of Succession," 198–241.
19. Offen, "Creating Mosquitia," 254–82.
20. Helms, "Purchase Society," 329.
21. Ayón, *Historia de Nicaragua*, 194.
22. Dolores Gámez, *Historia de la costa de Mosquitos*, 82.
23. Salvatierra, *Contribución*, 422.
24. Floyd, *Anglo-Spanish Struggle for Mosquitia*, 22.
25. Sorsby, "British Superintendency of the Mosquito Shore," 22.
26. Olien, "Miskito Kings and the Line of Succession," 205.
27. Potthast-Jutkeit, "Centroamérica y el contrabando," 508.
28. Offen, "Mapping Amerindian Captivity in Colonial Mosquitia."
29. Naylor, *Penny Ante Imperialism*, 30.
30. Ibarra, *Del arco y la flecha*, 214.
31. Dolores Gámez, *Historia de la costa de Mosquitos*, 82–84.
32. Salvatierra, *Contribución a la historia de Centroamérica*, 422, 426.
33. Chacón de Umaña, *Don Diego de la Haya Fernández*, 95–98.
34. Floyd, *Anglo-Spanish Struggle for Mosquitia*, 68.
35. Sorsby, "British Superintendency of the Mosquito Shore," 13, 183, 244.
36. Potthast-Jutkeit, "Centroamérica y el contrabando," 503.
37. Ibarra, *Del arco y la flecha*, xxxii.
38. Williams, "Living between Empires," 243.
39. Helms, "Cultural Ecology of a Colonial Tribe," 81–82.
40. Helms, "Miskito Slaving and Culture Contact," 191.
41. Offen, "Sambo and Tawira Miskitu."
42. Williams, "Living between Empires," 249; Dziennik, "Miskitu, Military Labour, and the San Juan Expedition," 162.
43. Mendiola, "El Reino Mosquito," 101–29; Mendiola, "Founding and Fracturing of the Mosquito Confederation."
44. Offen, "Sambo and Tawira Miskitu," 350–52.
45. Williams, "Living between Empires," 225.
46. Ibarra, *Del arco y la flecha*, 230.
47. Gabbert, "'God Save the King'," 79–80.

Epilogue

1. Juan Manuel de Cañas, Copia para el Ayuntamiento de Justicia y Regimiento de la Ciudad de Cartago, San José, October 31, 1819, ANCR MU 484, fols. 34r–35r.
2. Secretaría de la Asamblea, San José, May 24, 1829, ANCR AL 1428, fol. 1r–v.
3. Santiago Estanislau Bell (Mosquito Sheriff) to Costa Rica, Bluefields, August 17, 1844, ANCR AL 6342, fol. 1r.
4. Rivera and D González, "Reflexiones sobre las áreas protegidas."
5. Rupert Know et al., "Resistencia Miskitu."
6. Scott, *Art of Not Being Governed*, 11.
7. Cooper, *Colonialism in Question*; Immerwahr, *How to Hide an Empire*.
8. Villalobos, *Casa en Tierra Ajena*.
9. Hale, *Resistance and Contradiction*.

BIBLIOGRAPHY

List of Archives Consulted

Archivo General de Centro America (AGCA), Guatemala City, Guatemala
Archivo General de Indias (AGI), Seville, Spain
Archivo Nacional de Costa Rica (ANCR), San José, Costa Rica
The National Archives (TNA), London, England

Published Primary Sources

Exquemelin, A. O. *The Buccaneers of America: A True Account of the Most Remarkable Assaults Committed of Late Years upon the Coasts of the West Indies by the Buccaneers of Jamaica and Tortuga.* Translated by H. Powell. Cambridge: Cambridge University Press, 2010.
Fernández, León, ed. *Colección de documentos para la historia de Costa-Rica.* San José Costa Rica: Imprenta Nacional, 1881.
Hurtado y Plaza, Blas. *Memorial de mi vida.* Edited by Carlos Molina Argüello. Nicaragua: Banco de América, 1977.
Incer Barquero, Jaime. *Nicaragua, viajes, rutas y encuentros, 1502–1838: Historia de las exploraciones y descubrimientos, antes de ser Estado independiente, con observaciones sobre su geografía, etnia y naturaleza.* San José, Costa Rica: Libro Libre, 1990.
M. W. "A Familiar Description of the Mosqueto Kingdom in America, with a Relation of the Ftrange Cuftoms, Religion, Wars, Ect of Thofe Heathenifh People." In *A Collection of Voyages and Travels*, edited by Awnsham Churchill, vol. 6, 285–98. London, 1732.
Peralta, Manuel M. de, ed. *Costa Rica y costa de Mosquitos: Documentos para la historia de la jurisdicción territorial de Costa Rica y Colombia.* Paris: impr. de Lahure, 1898.
Sloane, Hans. *A Voyage to the Islands Madera, Barbados, Nieves, St. Christophers and Jamaica.* London, 1725.
Solorzano, Flor de Oro, and Germán Romero Vargas. "Declaración de Carlos Casarola negro esclavo bozal 1737." *Wani revista del Caribe Nicaragüense*, no. 10 (1991): 84–90.
Uring, Nathaniel. *The Voyages and Travels of Captain Nathaniel Uring.* Edited by Alfred Charles Dewar. London: Cassell, 1928.

Secondary Sources

Arguedas, Aaron. "The Kingdom of Guatemala: Under the Military Reform, 1755–1808." PhD diss., Texas Christian University, 2006.

Ayón, Tomás. *Historia de Nicaragua desde los tiempos más remotos hasta el año de 1852.* Granada, Nicaragua: Tipografía de El Centro-americano, 1882.

Bell, Charles Napier. *Tangweera: Life and Adventures among Gentle Savages.* Austin: University of Texas Press, 1989.

Burbank, Jane, and Frederick Cooper. *Empires in World History: Power and the Politics of Difference.* Princeton, N.J.: Princeton University Press, 2010.

Chacón de Umaña, Luz Alba. *Don Diego de la Haya Fernández.* San José: Editorial Costa Rica, 1968.

Clendinnen, Inga. *Ambivalent Conquests: Maya and Spaniard in Yucatan, 1517–1570.* Cambridge: Cambridge University Press, 1987.

Cooper, Frederick. *Colonialism in Question: Theory, Knowledge, History.* Berkeley: University of California Press, 2005.

Crooke, W. "Review of Tangweera: Life and Adventures Among Gentle Savages." *Journal of the Anthropological Institute of Great Britain and Ireland* 29, no. 3 (1899): 339–40.

Dawson, Frank Griffith. "William Pitt's Settlement at Black River on the Mosquito Shore: A Challenge to Spain in Central America, 1732–87." *Hispanic American Historical Review* 63, no. 4 (1983): 677–706.

Dennis, Philip A., and Michael D. Olien. "Kingship among the Miskito." *American Ethnologist* 11, no. 4 (November 1984): 718–37.

Dolores Gámez, José. *Historia de la costa de Mosquitos (hasta 1894) en relación con la conquista española, los piratas y corsarios en las costas centro-americanas, los avances y protecorado del gobierno inglés en la misma costa y la famosa cuestión inglesa con Nicaragua, Honduras y El Salvador.* Managua, Nicaragua: Talleres Nacionales, 1915.

Dziennik, Matthew P. "The Miskitu, Military Labour, and the San Juan Expedition of 1780." *Historical Journal* 61, no. 1 (2018): 155–79.

Floyd, Troy S. *The Anglo-Spanish Struggle for Mosquitia.* Albuquerque: University of New Mexico Press, 1967.

Fonseca, Elizabeth C., Ana Patricia Alvarenga Venutolo, and Juan Carlos Solórzano. *Costa Rica en el siglo XVIII.* San José: Editorial de la Universidad de Costa Rica, 2001.

Gabbert, Wolfgang. "'God Save the King of the Mosquito Nation!' Indigenous Leaders on the Fringe of the Spanish Empire." *Ethnohistory* 63, no. 1 (January 2016): 71–93.

García, Claudia. "Ambivalencia de las representaciones coloniales: Líderes Indios y Zambos de la costa de Mosquitos a fines del Siglo XVIII." *Revista de Indias* 67, no. 241 (2007): 673–94.

Gibson, Charles. *The Aztecs under Spanish Rule: A History of the Indians of the Valley of Mexico, 1519–1810.* Stanford, Calif.: Stanford University Press, 1964.

Hale, Charles R. *Resistance and Contradiction: Miskitu Indians and the Nicaraguan State, 1894–1987.* Stanford, Calif: Stanford University Press, 1994.

Hall, Carolyn, and Héctor Pérez Brignoli. *Historical Atlas of Central America.* Norman: University of Oklahoma Press, 2003.

Hämäläinen, Pekka. *The Comanche Empire.* New Haven: Yale University Press, 2008.

———. "The Shapes of Power: Indians, Europeans, and North American Worlds from the Seventeenth to the Nineteenth Century." In *Early American Studies: Contested Spaces of Early America*, edited by Juliana Barr and Edward Countryman, 31–68. Philadelphia: University of Pennsylvania Press, 2014.

Hanna, Mark G. *Pirate Nests and the Rise of the British Empire, 1570–1740*. Chapel Hill: University of North Carolina Press, 2015.

Hearn, Jonathan. *Theorizing Power*. New York: Palgrave Macmillan, 2012.

Helms, Mary W. "The Cultural Ecology of a Colonial Tribe." *Ethnology* 8, no. 1 (January 1969): 76–84.

———. *Middle America: A Culture History of Heartland and Frontiers*. Englewood Cliffs, N.J.: Prentice-Hall, 1975.

———. "Miskito Slaving and Culture Contact: Ethnicity and Opportunity in an Expanding Population." *Journal of Anthropological Research* 39, no. 2 (July 1983): 179–97.

———. "Of Kings and Contexts: Ethnohistorical Interpretations of Miskito Political Structure and Function," *American Ethnologist* 13, no. 3 (August 1986): 506–23.

———. "The Purchase Society: Adaptation to Economic Frontiers." *Anthropological Quarterly* 42, no. 4 (October 1969): 325–42.

Ibarra, Eugenia. *Del arco y la flecha a las armas de fuego: Los indios mosquitos y la historia centroamericana 1633–1786*. San José, Costa Rica: Editorial UCR, 2011.

Immerwahr, Daniel. *How to Hide an Empire: A History of the Greater United States*. New York: Farrar, Straus and Giroux, 2019.

Kellogg, Susan. *Weaving the Past: A History of Latin America's Indigenous Women from the Prehispanic Period to the Present*. New York: Oxford University Press, 2005.

Know, Rupert, Lucas Valderas, Esteban Madrigal, Eduardo Guerrero, and Francisca Stuardo. "Resistencia Miskitu: Una lucha por el territorio y la vida." Report, El Centro por la Justicia y el Derecho Internacional, San José, Costa Rica, 2019.

Kupperman, Karen Ordahl. "Errand to the Indies: Puritan Colonization from Providence Island through the Western Design." *William and Mary Quarterly* 45, no. 1 (1988): 70–99.

Lockhart, James. *The Nahuas after the Conquest: A Social and Cultural History of the Indians of Central Mexico, Sixteenth through Eighteenth Centuries*. Stanford, Calif.: Stanford University Press, 1992.

Lovell, W. George. *Strange Lands and Different Peoples: Spaniards and Indians in Colonial Guatemala*. Norman: University of Oklahoma Press, 2013.

Matthew, Laura E. *Memories of Conquest: Becoming Mexicano in Colonial Guatemala*. Chapel Hill: University of North Carolina Press, 2012.

Mendiola, Daniel. "Constructing Imperial Spaces: The Spanish and Mosquito Conquests of Eighteenth-century Central America." PhD diss., University of Houston, 2017.

———. "El Reino Mosquito: Nuevos descubrimientos desde el Archivo Nacional de Costa Rica, 1687–1791." *Revista del Archivo Nacional* 82, no. 1–12 (November 2018): 101–29.

———. "The Founding and Fracturing of the Mosquito Confederation: Zambos, Tawiras, and New Archival Evidence, 1711–1791." *Hispanic American Historical Review* 99, no. 4 (November 2019): 619–47.

———. "The Rise of the Mosquito Kingdom in Central America's Caribbean Borderlands: Sources, Questions, and Enduring Myths." *History Compass* 16, no. 1 (2018): 1–10.

Murga, Gustavo Palma. "Between Fidelity and Pragmatism: Guatemala's Commercial Elite Responds to Bourbon Reforms on Trade and Contraband." In *Politics, Economy, and Society in Bourbon Central America, 1759–1821*, edited by Jordana Dym and Christophe Belaubre, 101–27. Boulder: University Press of Colorado, 2007.

Naylor, Robert A. *Penny Ante Imperialism: The Mosquito Shore and the Bay of Honduras, 1600–1914: A Case Study in British Informal Empire*. Rutherford, N.J.: Fairleigh Dickinson University Press, 1989.

Offen, Karl. "British Logwood Extraction from the Mosquitia: The Origin of a Myth." *Hispanic American Historical Review* 80, no. 1 (February 2000): 113–36.

———. "Creating Mosquitia: Mapping Amerindian Spatial Practices in Eastern Central America, 1629–1779." *Journal of Historical Geography* 33, no. 2 (April 2007): 254–82.

———. "Mapping Amerindian Captivity in Colonial Mosquitia." *Journal of Latin American Geography* 14, no. 3 (2015): 35–65.

———. "The Sambo and Tawira Miskitu: The Colonial Origins and Geography of Intra-Miskitu Differentiation in Eastern Nicaragua and Honduras." *Ethnohistory* 49, no. 2 (April 2002): 319–72.

Olien, Michael D. "General, Governor, and Admiral: Three Miskito Lines of Succession." *Ethnohistory* 45, no. 2 (April 1998): 277–318.

———. "The Miskito Kings and the Line of Succession." *Journal of Anthropological Research* 39, no. 2 (July 1983): 198–241.

Pérez Brignoli, Héctor. *A Brief History of Central America*. Berkeley: University of California Press, 1989.

Pestana, Carla Gardina. "Early English Jamaica without Pirates." *William and Mary Quarterly* 71, no. 3 (2014): 321–60.

Potthast-Jutkeit, Barbara. "Centroamérica y el contrabando por la costa de Mosquitos en el siglo XVIII." *Mesoamérica* 36 (December 1998): 499–516.

Quezada, Sergio. *Maya Lords and Lordship: The Formation of Colonial Society in Yucatán, 1350–1600*. Norman: University of Oklahoma Press, 2014.

Restall, Matthew. *Maya Conquistador*. Boston: Beacon Press, 1998.

———. *When Montezuma Met Cortés: The True Story of the Meeting That Changed History*. New York: Harpers Collins Press, 2018.

Rivera, Brooklyn, and Donaldo Allen González. "Reflexiones sobre las áreas protegidas, la gobernanza, la territorialidad y el uso de la geografía y cartografía para los Miskitu y otros pueblos indígenas en América Central." Roundtable at Conference of Latin American Geography. San José, Costa Rica, 2018.

Romero Vargas, Germán. *Historia de la Costa Atlántica*. Managua: CIDCA-UCa, 1996.

———. *Las sociedades del Atlántico de Nicaragua en los siglos XVII y XVIII*. Colección cultural Banco Nicaragüense. Serie histórica. Managua: Fondo de Promoción Cultural-Banic, 1995.

Salvatierra, Sofonías. *Contribución a la historia de Centroamérica*. Managua: Tip. Progreso, 1939.

Scott, Heidi V. *Contested Territory: Mapping Peru in the Sixteenth and Seventeenth Centuries*. Notre Dame, Ind.: University of Notre Dame Press, 2009.

Scott, James C. *The Art of Not Being Governed: An Anarchist History of Upland Southeast Asia*. New Haven: Yale University Press, 2009.

Segovia Rivera, Mauricio Alejandro. "Los Mosquitos y La Provincia de Costa Rica:

Tres propuestas de paz, 1711–1726." Master's thesis, Centro de Investigaciones y Estudios Superiores en Antropología Social (CIESAS), 2018.

Sorsby, William Shuman. "The British Superintendency of the Mosquito Shore: 1749–1787." PhD diss., University of London, 1969.

———. "Spanish Colonization of the Mosquito Coast, 1787–1800." *Revista de Historia de América*, no. 73/74 (1972): 145–53.

Thornton, John K. "The Zambos and the Transformation of the Miskitu Kingdom, 1636–1740." *Hispanic American Historical Review* 97, no. 1 (February 2017): 1–28.

Villalobos, Ivannia, dir. *Casa en Tierra Ajena*. Consejo Nacional de Rectores, 2017.

Warren, James Francis. *Iranun and Balangingi: Globalization, Maritime Raiding, and the Birth of Ethnicity*. Singapore: Singapore University Press, 2002.

Williams, Caroline A. "Living between Empires: Diplomacy and Politics in the Late Eighteenth-Century Mosquitia." *Americas* 70, no. 2 (2013): 237–68.

Woodward, Ralph Lee. *Central America, a Nation Divided*. New York: Oxford University Press, 1976.

INDEX

Almar/Alomar/Almorar. *See* Dilson I (Admiral)
Andrade, Antonio, 34
Andres, 30–31
Anglo-Spanish Struggle for Mosquitia, The (Floyd), 15–16, 173, 175
Anglo-Spanish War (1779–1783), 23, 151–52, 157–58, 164–68. *See also* Spanish-English relations
anti-piracy campaign of Mosquito Confederation, 40, 50, 53–56, 65. *See also* piracy
Antonio, 61, 96
archival sources: archival sources on Mosquito Confederation, 15–20; silences in, 19–21
Art of Not Being Governed, The (Scott), 19–20
assassination plot (Tempest), 123–24, 126
Audiencia of Guatemala, 11
Ayón, Tomás, 15, 174–75, 177

Baraona, Antonio de Soto y, 67
Bell, Charles Napier, 171–74
Black River settlement: English claims and, 91–93, 103, 113–14, 118, 120; English defensive position at, 136, 165–66, 168; founding of, 88–89; slavery in, 14, 166, 168; Spanish-English trade agreements and, 103–4, 112; Spanish possession of, 160–61; Treaty of Aix-en-Chappelle and, 110–11. *See also* Mosquito Shore Intendency
Bluefields settlement, 134–35
Boaco attack, 97, 103, 111
Bonilla, Alferez, 67
Bonilla, Diego de, 58

Briones y Palacios, José Antonio Lacayo, 43
"British Superintendency of the Mosquito Shore" (Sorsby), 15–16, 178, 180
Briton, Colville (Governor): 1791 negotiation and, 182; Cartagena delegation of, 160; hosting of Spanish delegation, 148, 162; personal negotiations and killing of, 154, 160–61; regulation of slave trade and, 143, 146–47; rise of, 128; Terry treaty and proclamations of loyalty by, 149–51, 163
Briton, John (Governor), 75–77, 78–79, 98, 203n38
Briton, Timothy (Governor), 123–24, 125, 126–28
Briton, William (Governor), 97–98, 123
Briton letter (1773), 128
Burbank, Jane, 8

cacao, 106, 116. *See also* Mosquito-Matina relations; raiding, Mosquito
Cairns, Colville, 127, 167
captive-taking practices of the Mosquito Confederation: Amerindians and, 34, 50, 96; as ecological adaptation, 174, 178; kidnapping of Costa Rican governor and, 99–100; Matina raids and, 39, 65–66, 81, 84, 99, 101–2, 107, 109; negotiation and ransom in, 39–41, 43, 65–66, 69–70, 81; prevalence of, 28–29, 38, 48, 56, 59, 84, 97; slave trade restrictions and, 147; treatment of captives in, 44, 86, 105, 108, 145, 153, 159. *See also* diplomatic practices of the Mosquito Confederation; Mosquito-Matina relations

Caribbean borderlands of Central America: English settlers and, 13–14, 37, 142; power contests in, 4, 21, 26, 32–33, 72, 186–87; terrain challenges of, 32; Treaty of Madrid and, 36, 38. *See also* Black River settlement; Matina Valley, Costa Rica; Mosquito Shore Intendency

Cartago, Costa Rica, 100–101, 108–9, 125. *See also* Mosquito-Spanish relations

"Cession of the Mosquito Kingdom to Great Britain," 90

Chaverria, Joseph de, 39, 41

colonization efforts, English, 12–13, 36, 39, 113. *See also* Black River settlement; English conquest of Central America; Mosquito Shore Intendency; Providence Island

colonization efforts, Spanish, 12, 32. *See also* Spanish conquest of Central America

conquest, 3, 8–9, 14, 19–24, 185–87. *See also* English conquest of Central America; Mosquito conquest of Central America; Spanish conquest of Central America

constant warfare thesis, 177–80. *See also* theses of Mosquito decline

contraband trade: English, 82, 92, 106, 216n34; Mosquito-Spanish trade as, 42, 53, 63, 69–70, 104–7, 130–32, 183

Contribución a la historia de centroamérica (Salvatierra), 15

Cooper, Frederick, 8

Corella, Francisco, 40, 43–44, 46, 52–54, 57, 60–62

Corrin, Henry, 134

Costa Rica, 18, 21, 23, 25–25, 26. *See also* Cartago, Costa Rica; Matina Valley, Costa Rica; Mosquito-Matina relations; Mosquito-Spanish relations

council of Mosquito Confederation: centralization of, 4, 6–7, 21–23, 44–45, 76; empire-like program of, 46–47, 71, 78; friction in, 23, 75, 149–51, 170; leadership structure and, 28; political dominance claims and, 154–55. *See also* diplomatic practices of the Mosquito Confederation; fleet system of the Mosquito Confederation; internal conflict within the Mosquito Confederation; Mosquito Confederation; Mosquito-English relations; Mosquito-Spanish relations; *individual kings, governors, generals, and admirals*

"Creating Mosquitia" (Offen), 175

De la Haya Fernández, Diego, 52–53, 58–63, 66–70

Del arco y la flecha a las armas de fuego (Ibarra), 17, 173–74

De Nava, Joseph Joachin, 129–32

Dennis, Phillip, 16, 181

dependency thesis, 174–76. *See also* theses of Mosquito decline

Diez Navarro, Luis, 105–6, 125, 129, 131, 166

Dilly (Admiral), 79. *See also* Dilson I (Admiral)

Dilson conspiracy, 135–37

Dilson I (Admiral): alleged conspiracy of, 135–38; as Almar/Alomar/Almorar, 107–9, 208n16, 208n23, 210n50; Costa Rica incursions of, 100–102; as Dilly, 79; rise of, 98; Tempest plot and, 123–27; treaty negotiations of, 122, 130–32, 140

Dilson II (Admiral): Cartagena delegation of, 160; Cartago visit of, 151, 157, 162; Costa Rica delegation of, 148–49, 155–56, 162; council conflict and, 145–46; Fort Inmaculada attack and, 150–51; invasion of Matina, 152–53; personal negotiations and killing of, 154–55, 160–61; rise of, 127–28; Terry treaty and, 149–50

Dios Iglesias, Juan de, 108

diplomatic practices of the Mosquito Confederation, 27, 35–36, 179–80, 181–84. *See also* Mosquito-English relations; Mosquito-Matina relations; Mosquito-Spanish relations

Dolores Gámez, José, 15, 172, 174–75, 177, 179–80

Doyley, Edward, 36

Dutch, 100, 107

Edward (King), 79, 97

English conquest of Central America: evacuation of Mosquito Shore, 182–84; influence of Mosquito on, 186; overview of, 12–15; protection alliances and, 36–37; role of Black River in, 89; settlements and role of Mosquito in, 74; settler colonialism and, 14; Spanish territorial disputes and, 82; Treaty of Madrid and, 36. *See also* Mosquito-English relations; Mosquito Shore Intendency; Spanish-English relations

Esguerra, Joseph Antonio, 153, 159

ethnic rivalry thesis, 181–84. *See also* theses of Mosquito decline

ethnic rivalry within the Mosquito Confederation, 71, 76, 124, 125–27, 181–84. *See also* internal conflict within the Mosquito Confederation

factional alliances within the Mosquito Confederation, 7. *See also* council of Mosquito Confederation
Fernández de Pastora, Francisco, 99, 106–7
Fernández y Heredia, Alonso, 103–5, 112
firearms thesis, 172–74, 183. *See also* theses of Mosquito decline
fleet system of the Mosquito Confederation: 1719 expedition of, 38, 48–49, 59; 1720 expedition of, 49–50, 59; 1721–1722 expeditions of, 54–56, 60–62; 1723 expedition of, 57–58; 1724–1726 expeditions of, 64–66, 68–70; attack on Honduras by, 45, 64, 67; effects of smallpox on, 22, 73, 75, 78; growth of, 48; with Hodgson, 79–80, 90; joint Mosquito-English expeditions of, 80–81, 101, 151; Mosquito civil war and, 185; northern expeditions of, 50; piracy threats to, 40, 54, 56; power and, 26, 45, 72, 93, 96; territorial expansion and, 10, 21, 26–28, 30; Trujillo peace negotiations and, 78. *See also* captive-taking practices of the Mosquito Confederation; diplomatic practices of the Mosquito Confederation; Mosquito-English relations; Mosquito-Matina relations; Mosquito-Spanish relations
Floyd, Troy, 15, 173, 175, 178, 180
Fort Inmaculada Concepción, 90, 151–52, 157, 165
Fort San Fernando de Omoa, 151, 157
French pirates, 35, 50, 54–55, 60, 65
fugitives, 73, 78, 83, 86–87. *See also* captive-taking practices of the Mosquito Confederation

Gabbert, Wolfgang, 173, 183
Galbraith (Captain), 116
García, Claudia, 173
Garcia, Manuel, 75, 84
Garret y Arlovi, Benito, 42–43
Gemmir y Lleonhart, Juan, 85, 105
gender and archival silences, 20–21
geopolitical practices of the Mosquito Confederation: Caribbean borderlands and, 3–4, 25, 72, 118–19, 146, 185; central council and, 45, 127; as empire-like, 9, 21–22, 31, 97; Indigenous alliances and, 28; raiding and, 29–30, 177; restrictions on slave trade and, 147; Spanish America and, 26–27, 77, 93, 118–19, 131. *See also* diplomatic practices of the Mosquito Confederation; fleet system of the Mosquito Confederation; Mosquito-English relations; Mosquito-Matina relations; Mosquito-Spanish relations
George I (King), 97, 101, 123–24, 126–28
George II (King): attempts at political dominance, 154–55; council conflicts and, 148, 150; Fort Inmaculada attack and, 151, 157; Hodgson and, 141–43; manipulation of Dilson II invasion, 153; Matina delegation and, 157; rise of, 128; slave-raiding and, 145–47; Terry and, 149–50, 163
Gomez, Micaela, 28, 52
González, Donald Allen, 186
Granada negotiations, 154
Granada y Balbín, Lorenzo Antonio de, 41–42
Guadalupe, Christobal de, 1, 20, 58–59
gunboat diplomacy. *See* diplomatic practices of the Mosquito Confederation; fleet system of the Mosquito Confederation; geopolitical practices of the Mosquito Confederation; Mosquito-Matina relations
Guthierrez, Joseph, 42
Gutierrez, Thomasa/Tomasa, 96, 106

Haldane, George, 117
Hämäläinen, Pekka, 9
Handyside (General), 97, 123
Hannibal (Governor): 1724 Matina invasion and, 64–66; as Aníbel, 7; conflicting imperial alliances and, 87–88; demand for Spanish title, 55, 61; ethnic rivalry and, 182; leadership changes and, 75–76; Matina delegations, 40, 49–50, 54–56, 59–61, 69–71; M. W. account and, 28; Spanish delegation to, 61–62; Talamanca raid of, 55–56
Helms, Mary, 16, 173, 175, 176, 181, 182
Historia de la Costa de Mosquitos (Gámez), 15
Historia de Nicaragua (Ayón), 15
Hoare, Richard, 166
Hobby, Charles (General), 77, 78, 97
Hodgson, Robert: influence over Mosquito, 106, 116–17; Mosquito complaints about, 127–28; Mosquito-English alliance and, 78–79, 89–92; Mosquito Shore claims and, 110–12, 114; as Mosquito Shore superintendent, 92–93, 104, 111, 115–18; removal of, 161–62; scrutiny of, 114–18; trade proposals and, 112–13
Hodgson, Robert, Jr., 127–28, 131, 135–43, 217n34
Hodgson report on Dilson conspiracy, 136
Honduras: control of Mosquito Shore and, 110, 120; modern-day, 186; Mosquito peace

234　INDEX

Honduras (*continued*)
　treaties and, 78, 97; Mosquito slave raiding and, 33–34; Mosquito threat and, 50–52, 67, 82, 96, 158. *See also* Fort San Fernando de Omoa; Mosquito-Spanish relations

Ibarra, Eugenia, 17, 173–74, 179, 180, 183
imperialism, concept of, 8–9, 48
imperial system of the Mosquito Confederation: anti-piracy campaign and, 53–55; humanization of, 26–27; "imperialism" and, 8–9; Indigenous power relations and, 2; "influence" and "power" of, 10; influence on European imperial projects and, 4, 170; Jeremy I and, 27; Mosquito civil war and, 155, 170, 185; practices of, 5, 30, 45–48, 71–72; role of protection agreements in, 53–54; tribute demands and, 5. *See also* council of Mosquito Confederation; fleet system of the Mosquito Confederation; Matina truce; *individual Mosquito relations headings*
informants: gender and, 52, 106; sources and, 20–21; use of, 21, 28, 41, 47, 58
internal conflict within the Mosquito Confederation: breakdown of alliances and, 144–46, 153–54, 159–61; captive testimonies and, 145; dissent and, 122–23, 125–27; effects of, 23; foreign policy and, 153; leadership changes and, 128; negotiations and, 121–27, 134–35, 152–54, 159–60. *See also* assassination plot (Tempest); Dilson conspiracy; theses of Mosquito decline
Isaac (Duke), 145–46, 153, 159

Jamaica: English imperialism and, 13–14, 30, 36–38; Mosquito alliance and, 27; slave revolts and, 37, 87; Treaty of Madrid and, 113. *See also* English conquest of Central America; Mosquito-English relations; Trelawny, Edward
Jeremy I (King), 25–28, 30–31, 37–38, 40, 45, 182
Jeremy II (King): alliance-making of, 40, 45, 52–53, 59, 66, 70–71; as "Bernabé," 7; death of, 73, 75; expeditions of, 48–49; Jamaica and, 50; rise of, 30–32; runaway agreement and, 87
Jicaques, 28
Jimenez, Francisco, 39
Jones, Richard, 113, 123–24, 132–38
Jones report on Dilson conspiracy, 136–37

Kellogg, Susan, 20
kidnapping. *See* captive-taking practices of the Mosquito Confederation
kidnapping of Costa Rican governor by Mosquitos, 99–100
Knowles, Charles, 115–16

Lawes, Nicolas, 87
Lawrie, James, 113, 161, 163, 168
"Living between Empires" (Williams), 17
logwood, 88
London delegation (Mosquito), 141–42, 143
López, Melchor, 33

manpower and Mosquito imperial system, 2–4, 21, 31, 81, 96, 172–73. *See also* fleet system of the Mosquito Confederation; imperial system of the Mosquito Confederation
Margil de Jesús, Antonio, 33–34
Maria, 39
Marselo, Pedro, 108
Matias de Baraona, Juan, 84
Matina massacre, 100, 107, 117
Matina-Mosquito relations. *See* Mosquito-Matina relations
Matina truce, 49–53, 56–60, 63
Matina Valley, Costa Rica: as allied port, 25; fortifications and, 85–86; Fort San Fernando de Matina, 85; Mosquito occupation of, 64–65, 68–70; Mosquito territory and, 10; Spanish forces in, 30. *See also* Mosquito-Matina relations; Mosquito-Spanish relations
"Miskitu" (term), 5. *See also* Mosquito Confederation
missions, Spanish, 33–34, 43, 84. *See also* Fort Inmaculada Concepción; Fort San Fernando de Omoa
monopoly on violence, 54. *See also* imperial system of the Mosquito Confederation
Morales, Agustina, 96, 106
Mosquito civil war: background and context of, 23, 144, 146; events of, 154–55, 161, 169–70; scholarly treatment of, 181–84. *See also* ethnic rivalry within the Mosquito Confederation; internal conflict within the Mosquito Confederation; theses of Mosquito decline
Mosquito Coast/Shore: end of Anglo-Spanish War and, 158; English colonization and, 14,

89, 91–92; English evacuation of, 153, 159–60; European claims to, 102–5, 110–14, 168; Honduras and, 110; Mosquito raiding and, 111; Spanish control of, 216n34; Treaty of Madrid and, 89. *See also* Mosquito Shore Intendency

Mosquito Confederation: "admiral" position in, 98; alliance-making of, 45; Anglo-Spanish War and, 151–52, 157–58; anti-piracy campaign of, 40, 50, 53–56, 65; assumption about power and decline of, 4; as "enemies" of Spain, 52, 63, 83; English colonization efforts and, 12–13; English dependence on, 74; English subjecthood and, 38; ethnic features of, 31; ethnic rivalry and, 71, 76, 181–82; firearms and, 93; geography of territory of, 9–10; geopolitics of 1750s and 1760s, 118–19, 121; humanization of, 26; "imperialism" and, 8–9; independence of, 170; internal structure of, 28; killing of Colville Briton, 154; lack of ethnic tensions in, 169; leadership changes within, 75–76, 78–79, 97–98; mid-1740s raids of, 96–97; military alliances of, 6–7; modern-day concerns of, 186–87; negotiation privileges in, 40; as nonstate peoples, 20; organization of, 2, 6–7, 30, 31, 44–45, 79; origins of power of, 25–26; post-civil war, 185–87; raid and trade hypothesis about, 93–94; regulation of slave trade, 143, 147–48; role in Caribbean borderlands, 21; scholarship on, 15–19, 171–72; smallpox and, 75, 93; subsistence practices and foreign trade of, 128; Tebuppy meeting and, 148; Tempest assassination plot and, 123–24; terminology and, 4–5, 7–9; unity of, 71–72, 125–26, 127–28. *See also* diplomatic practices of the Mosquito Confederation; fleet system of the Mosquito Confederation; geopolitical practices of the Mosquito Confederation; imperial system of the Mosquito Confederation; internal conflict within the Mosquito Confederation; Mosquito civil war; piracy; theses of Mosquito decline

Mosquito conquest of Central America: contours of, 4–10; expansion and, 2–3, 5, 21; implications of, 96, 186. *See also* fleet system of the Mosquito Confederation; geopolitical practices of the Mosquito Confederation; imperial system of the Mosquito Confederation; slave raiding, Mosquito; *individual Mosquito relations headings*

Mosquito-English relations: alliance commitments in, 50, 77; Black River and, 88–89; Cartago attack and, 101, 108–9; colonization efforts and, 37, 38–39, 72, 74, 89–90, 91–92, 96; context of Mosquito civil war and, 146; control of Mosquito raiding and peacemaking in, 111–12, 118; debt coercion in, 122, 130, 147; Dilson II Costa Rica delegation and, 148–49, 155–56, 162; as economically and politically beneficial, 87, 94; English internal tensions and, 137–38; enslaved labor in, 166; Fort Inmaculada attack and, 151–52, 165; Hodgson treaty and, 78–79; importance of wartime alliances in, 164–67; interdependence and, 144; joint expeditions and, 22–23, 80–81, 84, 85–86, 90, 92, 152; Mosquito civil unrest and, 76–77, 126–27, 134–36; Mosquito London delegation and, 141–42, 143; Mosquito Shore evacuation and, 153–54, 168–69; Mosquito-Spanish alliance and, 47, 56–57, 87–88, 121, 126–27, 133–34, 139, 143–44; Mosquito unrest and, 167; reports on Mosquito threats and, 136–39; return of Matina cacao and, 116; scrutiny of Hodgson and, 115–18; scrutiny of Hodgson Jr. and, 141–42; slave trade and, 142–43, 147; Spanish coast guard incident and, 139–41; status of Mosquito in, 103, 113; Tebuppy meeting and, 148; Tempest assassination plot and, 123–24; territorial claims and, 38–39; Terry treaty and, 150, 162–64; War of Jenkins' Ear and, 89–91

Mosquito-European relations. *See* Mosquito-English relations; Mosquito-Matina relations; Mosquito-Spanish relations

Mosquito-Honduras relations, 78, 82–84

Mosquito Kingdom. *See* Mosquito Confederation

Mosquito-Matina relations: 1711 and 1713 treaty negotiations and, 39–44, 51, 179; 1724 occupation and, 64–65, 68–69, 71–72, 180; 1740 raid and, 84; 1750s raids and, 98–100, 106–7, 118–19; 1760s raids and, 100–102, 108; 1763 reconciliation and, 102–3, 109–10, 122, 129, 131; 1766 raid and, 121–22, 125, 130; 1769 treaty negotiations and, 125–27, 130–31, 134; 1781 raid and, 152–53, 158, 167; Christobal testimony and, 58–59; commissioning of Hannibal and, 60–61; constant warfare thesis and, 177–78;

Mosquito-Matina relations (*continued*)
Corella testimony in, 43–44; fugitives and, 78; gunboat diplomacy in, 65–66, 69–71, 77–78, 79–81, 86; Hannibal letter and, 69; Hannibal return trip and, 55–56, 61–62; Jeremy II peace delegation and, 52–53; joint English expeditions and, 84, 85–86, 90; kidnapping of Spanish governor and, 99–100, 106–7, 117; Mosquito as "enemies" in, 52, 63–64; Mosquito leadership change in, 98; post–civil war, 185; protection agreements and, 55; Spanish delegations to Mosquito territory and, 56–57, 61–62; Spanish reconciliation policy and, 129–30; trade proposals in, 39–41; tribute demands in, 102, 122, 124, 129–30, 140–41, 185. *See also* Mosquito-Spanish relations

Mosquito Shore Intendency: Mosquito activity and, 111, 133, 161–62; official recognition of, 91–93, 114–15, 168; role in English colonization effort, 118; slave trade and, 142. *See also* Hodgson, Robert

Mosquito-Spanish relations: 1759 Matina massacre and, 100; 1763 peace treaty and, 102–3, 109–10; 1763 treaty negotiations and, 102–3, 109–10; 1769 peace negotiations and, 124–26, 130–32; captive taking and slave raiding in, 34, 39, 70; Christobal testimony and, 58–60; coast guard incident and, 139; constant warfare thesis of, 177; context of Mosquito civil war and, 146; contraband trade and informal arrangements in, 47, 49, 70, 105–6, 132; Corella delegation and, 46; Dilson II reaffirmation of peace in, 148–49, 155–56; enemy status and resistance in, 83; English evacuation of Mosquito Shore and, 153–54; extermination of Mosquito and, 51, 52; Guatemala delegation to Black River and, 129; maintenance of protection agreements in, 152; Mosquito leadership claims and, 154–55; negotiation precedents in, 39–40, 93, 95–96, 97, 120–22; plans for attack on Cartago and, 101, 108–9; post–civil war, 185–86; reconciliation policies and, 22, 23, 143–44; Spanish imperial strategy and, 18, 26, 31; Spanish rejection of treaty proposals and, 42–43, 66–67; Spanish settlers on Mosquito Shore and, 160–61; subjecthood of Mosquito and, 103, 113; Tebuppy meeting and, 148; Terry treaty and, 149–51, 156–57, 162–63. *See also* Mosquito-Matina relations

Moya, Eufemio de, 84
M. W., 27–28, 37, 38

Naylor, Robert, 175, 179
negotiations. *See* diplomatic practices of the Mosquito Confederation
Nicaragua, 186–87. *See also* Fort San Fernando de Omoa; missions, Spanish; Mosquito-Spanish relations

Offen, Karl, 16–17, 144, 174–75, 178, 181–82
Olien, Michael, 16, 175, 178, 181
Oriamuno, Joseph Antonio de, 109–10
Ortega, Daniel, 186, 187
Otway, Joseph, 120, 133–34, 142–43

Payas, 33
Peter (General), 40, 64, 71, 75–77, 181–82
piracy: French, 35, 50, 54–55, 60, 65; Mosquito anti-piracy campaign, 40, 50, 53–56, 65; Mosquito involvement in, 6, 117, 125, 174; "pirate nests" and, 36, 89; Spanish concerns with, 33, 42. *See also* captive-taking practices of the Mosquito Confederation; raiding, Mosquito
Pitipie, 56, 57
Pitt, William, 88, 89, 97, 110, 113
Polson, John, 165, 167
Polson expedition, 165, 167
Potthast-Jutkeit, Barbara, 16–17, 178, 180
protection agreements: as imperial practice, 5, 22, 53, 74; Mosquito-English, 36–37, 111; Mosquito-Spanish, 39–40, 53, 58–59, 95, 111, 122, 152; private raiding and, 147
Providence Island, 6, 13
"Purchase Society, The" (Helms), 176
purchase society hypothesis, 176–77, 181. *See also* theses of Mosquito decline

raid and trade thesis, 93–94, 181. *See also* theses of Mosquito decline
raiding, Mosquito: firearm usage and, 174; frequency of, 23; impressment and, 86; privatized, 80–81; reassessment of, 173; role of, 177; scale of Mosquito, 28–29; Spanish mission and, 33–34. *See also* captive-taking practices of the Mosquito Confederation; diplomatic practices of the Mosquito Confederation; fleet system of the Mosquito Confederation; Mosquito-Matina relations; piracy

INDEX

raiding and constant warfare thesis, 177–80. *See also* theses of Mosquito decline
Rebullida, Pablo de, 34
Reimundo, 39
Restall, Matthew, 3
Rivera, Brooklyn, 186
Romero Vargas, Germán, 29
Ruiz, Pablo, 112, 113

Salvatierra, Sofanías, 15, 172, 177, 180
"Sambo and Tawira Miskito" (Offen), 181
Sandy Bay, 28
Scott, James C., 19–20
settler colonialism, 13, 14
1763 reconciliation (Mosquito-Matina), 102–3, 109–10, 122, 129, 131
slave raiding, Mosquito: prevalence and purpose of, 28–31; as privatized, 80, 147; Spanish missions and, 34; of Talamancans, 55–56. *See also* raiding, Mosquito; slave trade, Mosquito-English
slavery practices: in Anglo Caribbean, 14, 37; of Mosquito Confederation, 28–29
slave trade, Mosquito-English, 37–38, 142–43, 147
smallpox epidemic, 22, 73, 75–76
Solis y Miranda, Juan (*also* Joseph), 97, 104–5, 112, 113–14
Sorsby, William Shuman, 15–16, 178, 180
Spanish conquest of Central America: English territorial claims and, 102–3; Indigenous threats and, 33–34; influence of Mosquito Confederation on, 34–35, 186; jurisdiction and, 5–6, 10–11; logistical challenges for, 33, 35; Mosquito Shore project and, 160–61; motivations for, 32–33; overview of, 11–12, 14; policy and local actors in, 104–5; practices used in, 11, 32; Treaty of Madrid and, 36; weaknesses in, 82, 84–85
Spanish-English relations: 1769 negotiations and, 131–32; Anglo-Spanish War and, 151–52, 157–58, 164–68; Black River conflicts and, 166–67; control of Mosquito and, 111; English evacuation of Mosquito Shore and, 159–60; fear of Black River attack and, 113–14; Hodgson Jr. scrutiny and, 137; Hodgson management of coast guard incident and, 139–41; Mosquito cacao raids and, 106; Mosquito Shore claims and, 102–5, 110–14, 120, 162, 216n34; Treaty of Madrid and, 36. *See also* Anglo-Spanish War (1779–1783); War of Jenkins' Ear

Talamanca uprising, 109
Tangweera (Bell), 171
Tarbor, Isaac, 116, 117
Tawira-Mosquito: 1763 reconciliation and, 125, 184; ethnic rivalry and, 31, 76, 124, 126–27, 182; origins of, 6–7, 17, 31. *See also* Dilson I (Admiral); Dilson II (Admiral); ethnic rivalry thesis; Hannibal (Governor); internal conflict within the Mosquito Confederation; Mosquito civil war; Mosquito Confederation; *individual* "Briton" *headings*
Tebuppy meeting, 148, 217n42
technologies, European. *See* firearms thesis
Tempest (General), 123–24, 128, 150–51, 157, 164, 167
Tenorio, Martin, 68
territorial expansion of Mosquito Confederation: Costa Rican loyalty concerns and, 55; development of fleet system and, 48; expeditions and, 27–28, 48–50; piracy threats and, 53–55; power and influence in, 10. *See also* Mosquito conquest of Central America
Terry, Jeremiah, 141–42, 149–50, 156, 162–63
Terry treaty, 149–50, 156, 162–63, 180
theses of Mosquito decline: dependency thesis, 174–76; ethnic rivalry thesis, 181–82; firearms thesis, 172–74, 183; purchase society hypothesis, 176–77, 181; raid and trade thesis, 93–94; raiding and constant warfare thesis, 177–80
Thornton, John, 181–82
Tomas, 68
trade agreements: Matina negotiations and conflicts of, 43–44, 47, 49, 53; Mosquito-English, 37; Spanish-English proposals for, 104–5, 112
treaty negotiations. *See* diplomatic practices of the Mosquito Confederation; Mosquito-English relations; Mosquito-Matina relations; Mosquito-Spanish relations; Terry treaty
Treaty of Madrid, 13, 36–37, 89, 113
Trelawny, Edward, 89, 90–93, 110–11, 112–14, 142
tribute demands, 102, 122, 124, 129–30, 140–41, 185
Trujillo, Honduras. *See* Honduras; Mosquito-Honduras relations
turtle hunting/trade, 37–38, 45, 92

Umaña, Chacón de, 180

Uring, Nathaniel, 28, 31, 37–38

Valderrama, Balthasar Francisco, 70–71
Vargas, Joseph Antonio de, 132
Vasquez Prego, Joseph, 114
vassalage ceremony for Hannibal, 60–61, 63
Viceroyalty of New Spain, 10–11

War of Jenkins' Ear, 89–91. *See also* Spanish-English relations
Weaving the Past (Kellogg), 20
When Montezuma Met Cortés (Restall), 3
Williams, Caroline, 17, 180, 181, 182–83

Yanes, 57–58
Yasparral, 130
Yorosel, 57, 62–63

Zambo-Mosquito: 1763 reconciliation and, 125, 184; ethnic rivalry and, 31, 71, 76, 124, 126–27, 169, 182; joint English raid of Matina, 122; origins of, 6–7, 182. *See also* George I (King); George II (King); Hobby, Charles (General); Jeremy I (King); Jeremy II (King); Mosquito Confederation; Peter (General); Tawira-Mosquito; Tempest (General); theses of Mosquito decline
"Zambos and the Transformation of the Miskitu Kingdom" (Thornton), 181–82

EARLY AMERICAN PLACES

*On Slavery's Border: Missouri's Small
Slaveholding Households, 1815–1865*
BY DIANE MUTTI BURKE

*Sounds American: National Identity and the Music Cultures
of the Lower Mississippi River Valley, 1800–1860*
BY ANN OSTENDORF

*The Year of the Lash: Free People of Color in Cuba
and the Nineteenth-Century Atlantic World*
BY MICHELE REID-VAZQUEZ

*Ordinary Lives in the Early Caribbean: Religion,
Colonial Competition, and the Politics of Profit*
BY KIRSTEN BLOCK

*Creolization and Contraband: Curaçao in
the Early Modern Atlantic World*
BY LINDA M. RUPERT

*An Empire of Small Places: Mapping the
Southeastern Anglo-Indian Trade, 1732–1795*
BY ROBERT PAULETT

*Everyday Life in the Early English Caribbean: Irish,
Africans, and the Construction of Difference*
BY JENNY SHAW

*Natchez Country: Indians, Colonists, and the
Landscapes of Race in French Louisiana*
BY GEORGE EDWARD MILNE

Slavery, Childhood, and Abolition in Jamaica, 1788–1838
BY COLLEEN A. VASCONCELLOS

*Privateers of the Americas: Spanish American Privateering
from the United States in the Early Republic*
BY DAVID HEAD

*Charleston and the Emergence of Middle-
Class Culture in the Revolutionary Era*
BY JENNIFER L. GOLOBOY

*Anglo-Native Virginia: Trade, Conversion, and
Indian Slavery in the Old Dominion, 1646–1722*
BY KRISTALYN MARIE SHEFVELAND

*Slavery on the Periphery: The Kansas-Missouri
Border in the Antebellum and Civil War Eras*
BY KRISTEN EPPS

*In the Shadow of Dred Scott: St. Louis Freedom Suits and
the Legal Culture of Slavery in Antebellum America*
BY KELLY M. KENNINGTON

Brothers and Friends: Kinship in Early America
BY NATALIE R. INMAN

*George Washington's Washington: Visions for the
National Capital in the Early American Republic*
BY ADAM COSTANZO

*Borderless Empire: Dutch Guiana in
the Atlantic World, 1750–1800*
BY BRIAN HOONHOUT

*Complexions of Empire in Natchez: Race and
Slavery in the Mississippi Borderlands*
BY CHRISTIAN PINNEN

*Toward Cherokee Removal: Land, Violence,
and the White Man's Chance*
BY ADAM J. PRATT

*Generations of Freedom: Gender, Movement,
and Violence in Natchez, 1779–1865*
BY NIK RIBIANSZKY

A Weary Land: Slavery on the Ground in Arkansas
BY KELLY HOUSTON JONES

*Rebels in Arms: Black Resistance and the Fight
for Freedom in the Anglo-Atlantic*
BY JUSTIN IVERSON

*The Good Forest: The Salzburgers and
the Trustees' Plan for Georgia*
BY KAREN AUMAN

*From Empire to Revolution: Sir James Wright
and the Price of Loyalty in Georgia*
BY GREG BROOKING

*A Southern Underground Railroad: Black Georgians
and the Promise of Spanish Florida and Indian Country*
BY PAUL M. PRESSLY

*The Mosquito Confederation: A Borderlands
History of Colonial Central America*
BY DANIEL MENDIOLA

Printed in the United States
by Baker & Taylor Publisher Services